PHILOSOPHY OF THE BUDDHA

'*I think this book is excellent . . . a philosophical introduction to Buddhism is just what is needed, and I would very much welcome it. It is written by an accomplished moral philosopher, who treats the material in a careful, sensitive and philosophically rigorous manner.*' Jonardon Ganeri, Nottingham University

Philosophy of the Buddha is a philosophical introduction to the teaching of the Buddha. It carefully guides readers through the basic ideas and practices of the Buddha, including *kamma* (karma), rebirth, the not-self doctrine, the Four Noble Truths, the Eightfold Path, ethics, meditation, nonattachment, and *Nibbāna* (Nirvana).

The book includes an account of the life of the Buddha as well as comparisons of his teaching with practical and theoretical aspects of some Western philosophical outlooks, both ancient and modern. Most distinctively, *Philosophy of the Buddha* explores how Buddhist enlightenment could enable us to overcome suffering in our lives and reach our full potential for compassion and tranquillity.

This is one of the first books to introduce the philosophy of the Buddha to students of Western philosophy. Christopher Gowans' style is exceptionally clear and appropriate for anyone looking for a comprehensive introduction to this growing area of interest.

Christopher W. Gowans is professor of philosophy at Fordham University, USA. He is editor of *Moral Disagreements* (Routledge 2000), *Moral Dilemmas* (1987) and the author of *Innocence Lost: An examination of inescapable moral wrongdoing* (1994).

PHILOSOPHY OF THE BUDDHA

Christopher W. Gowans

Routledge
Taylor & Francis Group

LONDON AND NEW YORK

First published 2003
by Routledge
11 New Fetter Lane, London EC4P 4EE

Simultaneously published in the USA and Canada
by Routledge
29 West 35th Street, New York, NY 10001

Routledge is an imprint of the Taylor & Francis Group

Typeset in Times by
Florence Production Ltd, Stoodleigh, Devon
Printed and bound in Great Britain by
MPG Books Ltd, Bodmin

British Library Cataloguing in Publication Data
A catalogue record for this book is available
from the British Library

Library of Congress Cataloging in Publication Data
A catalogue record for this book has been requested

ISBN 0–415–27857–0 (hbk)
ISBN 0–415–27858–9 (pbk)

FOR MY WIFE, COLEEN

CONTENTS

CONTENTS

PREFACE

My purpose in writing this book is to provide a philosophical introduction to the teaching of the Buddha. It is intended neither as an apology nor as a critique, but as a thoughtful guide. I try to articulate the Buddha's teaching, explain how it could make sense, raise critical questions about it, and consider what he could say in response – all from the perspective of a philosopher trained in the West. I have the highest respect for the Buddha's teaching, and I take it seriously by reflectively engaging it. To a large extent, such critical reflection is encouraged by the Buddha himself. My hope is to motivate readers to take the Buddha seriously as well by thinking through his ideas and reaching their own conclusions about their value.

Many philosophers in the analytic tradition and elsewhere may view this as a quixotic enterprise at best. Yet there is now a well-established trend among some philosophers to look beyond the Western world in their research and especially their teaching. I wholeheartedly endorse this. But there are many dangers in this enterprise, and one of them is superficiality. I have endeavored here to focus on something rather specific, the teaching of the Buddha as represented in the *Sutta Piṭaka* of the *Pāli* canon, and to engage it in a serious philosophical way. It is still an introduction suitable for under-graduate students of philosophy. But the aim is to understand and reflect on the Buddha's teaching in a careful and detailed manner.

Aspects of Buddhism have been finding their way into the Western world for a couple of centuries. Increasingly in the last fifty years, a number of philosophers and scholars with a philosophical bent have been thinking in a sustained and insightful way about Buddhism and the possibilities for bringing Buddhist thought into dialogue with Western philosophy. I am greatly appreciative of their efforts and have benefited immensely from their work. A book of this sort does not lend itself to detailed scholarly disputation, but throughout I have learned much from others, both when I have agreed and not agreed with their interpretations and analyses. Many of these persons are referred to in the brief 'Suggested reading' section of each chapter. These are meant to guide readers to some pertinent philosophical discussions of the issues as well as to relevant sections of the *Sutta Piṭaka* (they are by no means exhaustive).

I have also profited a good deal from discussions of the Buddha's teaching in the *Theravāda* tradition. Though this book is not about that tradition, encounters with it have been natural insofar as it regards the *Sutta Piṭaka* of the *Pāli* canon as among its authoritative texts. Though I do not always accept traditional interpretations, I have always found it helpful to reflect on them. In general, I have tried to stay close to what is actually in the *Sutta Piṭaka* in contrast to what developed only later in the tradition. The one area where it was necessary to develop an interpretation at some length is the not-self doctrine (see part 2). What I say about it goes beyond but remains consonant with the spirit of the traditional understanding (and hence is contrary to revisions of this).

Sufficient quotations from the texts have been provided to give readers the flavor of the Buddha's teaching. But my main emphasis has been on explanation and evaluation. I urge readers to consult the original texts for themselves. Whenever possible, I have quoted more recent translations rather than the older ones of the Pali Text Society. The PTS translations are a tremendous resource and are always worth consulting. But their language is now rather out of date, and the newer translations are more available. For these reasons, the more recent translations are more suitable in an introductory guide. Likewise, my references are to the ordinary pagination rather than to the standardized pagination often used: the latter could be confusing to beginning students, while those already conversant with the texts should be able to move to other editions with comparative ease.

I have benefited greatly from comments on an earlier draft of the entire manuscript by Merold Westphal, Craig Condella, and an anonymous reviewer of this press. Dana Miller provided some insightful feedback on the chapters relating to Hellenistic philosophy, and Leo Lefebvre offered some helpful advice on my discussion of Buddhism and religion. A long conversation with Joseph Roccasalvo about Buddhism one afternoon was also of great value. Additionally, I have learned much from my students while teaching earlier versions of the manuscript in my sophomore philosophy classes the past two years.

Most of all, I was helped in a multitude of ways by my wife Coleen while preparing this book. She has read and commented on the entire manuscript, and we have had innumerable stimulating and illuminating conversations about Buddhism during the past several years. Her caring interest and encouragement, her knowledge and insight, her penetrating but respectful skeptical inquiries, and her numerous suggestions have all been of tremendous value. The book is dedicated to her. Without her loving and perceptive heart, I could not have written it. Finally, I am greatly appreciative of a rather different kind of support from my six-year-old daughter Hannah. Her regular energetic forays into my office while writing my book about 'Mr Buddha' have constantly reminded me of the life in terms of which these issues are so important.

ABBREVIATIONS

References are to page numbers, preceded by volume number in roman numerals when appropriate. Translations are sometimes altered slightly for the sake of uniformity.

L   *The Long Discourses of the Buddha*, translated by M. Walshe, Boston: Wisdom Publications, 1987.

M   *The Middle Length Discourses of the Buddha*, translated by Bhikkhu Ñāṇamoli and Bhikkhu Bodhi, Boston: Wisdom Publications, 1995.

C   *The Connected Discourses of the Buddha*, 2 vols, translated by Bhikkhu Bodhi, Boston: Wisdom Publications, 2000.

G   *The Book of the Gradual Sayings*, 5 vols, translated by F.L. Woodward, 1932–1936, Reprint, London: Pali Text Society, 1972–1979.

N   *Numerical Discourses of the Buddha: An Anthology of Suttas from the Aṅguttara Nikāya*, translated by N. Thera and Bhikkhu Bodhi, Walnut Creek, CA: AltaMira Press, 1999.

U/I *The Udāna: Inspired Utterances of the Buddha and The Itivuttaka: The Buddha's Sayings*, translated by J.D. Ireland, Kandy, Sri Lanka: Buddhist Publication Society, 1997.

Part 1

THE BUDDHA'S TEACHING AS A PHILOSOPHY

1

OBSERVING THE STREAM

Followers of the Buddha are increasingly visible to people in Western societies. Most Buddhists live in Southeast Asia, China, Korea or Japan, but there are also significant Buddhist populations in countries such as Tibet, Nepal, and Sri Lanka. Though accurate measurement is difficult, there are perhaps some 500 million Buddhists in Asia. Western awareness of Buddhists is not entirely new: Christian missionaries and colonial forces entered much of Asia centuries ago. But today, on account of increased ease of communication and transportation, and the general phenomenon of globalization, we in the West now have the opportunity, and sometimes the necessity, of interacting with Buddhists to an extent unprecedented in our past.

In fact, due to immigration and (to a much lesser extent) conversion, many Buddhists now live in Western countries. For example, there are probably at least one to two million Buddhists in the United States of America and significant numbers in European countries such as the United Kingdom and France. This too is not altogether a recent development: there were Chinese Buddhists in California shortly after the Gold Rush of 1849, and Buddhist societies began to spring up in some Western countries in the late nineteenth century. Moreover, closer to our time, books such as Eugen Herrigel's *Zen in the Art of Archery* (1953) and Hermann Hesse's *Siddhartha* (1951), along with the writings of D.T. Suzuki and Alan W. Watts, inspired a good deal of popular interest in Buddhism in the period after the Second World War. But in recent years, immigration to the West by Buddhists has increased, and so has interest in Buddhism among persons in the West, such as myself, who were not raised as Buddhists.

An indication of the current interest, and part of its cause, is the prominence of His Holiness the Dalai Lama, Tibet's spiritual head and political leader-in-exile. His efforts both on behalf of Tibetan independence from China and in support of inter-religious dialogue between Buddhism and Western religious traditions have attracted much attention. The Dalai Lama's book *The Art of Happiness* was on the *New York Times* 'best sellers' list for well over a year. There is also a small movement of 'Socially Engaged Buddhists' in some Western countries led partly by Westerners with a serious

3

commitment to Buddhism and partly by persons from traditional Buddhist countries such as Thich Nhat Hanh, the Vietnamese monk now living in France. Buddhism has even entered the arena of popular culture: in sports, advertising, television, movies, and rock music, occasional appearances of Buddhism may be found. Whether it is the golfer Tiger Woods, basketball coach Phil Jackson, actor Richard Gere, pop singer Tina Turner, or Adam Yauch of the rock group the *Beastie Boys*, it seems we have all heard of a celebrity who has proclaimed allegiance to some form of Buddhism.

In this context of increased awareness and interest, there are many reasons for persons in the West to inquire into Buddhism. One is to learn something about ourselves, to better understand our beliefs and values by comparing them with those of persons in cultures different from our own. A second is to understand something about those cultures, to comprehend how people in societies with Buddhist traditions live their lives. Related to this, a study of Buddhism may help us to interact better with Buddhists and Buddhist countries: it may enable us to approach these encounters in a more informed, responsible, and respectful way. Yet another reason is to see what we can learn from Buddhism, to ascertain whether an understanding of Buddhism might give us grounds for changing our own convictions and practices.

In some measure, this book may facilitate all these concerns, but its primary aim is the last, to reflect on what Buddhism can teach us. Specifically, the purpose is to help those with little or no knowledge of Buddhism to understand and evaluate the teaching of the Buddha from a philosophical perspective. Let us begin by reflecting on some key features of this approach.

1 The nature of this inquiry

We will focus on the teaching of Siddhattha Gotama, the person who became known as the Buddha (the enlightened one).[1] There are many ways of studying Buddhism that do not emphasize or go well beyond this teaching. For example, we might investigate the long history of Buddhism, both in its theoretical and practical aspects, in the Asian countries it has influenced. Or we might examine contemporary Buddhist cultures in those countries from the perspective of anthropology, sociology, or religious studies. These are all valuable approaches. But there is also merit in concentrating attention on what the Buddha himself taught. Both the history of Buddhism and its contemporary manifestations are large, complex, and diverse subjects: an introductory survey of them could be informative, but its sheer breadth would not tend to encourage in-depth reflection about what Buddhism might teach us. Though there are various ways of narrowing the field, an obvious approach is to focus on the source common to all Buddhist traditions – the teaching of the Buddha himself.

The Buddha said he taught all human beings a path for achieving enlightenment and well-being. As he approached his death, he laid particular emphasis on the importance of this teaching. To his attendant, Ānanda, he said:

> Ānanda, it may be that you will think: 'The Teacher's instruction has ceased, now we have no teacher!' It should not be seen like this, Ānanda, for what I have taught and explained to you as *Dhamma* and discipline will, at my passing, be your teacher.
>
> (L 269–70)

Buddhists everywhere revere as a source of wisdom and guidance the *Dhamma* of the Buddha, his teaching about the ultimate nature of reality and the way of life that accords with this. ('*Dhamma*' is the *Pāli* spelling followed here; the more familiar '*Dharma*' is in Sanskrit.) By examining this teaching, we will be studying the heart of all Buddhist traditions. Of course, these traditions have interpreted and developed the Buddha's teaching in strikingly different ways. For example, as we move from Sri Lanka to Tibet to Japan, the practice of Buddhism varies significantly. A full understanding of Buddhism would require investigation of these divergences, but they will not be our concern here. We will restrict ourselves to the teaching of the Buddha himself as we now know it.

Our aim is to understand and evaluate the Buddha's teaching. Some may object that evaluation is not a proper concern of non-Buddhists living in the West, that this is the prerogative of persons in Buddhist cultures. The Buddha himself provided an answer to this contention. He offered his teaching to all human beings, and he invited us all to reflect on what he taught and to learn from it. The intended audience of his message was not restricted to persons of a particular culture or tradition. In fact, the Buddha meant to radically challenge many of the values of his own culture. Moreover, from the northeastern corner of India where he taught some 2,500 years ago, the Buddha's teaching spread to societies such as China and Japan that were substantially different from his own. We accord the Buddha the highest tribute by accepting his invitation to seriously assess his teaching, not by flatly refusing to do so on the ground that it is the exclusive possession of another culture. By seeking to learn from the Buddha, we are not trying to tell others what they should believe: we are trying to ascertain what we should believe.

Finally, we will endeavor to grasp and appraise the Buddha's teaching from a philosophical point of view. That is, we will focus mainly on the philosophical aspects of the teaching, and we will seek to render these intelligible and to consider their worth by reflecting on them as a philosopher would. We will bring some characteristic perspectives, concerns, and habits of mind of philosophy to this teaching in order to illuminate it and examine what may be learned from it. Though there are several worthwhile avenues by which persons in the West might engage the teaching of the Buddha, philosophy is a natural one. Philosophy has played a central role in Western traditions, and

5

there is much in the Buddha's teaching that is philosophical in nature – for example, his ideas concerning the self, impermanence, and dependent origination. Moreover, his teaching gave rise to much explicit philosophical reflection in Asian cultures. Nonetheless, some may object that Western philosophical orientations are not suitable to comprehending and assessing the Buddha's teaching. The appropriateness and value of this approach will be explained at some length in chapters 4 and 5, but several preliminary points may be made here.

practice objection

One form of the objection is the claim that, above all else, the Buddha taught a practice – an ensemble of dispositions, skills, and activities aimed at achieving ultimate well-being – and it is a distortion of his teaching to distill a theory from this practice and then consider the theory alone. Indeed, this would be a mistake. However, the practice taught by the Buddha does have theoretical dimensions, and there is much to be learned by focusing on these, so long as we do not lose sight of their practical context. A tradition developed early on in Buddhism that emphasized its theoretical elements (the *Abhidhamma* literature), and there is at least one important branch of Western philosophy (the Hellenistic tradition) that stressed its practical significance. This suggests that lines of communication are available by which persons with a Western philosophical perspective might constructively encounter the teaching of the Buddha.

Religion objection

Another form of this objection is the assertion that the Buddha taught a religion and not a philosophy. The first part of this contention presumably is correct, depending on what we mean by the term 'religion'. The Buddha did not believe in God and hence did not regard his teaching as divine revelation. But in many respects it is appropriate to consider his teaching a religion – for example, it centrally involves a notion of transcendence. However, that the Buddha's teaching is a religion in these respects does not entail that it is not, or does not include, a philosophy. The terms 'Christian philosophy' or 'Jewish philosophy' are not ordinarily considered oxymorons, and the existence of God is an important part of the theories of many canonical figures in Western philosophy. Though the purpose of our inquiry is not primarily comparative, we will see that there are numerous points of contact between the teaching of the Buddha and Western philosophical traditions.

meditation objection

A final challenge to a philosophical approach is the claim that the primary mode of understanding in Western philosophy is reason, whereas for the Buddha enlightenment is achieved not by reason, but by meditation. This is the most interesting objection, and it raises a serious issue that will be one of our principal concerns. Rational thought and discourse have been fundamental to much Western philosophy (though not all of it), and Buddhist meditation has played no role in its traditions. However, both the Buddha and many Western philosophers held that objective knowledge of reality and of how to live may be achieved by human beings. The teaching of the

6

Buddha challenges the belief, so typical in Western philosophy, that rational reflection is the main means of attaining this knowledge. The Buddha thought reason was valuable but insufficient for enlightenment, and he thought meditation was crucial. The meditation techniques he taught were intended to develop our powers of concentration and, in a special sense, observation. They were meant to take us beyond ordinary modes of understanding, but not outside all understanding. The fundamental role of meditation in the Buddha's teaching should be seen not as precluding an inquiry into this teaching from a Western philosophical perspective, but as providing a key issue for consideration in this inquiry. As we seek to make sense of the teaching of the Buddha, one of our concerns will be to determine if we have something to learn from meditation. Perhaps the primacy of reason commonly asserted by Western philosophers is ill-advised.

2 Guidelines for learning from the Buddha

It will help to have some guidelines for comprehending and assessing the Buddha's teaching in a philosophical way. These guidelines are not beyond controversy. We will need to consider one critique from the Buddha himself. Nonetheless, it is important to begin our inquiry with an awareness of some of the methodological issues involved in seeking to understand and evaluate his teaching. These two activities cannot be completely separated: evaluation obviously presupposes understanding, but we cannot fully understand something without recourse to evaluation. However, we will proceed by first discussing some principles of interpretation and then turning to some standards of assessment. In the next section (see pages 11–13), we will reconsider these in light of the Buddha's own pronouncements apropos the comprehension and evaluation of his teaching.

Objectivity

Our first goal is an accurate and insightful understanding of the Buddha's teaching. We should assume neither that a perfectly objective account is possible nor that any interpretation is as good as another. As we strive to understand, we are influenced by our own perspective, an ensemble of outlooks, interests, feelings, and capacities rooted in the particulars of our historical, social, and personal circumstances. This is inevitable and not entirely cause for regret. Without some perspective, we could not comprehend anything – for example, we could not understand without language, and whatever languages we know are the products of specific cultures and traditions. Since each of our perspectives differ in important ways, none of us can expect a fully objective account. On the other hand, we should not infer from this that all interpretations are on a par. We need not suppose there is a single correct interpretation to realize that some accounts may be better than others.

Even if conflicting interpretations are sometimes equally or incommensurably good, our goal should be to seek an understanding that is well-founded and illuminating. One reason for being aware of our own perspective is to ascertain the ways it both enables and hinders us from achieving this goal. Though we cannot escape our perspective, we can gain some distance from it and perhaps modify it. This may enable us to overcome some of our limitations and to understand the Buddha in a more accurate and penetrating way.

Honesty

We should be careful not to presume either that the Buddha's teaching must be pretty much the same as what we already believe or that it has to be radically different from what we think. Both mistakes have been made by some Western interpreters. For example, if we assume that all religions are really saying the same thing in the end, we may fail to see the deep differences between Buddhism and Christianity. Or if we suppose that the 'Eastern mind' is essentially different from the 'Western mind,' and that 'never the twain shall meet,' we may miss the fact that the Buddha addressed concerns of great importance to us. We need to be honest about what he did and did not say. Our aim should be to carefully determine the differences and similarities that actually exist between his teaching and our own beliefs. We may discover that there are real disagreements that must be acknowledged, but we may also find out that there is more common ground than we suspected.

Translation

The Buddha's words were first recorded in the ancient language *Pāli*, and were later translated into other languages such as Chinese and Tibetan. We will rely on translations from the *Pāli* canon. We should assume neither that no adequate translations are possible nor that the translations we have are without drawbacks. There are fairly accurate translations of most *Pāli* words into English, but often these are only approximately correct. Nuances of a *Pāli* word may be lost in its English counterpart, or connotations of the English word may be inappropriate to the *Pāli* term it translates. For example, the crucial term '*dukkha*' is commonly translated as suffering (as it is here), but this is misleading since '*dukkha*' has broader implications suggesting lack of satisfaction, contentment, or fulfillment. We need to be aware of such limitations. For some central terms, any translation is potentially misleading. In some cases – especially '*kamma*' and '*Nibbāna*' ('*karma*' and '*Nirvāṇa*' in Sanskrit) – we will follow the custom of leaving the words untranslated and providing a commentary on their meaning. There is a glossary of some important *Pāli* terms beginning on page 202.

Context

We have to pay attention to the context of the Buddha's teaching in several respects. First, we need to know something about the culture in which he lived, the circumstances of his life, and the concerns and capacities he had. Second, each part of his teaching can be understood fully only by reference to the whole, and conversely a proper understanding of the whole requires an understanding of each of the parts. Hence, we need to alternate between an examination of the whole and an interpretation of the parts. Third, in our texts the Buddha usually addresses a specific audience (for example, many are followers, but some are critics). To understand a particular text, it may be important to know something about the identity of the Buddha's interlocutors. The first two issues will be facilitated to an extent in the next two chapters, which contain an account of the Buddha's life and an overview of his teaching. It is difficult to do justice to the final issue in an introductory discussion, but it will sometimes be significant.

Empathy and criticism

A good way to develop our understanding of the Buddha's teaching is to employ a dialectic of empathy and criticism. We should begin by trying to hear what the Buddha has to say. This requires attempting, as much as possible, to set aside our own perspective and to empathetically and imaginatively place ourselves in his perspective. The goal here is to figure out why the teaching made sense *to the Buddha*. The next step is to return to our standpoint and think critically about the teaching. Here the purpose is to raise some hard questions about, for example, the plausibility, coherence, or relevance of the Buddha's thought. Once these questions have been formulated, it is essential to go back to the mode of empathy to sympathetically determine the extent to which the Buddha may be able to answer our questions. This might lead us to realize there is more to his teaching than we first thought. For example, the search for coherence may lead us to discover something new. We should then return to the critical perspective, and so on and so forth. By moving back and forth between empathy and criticism, we hope to achieve a deeper understanding of the Buddha's teaching, one that gets beneath the surface meaning and goes to the heart of what is being proposed. There are two dangers: being critical too soon, so that we deprive ourselves of the opportunity to hear what is being said, and not being critical soon enough, so that we postpone asking penetrating questions that may bring out the real meaning of the teaching.

We see in this dialectic one reason why understanding and evaluation are not separate activities. Let us now consider some guidelines for assessing the Buddha's teaching.

Cosmopolitanism

We should not dogmatically assume our culture is best and provides not only the correct beliefs and values, but also the proper standards for evaluating these. Whatever 'our culture' refers to, it is something heterogeneous, contingent, changing, and influenced by other cultures. It is unlikely that it supplies definitive standards that are incapable of improvement. When we find disagreement with the Buddha, one possibility is that he is mistaken, but another is that we are. Though we cannot help but begin with our own outlook, we need not end up with the same outlook, at least not without modification. On the other hand, we should not make the opposite mistake and assume that everything distinctive in our culture is corrupt and in need of correction by, for example, the ancient and flawless wisdom of the Buddha. There is no substitute for reflecting on whether something is sound, whether it comes from our culture or another.

Open-mindedness

A related point is that we should not assume either that the teaching of the Buddha cannot possibly make sense because it seems so strange and difficult to comprehend, or that it must make sense because Buddhists have lived their lives in accordance with it for thousands of years. We need to be open to the possibility that there is great insight and value in the Buddha's message, but also to the possibility that it has limited worth.

Coherence

If the teaching of the Buddha appears to lack coherence, this should give us pause. In the most obvious case, if one part contradicts another part, the teaching as a whole cannot be entirely true. Faced with an apparent contradiction, we need to consider whether it can be resolved (for example, by showing that the two parts do not really contradict one another, or that we have mistakenly attributed one of them to the Buddha). Coherence does not guarantee truth, but lack of coherence is a sign that something is probably amiss. Hence, we need to reflect regularly on whether the Buddha's teaching is coherent. Here especially interpretation and evaluation should work hand in hand.

Fidelity to our experience

If there is something to learn from the Buddha, then at some point and in some way his teaching must connect with our own experience. It must show itself to be a relevant and compelling analysis of our lives – as the Buddha himself would be the first to insist. However, we should not suppose that what the Buddha says will be immediately obvious. In fact, he gives reasons for being suspicious of what we think is obvious. But sooner or later, if we are to discover something important in the Buddha, his teaching must illuminate our deepest concerns, values, aspirations, feelings, and the like.

Selectivity

Finally, we need not suppose that we must accept or reject the teaching of the Buddha as a whole. Perhaps we can learn from some aspects of it, but not others. Historically, as Buddhism entered different cultures, it developed in diverse and sometimes conflicting directions. Often the Buddha's teaching was integrated into a native tradition in such a way that the teaching modified the tradition and the tradition also modified what was thought worthwhile in the teaching. For example, Japanese Zen Buddhism is rooted in the Buddha's teaching, but it is a distinctive cultural formation that differs significantly from many other forms of Buddhism. We should not assume our situation is any different. Understanding parts of the teaching requires consideration of the whole, but we might discover that some parts are more valuable to us than others.

3 The guidelines, the Eightfold Path, and the stream-observer

The guidelines just outlined express principles that I believe are reasonable in light of contemporary Western debates about methodology (discussion of these issues is often called hermeneutics). It would take us too far afield to consider recent critiques of these guidelines, but it is pertinent to our inquiry to ask to what extent they comport with the teaching of the Buddha. He was much concerned that his teaching be properly understood and evaluated. For example, just before his death he said to his followers that, if someone attributed a particular teaching to him, then 'without approving or disapproving, his words and expressions should be carefully noted and compared with the *suttas* [his discourses] and reviewed in the light of the discipline.' He said the purported teaching should be considered 'the word of the Buddha' if and only if it conformed to the *suttas* and discipline (L 255). With respect to evaluation, the Buddha encouraged his followers to 'examine the meaning of [his] teachings with wisdom' in order to 'gain a reflective acceptance of them' (M 227).

These passages show an awareness of methodological issues, but the Buddha did not teach anything comparable to the guidelines stated in the last section. However, there is reason to think he might have accepted, or at least might not have had reason to reject, many of these guidelines. The passages just quoted express a concern for objective understanding and reflective evaluation that is spelled out in many of the guidelines. Moreover, several of these principles recommend a middle position between two extremes. This is in the spirit of a central motif in the Buddha, the idea that his teaching is a middle way. In addition, the contextual principle that interpretation of a passage may require reference to the Buddha's audience has long been a standard precept, taken to be implicit in his teaching, of 'Buddhist hermeneutics' (as it is called in the West). Of course, there are also some obvious differences. The Buddha did not have the concern about the influence of cultural and historical location on interpretation that is so common nowadays. Moreover, his convictions about the limitations of language in describing *Nibbāna* may challenge the extent to which coherence is a viable criterion in this respect. And he did not suggest that we might be selective in learning from his teaching.

Nonetheless, the central point to make in comparing the guidelines of the last section and the teaching of the Buddha is this: instead of proposing any such guidelines, the Buddha taught the Noble Eightfold Path (*ariya aṭṭhangika magga*) to enlightenment, and he believed that only someone fully enlightened could properly understand and evaluate his teaching. The Eightfold Path is a long, complex, and difficult regime that is intended to radically transform us by means of an array of intellectual, moral, and meditative disciplines. Undertaking the path requires a long-term commitment. We cannot try it out for a few weeks and quickly see how well it works. For someone new to the teaching who is wondering if there is something to learn from the Buddha, a central question is whether there is any reason to make such a commitment in the first place. This person is not helped by being told that the ultimate standpoint for understanding and evaluating the teaching is only available to someone who has followed the Eightfold Path and achieved enlightenment. A person initially encountering the Buddha's teaching needs some advance assurance that there is truth in this teaching if he or she is to go farther. It is for this person that the guidelines in the last section are important. Following these guidelines might provide someone with this advance assurance. If it did, this person would have reason to undertake the Eightfold Path, and the training of the path may be expected to supersede the guidelines. (An interesting question, however, is whether the modern perspective expressed in the guidelines might give a contemporary follower of the Buddha reason to modify the Eightfold Path or our interpretation of it.)

The Buddha agreed that some initial assurance was required before beginning the Eightfold Path. He did not propose that people undertake it on blind faith. There is reason to think he might have been in broad agreement with many of the guidelines, understood not as a substitute for the Eightfold Path, but as instruments for determining whether or not to begin it. It will be convenient to have a label for the person contemplating this. The Buddha classified persons already on the path according to four levels of achievement towards full enlightenment. He called the lowest of these the stream-enterer (*sotāpanna*) – someone who has begun the journey across the river whose opposite shore represents enlightenment. Since a stream-enterer is someone who already has confidence in the Buddha's teaching, let us call a person who is considering whether such confidence is warranted a *stream-observer*: this is someone standing on the shore wondering whether enlightenment is really the reward of the difficult journey across.

The concerns of stream-observers will vary according to the specific perspective each brings to the teaching of the Buddha. In this book, the stream-observers I have in mind are primarily those who are culturally part of the contemporary Western world and have no Buddhist upbringing. Of course, this is a large group of persons with many different and often conflicting viewpoints. Nonetheless, there are some characteristic questions such persons may be expected to ask. I will endeavor to formulate these questions and consider what the Buddha might be able to say in response. My purpose is not to argue that Western stream-observers should or should not strive to become stream-enterers, but to provide them with some guidance for making this decision for themselves, and more broadly for determining what they might learn from the Buddha.

The promise and great attraction of the Buddha's teaching is a life of happiness, compassion, and tranquillity. But for stream-observers there are likely to be many serious obstacles to understanding and appreciating this teaching. These include the moral rigors of the Eightfold Path, the practice of meditation, and ideas such as rebirth, impermanence, non-attachment, *Nibbāna*, and especially the not-self doctrine. We need to consider whether, or to what extent, such obstacles can be overcome.

4 A word about sources

A brief account of the sources of our knowledge of the Buddha's teaching is in order. The Buddha wrote nothing: his teaching was communicated orally over a period of 45 years some 2,500 years ago. According to tradition, shortly after the Buddha's death, 500 enlightened followers (*arahants*) met in Rājagaha, India for a communal recitation of his teaching. This was divided into two parts now known as the *Vinaya Piṭaka* ('Discipline basket') and the *Sutta Piṭaka* ('Discourse basket'). The recitations were led respectively by Upāli and Ānanda, thought to be especially well-qualified to accurately remember what the Buddha taught. The *Vinaya Piṭaka* contains detailed rules of conduct governing the monastic community the Buddha founded. The *Sutta Piṭaka* consists mainly of discourses the Buddha delivered to explain his teaching. These rules and discourses were committed to memory and transmitted orally from generation to generation. About a century later, various factions began to emerge, each with its own somewhat different understanding of the Buddha's teaching. During this time, a third genre of the teaching developed, the *Abhidhamma Piṭaka* ('Higher teaching basket'). This contains a more systematic and abstract exposition and interpretation of what the Buddha taught. With this, the entire body of teaching – the *Vinaya*, *Sutta* and *Abhidhamma*

Piṭakas – came to be known as the *Tipiṭaka* ('Three baskets'). However, it was not until later, perhaps the first century BCE, that this teaching was first committed to written form, and it was much later yet that modifications of this canon came to an end. There now exist several versions of the *Tipiṭaka* in different languages, and while they substantially overlap, they are not identical.

In short, we do not have direct knowledge of the teaching of the Buddha. Instead, we have a large and diverse body of texts that purport to represent his teaching, but which are the product of a long period of oral transmission from memory as well as translation from one language to another. The distance from the Buddha's mouth to the texts we now possess is considerable (more so than in the case of written accounts of the teaching of Socrates or Jesus), and there is much room for modification and misunderstanding. To a limited extent, modern scholarship may inform us when texts are more or less likely to accurately represent what the Buddha really thought. But there is little prospect that we will ever know in detail how closely extant texts correspond to his actual teaching.

However, for our purposes we will follow tradition and consider the teaching of the Buddha to be the teaching expressed in these texts. We have no other access to what he said, and these texts probably accurately represent his instruction on the whole. Moreover, it is the teaching conveyed in the *Tipiṭaka* that has been influential in the world: what we now call Buddhism is fundamentally rooted in these texts and the various traditions that have interpreted them. (It should be recognized, though, that some traditions such as *Mahāyāna* Buddhism emphasize later texts, and Ch'an (Zen) Buddhism is skeptical about the value of texts.)

The main versions of the *Tipiṭaka* available today are the *Pāli*, Chinese, and Tibetan canons. We will rely on the *Pāli* canon. In overall comparison with the other two, it is probably older, less interpretive, and closer to the language of the Buddha (it is not known exactly what language he spoke, but *Pāli*, a Middle Indo-Aryan language related to Sanskrit, has historical connections with it). Moreover, unlike the other canons, we have full, and for the most part readily available, translations into English of the relevant *Pāli* texts. The *Pāli* canon is the authoritative canon of the *Theravāda* tradition that prevails in Sri Lanka and parts of Southeast Asia. The purpose is not to side with this tradition in contrast with other Buddhist traditions, but to employ the texts of its canon to understand and evaluate the Buddha's teaching. In an introductory inquiry, this is the most sensible course. But it is not perfectly neutral. Though the *Theravāda* tradition takes the *Pāli* canon to express the original teaching of the Buddha, it is still the result of a long, interpretive history.

Of the three parts of the *Tipiṭaka*, we will focus on the *Sutta Piṭaka*. The *Vinaya Piṭaka* has great practical significance for Buddhist monastic communities, but it is comparatively less important for understanding the philosophical aspects of the Buddha's teaching. By contrast, the *Abhidhamma Piṭaka* contains what in some respects are the most philosophical presentations of the *Tipiṭaka*. However, the detailed, systematic, and abstract formulations of these texts, and their concern with doctrinal disputes, are the product of interpretations subsequent to the Buddha's life. Though they are considered by the *Theravāda* tradition to be the word of the Buddha, they are less close to his actual teaching than the other parts of the *Tipiṭaka* and essentially mark the beginning of commentaries that have continued to this day.

The *Sutta Piṭaka* purports to represent the actual teaching of the Buddha, for the most part on specific occasions to particular persons. Typically a *sutta* (discourse) begins with the phrase, purportedly of Ānanda at the first recitation, 'Thus I have heard,' followed by a description of a place and an audience. The main body of the text consists of a teaching of the Buddha, usually expressed by the Buddha himself, but sometimes by one of his chief disciples such as Sāriputta. Often at the end, there is a declaration by the person addressed expressing confidence in the truth of the teaching. Though the *suttas* as we have them are partly the product of later interpretation, they are probably the texts available to us that come closest to expressing the philosophical aspects of the actual teaching of the Buddha. The *Sutta Piṭaka* is divided into the following five collections of texts called *Nikāyas* ('Groups'):

*   *Dīgha Nikāya* ('*Long Discourses*')
*   *Majjhima Nikāya* ('*Middle Length Discourses*')
*   *Saṃyutta Nikāya* ('*Connected Discourses*')
*   *Aṅguttara Nikāya* ('*Numerical Discourses*')
*   *Khuddaka Nikāya* (fifteen short texts with various titles).

Information about translations of these texts may be found in the Bibliography. We will mainly be concerned with the first four of these. The *Khuddaka Nikāya* consists of a miscellaneous group of texts, though these include popular works such as *The Dhammapada*, and also the *Therīgāthā*, an important representation of the voices of women followers of the Buddha.

Taken as a whole, the *Sutta Piṭaka* is incredibly long and repetitious. Moreover, except for the *Saṃyutta Nikāya*, the method of organization is largely non-thematic and hence not user-friendly. The beginning student of the Buddha who reads these texts without guidance is likely to become discouraged very quickly. To mitigate this problem, at the end of each chapter I recommend some *suttas* as particularly relevant to that chapter (see the 'Suggested reading' sections). Readers are strongly urged to study these *suttas* in conjunction with this book. To the extent feasible, I have chosen these recommendations from the *Majjhima Nikāya*: if there were one substantial text with which to begin, this would probably be it. (However, the English translation runs over 1,100 pages.) I have also cited passages from the *Majjhima Nikāya* in preference to parallel passages elsewhere whenever possible. But texts from other parts of the *Sutta Piṭaka* have been recommended and cited when necessary.

SUGGESTED READING

No specific *sutta* is uniquely appropriate to this introductory chapter, but the reader might start with *The Dhammapada*, especially chapters 9, 14, 15, 16, 20, 24, and 26. For our purposes, this inspirational anthology of sayings has limited value, but it does provide an initial taste of the practice the Buddha taught. There are numerous translations (see Bibliography for references to two of these – page 206). For an introduction to this work, see Kupperman (2001). Dissanayake (1993) offers an interesting analysis.

Accounts of the emergence of Buddhism in the West can be found in Batchelor (1994), Fields (1992), Harvey (1990: chapter 13), Keown (1996: chapter 9), Mitchell (2002: chapter 11), and Strong (2002: chapter 10).

For discussion of methodological issues, see Larson and Deutsch (1988), Mueller-Vollmer (1985), and Nussbaum (1997: chapter 4). Methodological questions in the study of Buddhism are considered in Garfield (2002: chapters 13 and 14), Hoffman (1991), Lopez (1988), and Maraldo (1986). A useful resource for important terms in the *Pāli* canon is Nyanatiloka (1988).

NOTE

1   Mahāyana Buddhism speaks of numerous Buddhas who exist in various 'Buddha fields.' However, the term 'the Buddha' ordinarily refers to Siddhattha Gotama (also called Śākyamuni Buddha).

2

THE LIFE OF THE BUDDHA

The life of the Buddha is a constitutive part of his teaching. In this respect, it is natural to compare the Buddha with other primordial figures such as Socrates and Jesus, teachers who conveyed their beliefs with the whole of their lives, but wrote nothing. In all three cases, there was much oral communication that was preserved by memory and subsequently recorded by enthusiastic followers. But these three personages intended to teach with their actions as well as their words, and we cannot properly understand these words, in the canonical texts of their adherents, without placing them in the context of the lives of those who expressed them.

The Buddha's life, as it has been passed down to us in Buddhist traditions, is surely rooted in historical fact, but it has been embellished by the imaginative inventions of devoted disciples. There is little prospect of clearly and fully separating literal truth from supplemental fiction in these accounts, and in any case the apparent amendments are often symbolically significant even if historically false. In order to learn from the Buddha, stream-observers first need to listen sympathetically to the story of his life and attempt to feel its power as countless generations of persons in Buddhist cultures have felt it. Subsequently they should reflect critically on its meaning.

The narrative recounted here contains the main features standardly included in traditional accounts, with an emphasis on those aspects especially important to understanding the Buddha's teaching. His life had three distinct phases: the early years culminating in the realization of human suffering, the search for and attainment of enlightenment concerning this suffering, and the fulfillment of his commitment to devote the remainder of his life to instructing others how to achieve enlightenment for themselves.

1 The discovery of human suffering

The person we know as the Buddha was born in the Lumbinī grove, in the vicinity of Kapilavatthu, near the present-day border of India and Nepal, sometime between the seventh and the fifth centuries BCE. He was called Siddhattha Gotama (Siddhārtha Gautama in Sanskrit). In view of the doctrine of rebirth, it should not surprise us that this was not his first birth, though it was to be his last. In one of his previous lives, when he was called Sumedha, he met someone already enlightened, already a Buddha. Sumedha vowed to strive for enlightenment himself. He became a *bodhisatta*, a being devoted to seeking enlightenment. But he was to achieve enlightenment only after many rebirths during his life as Siddhattha. (The name 'Siddhattha' means 'One who achieves his goal'.)

Siddhattha's father, Śuddhodana, was a relatively powerful and wealthy leader of a small tribe called the Sakka, structured more as a republic than a kingdom, and located in the Ganges river basin near the foothills of the Himalayan mountains (Kapilavatthu was its capital). His mother Mahāmāyā died a week after his birth, and he was raised by Mahāpajāpatī, an aunt who became his father's second wife. Little is known of Siddhattha's early life. Presumably he was raised in considerable prosperity and received a good education by the standards of the time. He was also reputed to have been extremely attractive physically. Aged sixteen, he married the beautiful Yaśodharā. Several years later, when he was twenty-nine, she gave birth to their first (and, it would turn out, only) child, their son Rāhula. That Siddhattha was married, had a son, and was probably in line to acquire the power and wealth of his father no doubt made him a very fortunate and much envied young man in Sakka.

At the time of his birth, religious authorities observed that Siddhattha possessed the 'thirty-two marks peculiar to a Great Man' (L 441) and they predicted that he would become an important world figure, either a just ruler or an enlightened spiritual leader. His father was determined that he should become a ruler, and to ensure this outcome he protected his son from everything unpleasant in life. An early omen should have warned Śuddhodana that his son had a different destiny. At the age of twelve, Siddhattha was found meditating under a tree during a festival. Eventually, he discovered what everyone comes to know – that there is suffering in human life. One day he left the palace and saw a decrepit, bent-over old man walking with a stick to support him. Thus Siddhattha realized that human beings are not forever young: we all age and grow old. On a second outing, he saw a man who was extremely ill. Thus Siddhattha realized that human beings are not forever healthy: we are all liable to sickness. On a third excursion, he saw a dead man in a funeral procession. Thus Siddhattha realized that human beings do not live forever: we all die eventually.

The threefold discovery that aging, illness and death are facts of every human life was a shock to Siddhattha. He was overcome with disgust and shame (N 54). He wondered: What is the meaning of human suffering? What is its cause? Can it be overcome? How can such questions be answered? On a fourth outing, Siddhattha saw a man who had left home, shaved his head, and donned yellow robes: he was seeking a life of wisdom, virtue and tranquillity outside the conventional life of society, and he became an initial role-model for Siddhattha. The Buddha said later:

While still young, a black-haired young man endowed with the blessing of youth, in the prime of life, though my mother and father wished otherwise and wept with tearful faces, I shaved off my hair and beard, put on the yellow robe, and went forth from the home life into homelessness.

(M 256)

This was the beginning of Siddhattha's effort to understand human suffering. He was twenty-nine years old and would persist for six years before attaining enlightenment.

2 The quest for enlightenment

Siddhattha began his search by seeking instruction from persons who were reputed to be wise. The dominant religion in his society was Brahmanism, a forerunner of Hinduism based on a set of oral teachings known as the *Vedas* (their origin goes back as far as around 1,500 BCE). There are three features of Brahmanism worth noting here. First, it maintained that all persons were determined by birth to fall into exactly one class in a hierarchy of four: the religious leaders known as brahmins, rulers and warriors, farmers and traders, and servants (this is the ancestor of the later caste system in India). Second, Brahmanism accepted polytheism and supposed that benefits from the gods could be obtained by sacrificial rituals. Third, it emphasized the value of ascetic practices as well as meditation techniques known as yoga. As the Buddha, Siddhattha would be critical of the first two of these tenets, but he would incorporate and transform both features of the third. It is especially significant that, as he began his quest, he found himself in a world in which meditation was already regarded as an important spiritual discipline. It was with two teachers of meditation that he embarked on his quest for understanding.

The first was Āḷāra Kālāma. Siddhattha quickly learned Kālāma's teaching and attained the highest meditation level in his system – what he called 'the base of nothingness' (M 257). In fact, Kālāma was so impressed by Siddhattha's achievements that he offered him co-leadership of his community. But Siddhattha was not satisfied with what he had achieved. This teaching, he said, 'does not lead to disenchantment, to dispassion, to cessation, to peace, to direct knowledge, to enlightenment, to *Nibbāna*' (M 258).

His second teacher was Uddaka Rāmaputta. Once again, Siddhattha rapidly understood his teaching and achieved the highest level of concentration, the 'base of neither-perception-nor-non-perception' (M 258). This time his teacher was so taken with his accomplishments that he offered him leadership of his group. But as before, Siddhattha was similarly dissatisfied. He moved on, though the two aforementioned levels of concentration were later included in his own system of meditation.

Siddhattha lived during a period of spiritual unrest. The ideas of the *Upaniṣads* were emerging and there were many who challenged Brahmanism on a variety of philosophical fronts (the first *sutta* of the *Dīgha Nikāya* describes sixty-two different philosophical views). The Jains accepted a doctrine of *kamma*, rebirth, and liberation from rebirth; they also claimed that all things are alive and opposed every form of violence. The Ājīvikas were fatalists who believed our future lives were predetermined and beyond our control. There were also materialists who denied any life beyond this one. The Buddha would call this view annihilationism (*ucchedavāda*) in contrast to the eternalism (*sassatavāda*) of the previous two positions. And there were skeptics, described by the Buddha as 'eel-wrigglers,' who concluded we could not know which of the competing views was correct and advocated believing none of them. The Buddha would challenge each of these positions, but he would also draw on aspects of some of them, especially those of the Jains. What is significant at this juncture is that some proponents of these outlooks left their communities, lived on alms, and practiced extraordinarily severe regimes of asceticism and meditation. They were known as *samaṇas* – reclusive spiritual strivers. It was his observation of one of the *samaṇas* that inspired Siddhattha's own quest for enlightenment after his fourth excursion from the palace.

Having departed from his two more conventional teachers, Siddhattha joined company with five *samaṇas*. Among them he practiced asceticism with a vengeance, bringing himself to 'a state of extreme emaciation' and nearly to the point of death by eating almost nothing (M 339). In addition, he undertook a 'breathless meditation' he described in these words: 'I stopped the in-breaths and out-breaths through my mouth, nose, and ears. While I did so, violent winds cut through my head. Just as if a strong man were splitting my head open with a sharp sword' (M 337–8). But it was all to no avail. Eventually, after nearly six years, Siddhattha reached the conclusion that 'by this racking practice of austerities I have not attained any superhuman states, any distinction in knowledge and vision worthy of the noble ones.' He asked, 'could there be another path to enlightenment?' Thinking there must be, he began to eat food provided by a young woman named Sujātā, and his five ascetic companions left him, disgusted that he had 'reverted to luxury' (M 340).

Once nourished, Siddhattha sat under a tree later known as the 'Bodhi-tree' (tree of awakening) and he began to reflect and meditate, determined to achieve enlightenment on his own. According to later accounts, a final obstacle remained. Māra, a tempter somewhat like Satan, but representing not so much evil as the forces of desire and their propulsion of us into repeated rounds of death and rebirth, strove mightily to divert Siddhattha with the promise of sensual enchantments and the threat of physical torments. Siddhattha held firm. Māra then challenged Siddhattha's belief that he was now prepared for enlightenment. Siddhattha insisted that his good works and spiritual attainments were sufficient preparation, and he touched the ground with his right hand to bid the earth to bear witness to his claim. The earth shook. Māra fled in defeat. Siddhattha was now ready.

He promptly passed through four levels of concentration, the four *jhānas* that are a key part of Buddhist meditation. Siddhattha's mind was thereby 'purified, bright, unblemished, rid of imperfection.' He then attained three kinds of knowledge. The first was specific knowledge of his own past lives. The second was knowledge of the passing away and reappearance of beings, those who lived well in a 'good destination,' and those who did not in a 'state of deprivation.' The third and most important was knowledge of the nature of suffering, its origin, its cessation, and the way leading to its cessation – what he would call the Four Noble Truths (*ariya sacca*), the heart of his teaching. Thus his mind was liberated from the taints (*āsava*) of sensual desire, being, and ignorance. He had achieved enlightenment: 'Ignorance was banished and true knowledge arose, darkness was banished and light arose.' Siddhattha was now a buddha, an enlightened one who had rediscovered liberation from the cycle of rebirth and suffering. He declared, 'I directly knew: "birth is destroyed, the holy life has been lived, what had to be done has been done, there is no more coming to any state of being"' – a somewhat cryptic allusion to *Nibbāna* we will come to understand (M 105–6).

3 The life of teaching

For the most part, the Buddha – as we may now call Siddhattha – is not portrayed as growing in wisdom or virtue after his enlightenment. The transformation under the Bodhi-tree was radical and complete, and these qualities could not be improved upon further. But there was one moment immediately after his awakening when the Buddha did undergo a significant change. He first believed that the *Dhamma*, the understanding of the ultimate reality and correspondingly correct way of life he had now achieved, was too difficult for people to grasp in their present condition and that it would not be worthwhile to teach them:

> This *Dhamma* that I have attained is profound, hard to see and hard to understand, peaceful and sublime, unattainable by mere reasoning, subtle, to be experienced by the wise. But this generation delights in adhesion [to sense pleasures], takes delight in adhesion, rejoices in adhesion. It is hard for such a generation to see this truth . . . . If I were to teach the *Dhamma*, others would not understand me, and that would be wearying and troublesome for me.
>
> (M 260)

Hence, the Buddha was 'inclined to inaction rather than to teaching the *Dhamma*.' At that moment, however, the Brahmā Sahampati appeared and declared to the Buddha: 'There are beings with little dust in their eyes who are wasting through not hearing the *Dhamma*. There will be those who will understand the *Dhamma*.' In response to this appeal, the Buddha decided to teach what he had learned 'out of compassion for beings' (M 260–1). He was aged thirty-five and would spend the remaining forty-five years of his life teaching the *Dhamma* to all who would listen so that they themselves might achieve enlightenment and overcome suffering.

The Buddha's initial thought was to return to his first two teachers, Kālāma and Rāmaputta, but they had both died recently. He then sought out the five ascetic *samaṇas* he had abandoned earlier. They were suspicious at first. After all, they thought, their former companion had succumbed to luxury and so could not be a true spiritual striver. They refused to pay him homage but did allow him to sit down. The Buddha declared that he had not given in to luxury, that he had not abandoned striving, and that in fact he had achieved enlightenment. It was to this group of five that the Buddha gave his first *sutta*, 'Setting in motion the wheel of *Dhamma*.' Its focus was the Four Noble Truths, culminating in the Eightfold Path leading to the cessation of suffering. The Buddha described this path as a 'middle way' (*majjhimā paṭipadā*) between the worldliness of most persons and the asceticism of the *samaṇas*. In short order all five were convinced. They became *arahants*, fully enlightened ones, and they were the Buddha's first followers.

He soon attracted a large group of male disciples called *bhikkhus*. Like the Buddha, they had left home and family to seek enlightenment, and with the Buddha, many found it. They lived together in the *Sangha*, a highly disciplined, celibate community that was supported by alms. The common translations of the terms '*bhikkhu*' and '*Sangha*' as monk and monastic order respectively are not inappropriate if we keep in mind qualifications to be made in understanding Buddhism as a religion (see chapters 4 and 5). Five years later, upon the urging of his step-mother Mahāpajāpatī and his attendant Ānanda, the Buddha established a community of female disciples, the *bhikkhunīs*, or nuns. This was a second important post-enlightenment development in the Buddha's thinking. In addition to the *bhikkhus* and *bhikkhunīs*, there were male and female lay followers – *upāsakas* and *upāsikās* – who did not leave home but nonetheless strove to live according to the teaching of the Buddha.

The Buddha spent the remainder of his life travelling on foot in the vicinity of the Ganges river basin, in the company of many disciples, teaching to whomever would listen, irrespective of class or gender. In his eightieth year, he fell ill (possibly from food poisoning) and realized he was dying. The *Tathāgata*, a common epithet for the Buddha meaning literally 'thus come one, thus gone one,' first informed Ānanda:

> Have I not told you before: All those things that are dear and pleasant to us must suffer change, separation and alteration? So how could this be possible? Whatever is born, become, compounded, is liable

to decay – that it should not decay is impossible. And that has been renounced, given up, rejected, abandoned, forsaken: the *Tathāgata* has renounced the life-principle. The *Tathāgata* has said once for all: 'The *Tathāgata's* final passing will not be long delayed. Three months from now the *Tathāgata* will take final *Nibbāna*.'

(L 252–3)

The Buddha appointed no successor. Through Ānanda, he instructed the *bhikkhus* to 'live as islands unto yourselves, being your own refuge, with no one else as your refuge, with the *Dhamma* as an island, with the *Dhamma* as your refuge, with no other refuge' (L 245). He also said to them that his teaching 'should be thoroughly learnt by you, practiced, developed, and cultivated, so that this holy life may endure for a long time, that it may be for the benefit and happiness of the multitude, out of compassion for the world' (L 253).

On the night of the Buddha's death, in the small village of Kusinārā, a wanderer named Subhadda asked to speak with him. He had a doubt he hoped the Buddha could dispel. Over the objection of Ānanda, the Buddha agreed to see him. The Buddha emphasized to Subhadda, as he had earlier to so many others, the importance of the Eightfold Path as the distinctive feature of his teaching. Subhadda declared, as had so many before, 'It is as if someone were . . . to point out the way to one who had got lost, or to bring an oil lamp into a dark place, so that those with eyes could see what was there' (L 268–9). Thereupon Subhadda became an *arahant*, the final personal disciple of the Buddha.

The Buddha was now confident all questions among the *bhikkhus* were resolved. To them he addressed his final words: 'All conditioned things are of a nature to decay – strive on untiringly' (L 270). With this, the Buddha passed to final *Nibbāna*. Those *bhikkhus* 'who had not yet overcome their passions wept and tore their hair, raising their arms, throwing themselves down and twisting and turning.' But those *bhikkhus* 'who were free from craving endured mindfully and clearly aware, saying: "All compounded things are impermanent – what is the use of this?"' (L 272). Following instructions he had left behind, seven days after his death, the body of the Buddha was cremated on a stupa in the manner of a king.

4 Reflecting on the Buddha's life

We will probably never know to what extent our understanding of the Buddha's life is historically accurate. No biography was written during or near his lifetime. Most of the details just recounted are found in the *Sutta Piṭaka*, but some appear only later. Moreover, these texts are the product of an oral tradition lasting several generations before they were written down, and they include obvious fabrications. My favorite tells us that at birth Siddhattha walked north seven steps, surveyed the world, and declared: 'I am the highest in the world; I am the best in the world; I am the foremost in the world. This is my last birth; now there is no renewal of being for me' (M 983). And you think your child is precocious.

We do not even know in which centuries the Buddha lived. Everyone seems to agree that his life lasted eighty years, but there is considerable disagreement about the date of his birth. Dates ranging from the late seventh to the late fifth centuries BCE have been proposed. Most Western scholars think he was born somewhere around 500 BCE. If this were correct, then the Buddha would have lived most of his life in the fifth century BCE. This would mean he lived many centuries after Abraham, around the same time as Confucius, about a century before Socrates, five centuries before Jesus, and eleven centuries before Muhammad. For simplicity, it will be convenient to remember that the Buddha lived approximately 2,500 years before us.

For our purposes, these issues do not matter much. Whatever the precise details of the Buddha's life, there is broad agreement about its general outline, and it is this life – the life that has been passed down through generations of Buddhists – that is important. For it is this life that is a constitutive part of the teaching of the Buddha as we know it, and it is about this life that we are invited to reflect.

The life of the Buddha might be described in a variety of ways – as a story about someone who lost his mother at birth, who abandoned his wife and child, who rebelled against his father, who forsook worldly for spiritual power, and so on. From these perspectives, there are many questions stream-observers might ask about the Buddha. How did the death of his mother affect him? Were there other perhaps less noble motivations in leaving home? Did he yearn for his wife and child during his long search for enlightenment? Did he ever seek reconciliation with his father? From a personal standpoint, these questions appear especially interesting and important. But they are not the questions the traditional story primarily is meant to raise. This is not because our answers could only be speculative (which is mostly true), but because the story is intended to speak to us in universal terms that do not depend on the specifics of particular personal relationships.

What is important, we are supposed to believe, is that the Buddha had virtually all those things most people seek and suppose will bring them happiness – good looks, wealth, power, prestige, a fruitful marriage, and so on – and he realized that, in fact, these things were insufficient for real happiness. No matter how successful we are in pursuing these apparent goods, it remains the case that each of us will grow old, become ill, and die (unless we die sooner from accidents, natural disasters, or acts of violence). Old age, illness, and death are basic facts of life, and they appear to be inevitable sources of suffering for each of us and for those we love. The Buddha saw this as emblematic of a more general truth: that the goods most persons devote their energies to acquiring are impermanent and so are not by themselves genuine sources of happiness. Hence he looked elsewhere. This is one meaning of his 'great renunciation,' his departure from home and family to seek enlightenment.

After a long and arduous struggle, the Buddha believed he discovered that true happiness is achieved precisely where we might think it least likely to be found – in freedom from craving, clinging, and attachment to what we desire. The state of non-attachment is the primary fruit of enlightenment. It is the promised culmination of a difficult and complex journey, an intellectual, moral, and meditative undertaking – the Eightfold Path – that, successfully completed, releases two powerful forces within us: compassion for other living beings and joyful appreciation of each moment of our lives irrespective of what happens to us. These forces have a latent presence in each of us, the Buddha taught, but for most of us, because of our attachments, they manifest themselves only weakly and sporadically. Still, by attaining the state of non-attachment, compassion and joy are made available to each of us, and with these comes tranquillity, the mark of genuine happiness. This is one meaning of the Buddha's life of homelessness: real happiness is to be found not in the fulfillment of our conventional pursuits, but in a fundamental reorientation of our attitudes towards those pursuits – that is, in freedom from the craving and attachment typically associated with our desires for success.

No doubt stream-observers noticed that, in the end, the Buddha grew old, got sick, and died. He did not purport to have found a way to eliminate these sources of suffering in life as we know it. He did not announce the discovery of a fountain of youth. Rather, he proclaimed that full enlightenment would enable us to achieve happiness in this life despite aging, sickness, and death, and that it would release us from the cycle of rebirth into similar lives so as to attain another form of being free from all suffering. Though it is said to be beyond adequate description in our language, *Nibbāna* is a state we can achieve while living this life as well as one beyond life as we ordinarily know it.

This is the central message the life of the Buddha is meant to convey: true happiness may be achieved not by gaining what we seek to possess, but by cultivating a state of non-attachment with regard to our desires. This is the message we are meant to apply to our own lives. It is at once powerful and perplexing, powerful because it offers a road to well-being immune to vicissitudes we all recognize, and perplexing – for many, I suspect – for a variety of psychological and philosophical reasons. The Buddha encouraged his followers to understand his teaching for themselves. Stream-observers can do this only by confronting what perplexes them and reflecting on the extent to which this teaching has resources to resolve their concerns. It is thus appropriate to close this chapter by considering one question directly raised by the story of the Buddha's life.

5 The integration question

After achieving enlightenment, the Buddha wondered whether or not to teach what he had learned, and he decided to teach 'out of compassion for beings.'

But he did not wonder whether or not to return to Yaśodharā and Rāhula, the wife and child he had left behind six years earlier. He is not portrayed so much as having considered this option. He seemed just to assume he would not return. I do not mean to suggest that we should condemn the Buddha for forever abandoning his wife and child. We should be hesitant about applying our moral standards too quickly and simply to a situation so remote in time and place from our own. In the traditional story, the Buddha presumably is understood as fulfilling a higher calling, for the good of all persons, and it may be observed that his wife and child were taken care of properly (later Rāhula became a disciple).

Nonetheless, there is an issue for us in connection with this aspect of the Buddha's life. In his teaching, there is a sharp dichotomy between members of the *Sangha* and lay followers. There is also a reciprocal relationship between them: the *Sangha* offers spiritual guidance to the lay community, and that community in turn provides material support for the *Sangha*. But it is the sharpness of this dichotomy that is important here. Because of it, the Buddha could not both lead the *Sangha* and return to his wife and child. He did not consider such integration to be possible. Why not?

The answer, in brief, lies in the fact that the Buddha tended to regard life in the *Sangha* as the express train to enlightenment. He often said: 'Household life is crowded and dusty . . . it is not easy, while living in a home, to lead the holy-life utterly perfect and pure as a polished shell' (M 448). Seeking enlightenment in a household life is like taking the local train: you may make progress towards your destination, but it will take longer and it is likely there will be many stops – that is, rebirths – along the way; moreover, at one of these stops, you probably will have to change to the express if you are to reach your destination. On this view, enlightenment requires a radical transformation of the person, and for this radical means are necessary – means that typically are possible only in a literal withdrawal, sooner or later, from the ordinary pursuits of family, work, and the like.

No doubt life in the *Sangha* is an attractive and admirable ideal for some persons. But if this were all there was to say, it would be unlikely that the teaching of the Buddha could have much personal meaning for most people, especially stream-observers in the West. Even among persons impressed by this teaching, very few are prepared to enter the *Sangha*. If monastic life were the only way to truly follow the Eightfold Path, to genuinely seek enlightenment, this path is one nearly all would forego (at least in this lifetime!), regardless of its promise of real happiness. In fact, much of the teaching of the Buddha was directed primarily to members of the *Sangha*. In this respect, his lack of interest in returning home appears to carry great significance.

But perhaps there is more to say. The Buddha did teach that enlightenment was possible for all persons, he did welcome and encourage lay disciples, and he did say, shortly before his death, that 'more than fifty lay-followers have . . . been spontaneously reborn, and will gain *Nibbāna* from that state without returning to this world' (L 240). This indicates that significant progress towards enlightenment is possible in this lifetime for those who do not enter the *Sangha*. The Buddha presented the Eightfold Path as a middle way between the extreme asceticism of the *samaṇas* and the worldly lives of most people. Yet life in the *Sangha* is likely to look quite ascetic to most people. However, to revert to the earlier metaphor, perhaps the middle way is not an express track to which local tracks are mere means of eventual access, but a wide multilane highway in which some lanes are relatively withdrawn from the affairs of the world while others are more integrated with them via a network of connecting roads. Maybe, as indeed some Buddhists believe, it is possible to attain, or at least significantly progress towards, enlightenment not by literally withdrawing from the everyday world and forming an alternative community, but by changing that world from within.

The life of the Buddha does not provide us with a model of such integration. But if the teaching of the Buddha is to have value for all persons here and now, we need to see if the middle way is wide enough to make the search for enlightenment relevant to the kinds of lives most of us live. The Buddha did not emphasize this possibility, but that does not necessarily mean we should not emphasize it. We live in a very different world from that of the Buddha. The key to this possibility is the extent to which the everyday lives of work and family that most persons lead could be transformed into a meaningful search for enlightenment, and the degree to which such lives could be informed by the ideal of non-attachment.

SUGGESTED READING

Suggested reading in the *suttas* is usually indicated by title, work in the *Sutta Piṭaka*, and number of the *sutta* (#). On the life of the Buddha, see the *Ariyapariyesanā Sutta* ('The Noble Search'), M #26. See also the *Bhayabherava Sutta* ('Fear and Dread'), M #4, the *Mahāsaccaka Sutta* ('The Greater Discourse to Saccaka'), M #36, and the *Mahāpadāna Sutta* ('The Great Discourse on the Lineage'), L #14. The end of the Buddha's life is depicted in the *Mahāparinibbāna Sutta* ('The Great Passing: The Buddha's Last Days'), L #16.

For brief accounts of the Buddha's life and teaching, see Armstrong (2001) and especially Carrithers (1983). More detailed accounts can be found in Nakamura (2000) and Ñāṇamoli (2001). For background on the Indian philosophical traditions from which the Buddha emerged, see Hamilton (2001) and R. King (1999).

3

THE TEACHING IN BRIEF

There is every indication that the Buddha had a powerful and magnetic personality. In our terms, he must have had tremendous charisma that greatly moved many of those he encountered. Surely he was also a skilled leader with impressive organizational abilities that were employed in bringing together and maintaining the large *Sangha* over several decades. Much of the influence of the Buddha during and immediately after his lifetime may be attributed in part to these characteristics. But the teaching of the Buddha has lasted for two and a half millennia. Its capacity to affect people's lives cannot be attributed solely to the fact that the Buddha was a charismatic and skilled leader. For a very long time, no Buddhists have had direct personal experience of the Buddha himself. The endurance of Buddhism and its power to guide people's lives must substantially result from the nature of his message. Indeed, the Buddha emphasized the relative importance of his teaching in comparison with himself. It is this teaching that is our primary concern.

For forty-five years the Buddha articulated a complex set of closely inter-related practices and doctrines. It is difficult to understand any one aspect of his teaching without comprehending its connections to the whole. Hence, before undertaking a more detailed examination of the different facets of the message of the Buddha, it will be helpful to have in front of us a brief description of his overall outlook. The purpose of the present chapter is to provide this. The heart of his teaching is contained in the Four Noble Truths, and these will provide much of the structure of both this chapter and the second half of the book (see parts 3 and 4). Before describing these purported truths, we need to attend to some preliminaries.

1 A morally ordered universe

The Buddha's teaching was a radical challenge to the beliefs and practices of people in his social milieu – and to ours as well. This is not to deny that he was influenced by his environment. Human thought necessarily develops out of an historical context, and the thinking of the Buddha is no exception. Nonetheless, from the materials he found in his culture, he developed a unique and extraordinary message that deeply contested the intellectual, moral, and religious outlook of people then living in the Ganges river basin.

One important respect in which this was true concerned the fourfold division of persons into brahmins, rulers and warriors, farmers and traders, and servants. This rigid, hierarchical system of classification held that virtually everything important about a person – most significantly, a person's obligations and opportunities – was determined by birth. For example, the brahmins were supposed to have been born with a capacity for wisdom and virtue that no members of another class could achieve no matter what they did. The Buddha rejected this system. He declared that 'anyone from the four castes' could 'become emancipated through super-knowledge' (L 408). An important aspect of the Buddha's teaching is its *universalism*: it is put forth as an outlook that is true of, and has relevance for, all human beings – including us. The understanding, compassion, joy, and tranquillity that come with enlightenment are said to be available to anyone who undertakes the Eightfold Path (complications in this universalism, with respect to women and lay followers, will be considered in chapter 14).

The Buddha believed every human being could achieve enlightenment because he thought human nature and the universe have certain objective features we can know. There is no motif more central to the *Sutta Piṭaka* than that the Buddha acquired knowledge of reality that resulted in liberation – and that any of us, with great effort, can do the same thing. It is true that the Buddha's teaching stresses the impermanence of things, but this goes hand-in-hand with an emphasis on the law-governed nature of the universe. Though the world is in constant change, it is very far from being in a state of chaos. Knowledge of the order of the universe is the key to enlightenment.

The world depicted by modern science is often said to be morally neutral or meaningless. By contrast, the universe portrayed by the Buddha is morally ordered. This need not mean the Buddha's teaching is incompatible with modern science, but it does mean the Buddha would regard the world of modern science as incomplete insofar as this world was taken to be morally neutral. For the Buddha, the moral order of the universe is contained first and foremost in the doctrines of *kamma* and rebirth. These doctrines are not original with him. In some form, they were held by many others in his culture. On the other hand, there were those, such as the materialists and skeptics, who did not accept them. Hence, it was not culturally inevitable that the Buddha maintained these doctrines, and he thought he had good reason to do so. They are essential to the three kinds of knowledge he is said to have attained on the night of his enlightenment.

The doctrine of *kamma* is a simple idea: each action is good or bad, primarily on account of the moral quality of the intention it expresses; and, sooner or later, a good action brings well-being to the person who performs it, while a bad action brings the opposite. Put in these terms, the idea is one form of a commonly accepted belief in cosmic justice, and as such it is compatible with many religious traditions. What distinguishes the Buddha's doctrine of *kamma* from classical monotheistic traditions, however, is that the causal relationship between good or bad actions and happy or unhappy results is not understood as the effect of a just god dispensing rewards and punishments. For the Buddha, this causal relationship is an impersonal feature of the natural world: even as a plant flourishes when it receives appropriate amounts of light, moisture and nutrition, so our lives flourish when we perform morally good actions. Our present state of well-being is always a causal result of our past actions. However, past actions do not determine future actions: we are always free to choose well or poorly in our current situation. Past actions determine how happy we are, and to some extent our character, but they do not directly determine the morality of what we do.

The Buddha also believed that each person lives a series of lives that extends indefinitely into the past and could extend indefinitely into the future. These lives could take the form not only of human lives, but also of animals at the lower end of the spectrum and of deities at the other end. The causality of *kamma* operates through the entire series. Hence, my happiness in this life is the result of my past actions in this and all previous lives; and my actions in this life will affect my future happiness in this and all lives to come. The doctrines of *kamma* and rebirth are closely connected, and they are the framework of much popular Buddhist belief in the world today. But the Buddha also thought it was possible to escape the series of rebirths: achieving full enlightenment in any one life permanently brings the series to an end. This is *Nibbāna* – the ultimate state of happiness. The central instruction of the Buddha focused on attaining *Nibbāna* and thereby escaping rebirth.

2 Suffering and its cause

The Buddha's teaching is primarily practical rather than theoretical in its orientation. The aim is to show persons how to overcome suffering and attain *Nibbāna*. The purpose is not to persuade them to accept certain doctrines as such. This practical approach is famously illustrated by a story the Buddha told Mālunkyāputta, a skeptically minded disciple, when he persisted in demanding answers to a series of philosophical questions the Buddha refused to answer. The Buddha described someone wounded by a poison arrow who would not allow a surgeon to treat him until he knew the name and class of the man who wounded him, his height and complexion, where he lived, and so on. The Buddha pointed out that the man would die before finding out the answers to all his questions, and that he did not need these answers in order for the surgeon to operate successfully to save his life. For the practical purpose of healing his wound, there was no reason to answer the questions. The point of the story is that the Buddha had not declared answers to Mālunkyāputta's questions because there was no practical need to do so. Answering these questions would have been 'unbeneficial' and would not have led 'to peace, to direct knowledge, to enlightenment, to *Nibbāna.*' The teaching of the Buddha does not consist of answers to any and all philosophical questions that might occur to us. Rather, it consists of answers that are needed for a practical purpose. The Buddha then gave the moral of the story: 'And what have I declared? "This is suffering" – I have declared. "This is the origin of suffering" – I have declared. "This is the cessation of suffering" – I have declared. "This is the way leading to the cessation of suffering" – I have declared.' The Buddha put forward these answers – the Four Noble Truths – because they were 'beneficial,' because they did lead 'to peace, to direct knowledge, to enlightenment, to *Nibbāna*' (M 536). The practical orientation of the Buddha's teaching does not mean it includes no theoretical doctrines, nor that it is unconcerned with the truth of these doctrines. It plainly contains such doctrines, and they are put forward as true and known to be true. Nonetheless, the Buddha would not have taught these doctrines unless they served the practical aim of overcoming human suffering.

The Four Noble Truths are the centerpiece of the Buddha's message. An important commentary in the *Theravāda* tradition, Buddhaghosa's *The Path of Purification*, makes explicit what is clearly implicit in the presentation of these truths: 'The truth of suffering is like a disease, the truth of origin is like the cause of the disease, the truth of cessation is like the cure of the disease, and the truth of the path is like the medicine' (Buddhaghosa 1999: 520; cf. M 615–16 and 867). The Buddha's central teaching has the form of a medical diagnosis and plan of treatment: it describes a disease and its symptoms, identifies its cause, outlines what freedom from this disease would be like, and prescribes the course of treatment required to attain this healthy state. The story of the wounded man should be read in this light. We are to think of the Buddha as a physician who cures not strictly physical ailments, but broadly psychological ones, who shows 'wounded' human beings the way to the highest form of happiness.

The Buddha first described the Four Noble Truths in the *sutta* he addressed to the five *samaṇas* he had earlier abandoned, 'Setting in Motion the Wheel of *Dhamma*.' This initial speech may serve as an introduction for us as well. Here is the description of the disease and its symptoms:

> *First Noble Truth.* Now this, *bhikkhus*, is the noble truth of suffering: birth is suffering, aging is suffering, illness is suffering, death is suffering; union with what is displeasing is suffering; separation from what is pleasing is suffering; not to get what one wants is suffering; in brief, the five aggregates subject to clinging are suffering.
>
> (C II 1844)

The key term here and throughout is *dukkha*. It is ordinarily translated into English as 'suffering'. This is correct in part, but it is misleading. The description above features aging, sickness and death (the observation of which first led Siddhattha to seek enlightenment) and we naturally associate these with suffering. But for the other items listed – union with what is displeasing, separation from what is pleasing, and not getting what one wants – 'suffering' sometimes is the right term and sometimes seems too strong. The Buddha clearly has in mind a broad range of ways in which our lives may be unsatisfactory. For the time being, we may summarize the first Noble Truth as the claim that human lives regularly lack contentment, fulfillment, perfection, security, and the like.

Stream-observers might regard this as a rather pessimistic diagnosis. They might be inclined to think that many (if not most) human lives are not so bad, that the positive aspects of life outweigh the negative ones. The Buddha would not have been surprised by this response and did not deny that many persons would question his analysis. His point may be illustrated by an analogy: if an alcoholic is told his life is in bad shape, he will probably point out, perhaps correctly, that he has lots of good times; nonetheless, he has a serious problem and could have a far better life without alcohol and the 'good times' it brings. Similarly, the Buddha thought, most of us can point to some positive features of life: he is not saying we are miserable all the time. However, there is something not fully satisfactory about the lives most of us live. We seek enduring happiness by trying to attach ourselves to things that are in constant change. This sometimes brings temporary and partial fulfillment, but long-term result is frustration and anxiety. Because of the impermanence of the world, we do not achieve the real happiness we implicitly seek. The Buddha thought we could all sense the truth of this with a moderate amount of honest reflection on the realities of human life, but he also believed that full understanding of the first Truth was difficult to achieve and would require significant progress towards enlightenment.

The next Noble Truth is a claim about the cause of discontentment in human life. Here is how the Buddha explained it:

> *Second Noble Truth*. Now this, *bhikkhus*, is the noble truth of the origin of suffering: it is this craving which leads to renewed existence, accompanied by delight and lust, seeking delight here and there; that is, craving for sensual pleasures, craving for existence, craving for extermination.

> (C II 1844)

There is much in this passage that is likely to perplex us. For now, what is important is the contention that suffering and other forms of distress have a cause associated with various kinds of desire – craving, clinging, attachment, impulse, greed, lust, thirst, and so on are terms frequently employed in this connection. The Second Noble Truth states that the source of our discontentment is found not simply in our desires, but in the connection we forge between desires and happiness. In its simplest form, it asserts that

32

we are typically unhappy because we do not get what we desire to have, or we do get what we desire not to have. We do not get the promotion we wanted, and we do get the disease we feared. Outcomes such as these are common in human life. These outcomes, and the anxieties their prospect produces, are causes of our discontentment.

So far the diagnosis of the Buddha may appear fairly straightforward: suffering or discontentment is the disease, and its cause has to do with frustrated desires in an ever-changing world. However, in order to better understand this diagnosis, as well as the treatment prescribed for it, we need to make what initially will appear to be a digression but will actually take us to the philosophical heart of the Four Noble Truths.

3 The not-self doctrine

The most distinctive and yet counter-intuitive feature of the Buddha's message is the doctrine that there is no self (*anattā*). According to the Buddha, every doctrine of self results in suffering, and we must abandon all these doctrines if we are to attain *Nibbāna*: 'It cannot happen that a person possessing right view could treat anything as self – there is no such possibility' (M 928). In declaring this, he launched his greatest challenge to the beliefs of his contemporaries and, of course, to ours as well. As we will see in chapter 6, there is controversy over the proper interpretation of the Buddha in this regard, but there is no question that a not-self doctrine was central to his teaching.

Our first reaction to this doctrine is likely to be that it is obvious we are selves. Once again, the Buddha anticipated this reaction, and an analogy from modern science can illustrate his point. Everything in our ordinary experience tells us that the sun rises each morning in the east, travels across the sky through the day, and sets in the evening in the west. This is as obvious as can be. It is a matter of common sense. But it is also completely false. The sun only appears to be going through these motions because, unbeknown to ordinary experience, the earth revolves. Likewise, the Buddha maintained, it seems obvious that we are selves, but this belief is an illusion.

In denying that there is a self, the Buddha did not mean that what we take to be a self is nothing at all. Rather, his claim is that what reality there is does not correspond to what we mean by a self. In calling this reality a self, we misdescribe it (just as we misdescribe what is real by saying the sun rises). What, then, do we mean by a self? This is not an easy question to answer, but in the West a common philosophical representation of the 'ordinary' understanding of the self is as follows. A self is a being that is ontologically distinct from other beings and has as its identity some essential properties that do not change. These properties include the regularly exercised capacities to experience, remember, imagine, feel, desire, think, decide, act, and so on. The self is in control of the exercise of some of these capacities. Finally, a self is capable of being aware of itself as a self. (See chapter 6 for elaboration.)

The Buddha denies that anything in reality matches this description. In particular, there are no selves that are ontologically distinct from one another and persist through time in some respects unchanged.

Why did the Buddha think this? The full answer is complex, but we can gain an initial understanding by considering one crucial argument for the not-self teaching. The Buddha believed that, if we observe carefully, we will realize that what we call the self is really nothing other than the following five aggregates (*khandhas*): material form (especially our sense organs), feelings or sensations (as pleasant, unpleasant, or neutral), perceptions or cognitions (involving judgments about the world), mental formations (desires, wishes, and volitions), and consciousness (awareness). If we inspect each of these carefully, the Buddha maintained, we will see that none of them is permanent: each of them is in a constant process of change. But if what we call the self is nothing more than these aggregates, and these aggregates constantly change, then what we call the self cannot be a being that persists through time in some respects unchanged. There is no self in that sense.

We will assess this argument (and others) in more detail in chapter 7. For now, let us note two things the argument reveals about the teaching of the Buddha. First, he was, in a wide sense of the term, a kind of *empiricist*: he thought we come to understand reality on the basis of experience broadly construed to include not only ordinary sense-experience but also the experience of meditation. Second, he believed that experience shows that everything in the universe is ontologically interconnected and in a state of change (except *Nibbāna*). There are no beings at all that are ontologically distinct from one another and persist through time unchanged. The world is more accurately thought of as a complex of mutually interdependent processes of change. The not-self doctrine is part of this more general position. An analogical depiction of this doctrine may be helpful. There is a reality that corresponds to what we call a sandbar, but that reality is not a distinct, unchanging thing. Rather, it is an aspect of a mixture of interdependent and ever-changing processes. So too is what we call the self.

There is much in the Buddha's not-self teaching that should concern and perplex stream-observers. First, we take our selves to be essential to who we are, perhaps to be the most important and valuable feature of who we are. For this reason, the not-self teaching appears threatening. The Buddha will have to show us he is correct in claiming, to the contrary, that a deep understanding of this teaching is liberating and crucial to achieving the highest form of happiness. Second, despite the analogy of the sun, it seems obvious that we are selves. The Buddha will need to convince us otherwise. In particular, he will need to demonstrate that the not-self teaching is the best explanation of our experience. Finally, as stream-observers no doubt noticed, the doctrines of *kamma* and rebirth seem to presuppose that there are selves: if there are no selves, then what is reborn? The Buddha will have to show how the not-self teaching can be reconciled with these other doctrines. These issues will occupy much of our attention in Part 2.

Before returning to the Four Noble Truths, it is important to emphasize a key idea raised by the not-self teaching. The Buddha maintained that everything in the world we experience is in a process of change, but this is not to say that everything is random or chaotic. For the Buddha, there are no beings or entities that exist without change. However, there are permanent causal laws that dictate the processes of change. The stability of the universe consists not of the stability of things, but of the stability of these processes. The Buddha referred to this general phenomenon as dependent origination (*paṭicca samuppāda*). In a brief expression of this doctrine, he said: 'When this exists, that comes to be; with the arising of this, that arises. When this does not exist, that does not come to be; with the cessation of this, that ceases' (M 655). Sāriputta, the Buddha's disciple known for his wisdom, declared that 'one who sees dependent origination sees the *Dhamma*; one who sees the *Dhamma* sees dependent origination' (M 283). The idea of *kamma* is an important aspect of dependent origination. Another more comprehensive account is the twelve-fold formula of conditioning links in which suffering is shown to have craving as an intermediate cause (as seen on pages 32–3) and ignorance as a more fundamental cause. We will see that the belief that we are selves is the central case of this ignorance.

The causal nature of the universe is a fundamental feature of the Buddha's teaching. It is that which makes possible the diagnosis and treatment described in the Four Noble Truths. Suffering is the disease, and the cause of this disease includes craving and ignorance. Once we understand this, we can modify the causes and thereby overcome suffering. To see how this works, we need to examine the third and fourth Truths.

4 *Nibbāna*

Many people would agree that suffering or unhappiness is rooted in desire, that it consists of not getting what we want and getting what we do not want. It may seem natural to infer from this that happiness consists of the opposite, in getting what we want and not getting what we do not want. Happiness, in this view, is acquisition of all that we try to gain and security from all that we seek to avoid.

The Buddha taught that this understanding of happiness is a mistake. We can never achieve true and complete happiness in these terms, and there is another, far better form of happiness that we can achieve. To revert to our earlier analogy, someone who holds the first view is like an alcoholic who reasons that, since he is unhappy when he is not drinking, he will be truly happy only if he is always drinking. However, what will really make him happy is to find a way to stop the obsessive craving to drink, to stop looking for happiness in drinking. The Buddha's striking assertion is a similar but broader claim. Obtaining what we are hoping to gain and safety from what we are trying to avoid will not bring us real happiness. This can only be achieved by a radical transformation of our desires and aversions – and especially of our attitudes towards them. We have arrived at the next Truth:

> *Third Noble Truth*. Now this, *bhikkhus*, is the noble truth of the cessa-
> tion of suffering: it is the remainderless fading away and cessation
> of that same craving, the giving up and relinquishing of it, freedom
> from it, nonreliance on it.
>
> (C II 1844)

True happiness in life, the opposite of suffering, is brought about by reaching a state in which, on my reading, we eliminate many of our desires and stop clinging or attaching ourselves to all of them. The Buddha referred to this state with the term '*Nibbāna*'.

Why not seek happiness in the fulfillment of our desires, in striving to get what we want and to avoid what we do not want? The Buddha did not deny that a measure of happiness may be obtained from such striving, but he believed it would always be unsatisfactory in some respects. In part, the reason is that a life seeking such happiness will always be precarious because of the impermanent nature of the universe. What would fulfill our typical desires – for status, power, wealth, friends, and so on – is always subject to change. Even if we were fortunate and got all that we wanted (and can anyone truthfully say this?), old age, disease, and death would always stand ready to take these things from us. No matter what we have, we can never be secure that we will continue to possess it, and so we will never be truly happy. Another reason is that fulfilling our desires does not always make us happy. 'In this world there are only two tragedies,' said Oscar Wilde. 'One is not getting what one wants, and the other is getting it' (*Lady Windermere's Fan*: act 3).

For the Buddha, a better strategy than seeking to fulfill desires would be to live a morally good life: on account of *kamma*, this would eventually produce greater happiness. However, the Buddha thought such happiness still would be temporary and imperfect, and he thought it would always be a struggle to live a truly good life as long as the belief that one is a self persisted. At best, this strategy might bring improvement, but ultimately it would only perpetuate the cycle of rebirth and its inherent suffering.

Considerations of this sort might be taken to show that these are inadequate roads to real happiness. But why suppose there is another form of happiness – *Nibbāna* – that is not only possible to achieve but better? The answer is the key to the Buddha's teaching and it involves the not-self doctrine. Sometimes it sounds as if *Nibbāna* involves the complete cessation of all desires (the word '*nibbāna*' literally means extinction or cessation), but this is not generally true of a person who has achieved enlightenment. This person does eliminate many desires, specifically all those that presuppose the belief that oneself has primary importance. This belief gives rise to an orientation to life in terms of what is mine and hence is more valuable, in contrast to what is not mine and hence is less valuable. The resulting thoughts and desires are the source of hatred, intolerance, anger, pride, greed, thirst for power and fame, and so on. These states bring unhappiness not only to others, but to those who possess them: a person full of hate does not have a happy life. On the other hand, full realization that I am not a distinct self would undermine the tendency to think myself has primary importance. The Buddha thought this would put an end to all desires associated with hatred and the like, and in fact would release my capacity for universal compassion. The result would be increased happiness for all concerned.

However, enlightenment does not mean the elimination of all desires – at least, not in a sustained way during this life (during meditative experiences of *Nibbāna*, and with the attainment of *Nibbāna* beyond death, desires are absent). For one thing, compassion clearly involves desire in some sense – namely, the desire that others fare well. Moreover, no human life is possible that does not involve some elementary desires such as for food or sleep. Surely the Buddha did not mean to deny this (in fact, the extreme asceticism he rejected would seem to have been an endeavor to achieve freedom from any desires in this life). But the Buddha did think the realization that we are not selves would bring about a fundamental change in our attitude towards those desires that would remain. This realization would eliminate clinging or attachment to the satisfaction of these desires, and it would thereby cut through the bond we ordinarily forge between this satisfaction and happiness.

On my interpretation, there are at least two aspects of this difficult idea. First, in the absence of the belief that I am a self distinct from other selves, I would no longer think of some desires as mine, as things with which I deeply identify and so need to satisfy to achieve my well-being. As a result, there would no longer be an unhealthy drive or obsession to fulfill these desires. Second, in the absence of the belief that I am a self with identity, a substance persisting through time in some respects unchanged, I would no longer be preoccupied with regrets about the past unfulfillment of my desires and worries about the prospects for their future fulfillment. Liberated in these ways from attachment to desires as mine, from pinning my happiness on their satisfaction, there would be freedom to focus attention on the present moment at all times. The implicit message of the Buddha is that, in this state of awareness, no matter what happened, there would always be something of value, something good, in what was experienced. Not clinging to the fulfillment of our desires would release a capacity for joy at each moment in our lives.

For a person who has attained *Nibbāna*, life is a process of living selflessly in which, unencumbered by the false belief that we are selves, we are enabled to live compassionate and joyful lives. To this it may be added that our lives would also possess great peace and tranquility. They would be lives of perfect contentment and true happiness.

In addition to *Nibbāna* in this life, the Buddha described *Nibbāna* as a state beyond this life and the entire cycle of rebirth (henceforth, when it is important to distinguish these, I will refer to them respectively as *Nibbāna*-in-life and *Nibbāna*-after-death). Though he thought it could not be described adequately in our concepts, we may say by way of a preliminary that he believed *Nibbāna*-after-death is neither a state in which one exists as a self nor a state of absolute nothingness. It is a form of selfless existence in which there is realization of some union with *Nibbāna* understood as ultimate reality beyond change and conditioning. This is a state in which suffering, and all that causes suffering, is entirely absent. *Nibbāna* both in this life and beyond is a state of perfect well-being and tranquility, one that all conscious beings have reason to seek.

5 Wisdom, virtue, and concentration

Even if we were convinced that *Nibbāna* would be the ultimate happiness, we might well wonder whether it would be possible for us to attain it. The Buddha's practical orientation made this a primary concern. He believed it is possible to achieve *Nibbāna*, but very difficult to do so. We have come to the final Truth:

> *Fourth Noble Truth*. Now this, *bhikkhus*, is the noble truth of the way leading to the cessation of suffering. It is this Noble Eightfold Path; that is right view, right intention, right speech, right action, right livelihood, right effort, right mindfulness, right concentration.
>
> (C II 1844)

In the first discourse, addressed to the ascetic *samaṇas*, the Buddha described the Eightfold Path as a 'middle way' that avoids two extremes: 'The pursuit of sensual happiness in sensual pleasures, which is low, vulgar, the way of worldlings, ignoble, unbeneficial; and the pursuit of self-mortification, which is painful, ignoble, unbeneficial.' Though the Buddha portrayed the Eightfold Path as a middle way between seeking sensual happiness and undergoing self-mortification, it clearly involves a rigorous regime that is supposed to radically transform us. This path, the Buddha said, 'leads to peace, to direct knowledge, to enlightenment, to *Nibbāna*' (C II 1844).

The eight steps of the path are to be pursued not in sequence, but all together, with each step reinforcing the others (though the last two, right mindfulness and right concentration, are the culmination). The Buddha divided these steps into three parts: *wisdom* pertains primarily to intellectual development and conviction (right view and intention), *virtue* concerns moral or ethical training (right speech, action, and livelihood), and *concentration* – often rendered as 'meditation' – involves a set of mental disciplines (right effort, mindfulness, and concentration).

The first part, wisdom, instructs us to acquire a thorough comprehension of the Four Noble Truths and all that they involve. However, it does not require us to answer philosophical questions unrelated to attaining *Nibbāna*. In fact, this is discouraged, as we saw in the story of the man wounded by the arrow (pages 30–1). Mālunkyāputta wanted the Buddha to tell him whether the world is eternal, whether it is finite, whether body and soul are one, and whether the *Tathāgata* exists after death. The Buddha refused to answer these questions on the ground that attempts to do so would only hinder efforts to understand the Four Noble Truths. (It might seem that the existence of the *Tathāgata* after death is a relevant question; we will see in chapter 13 why the Buddha thought it was not).

Comprehension of the Four Noble Truths requires more than intellectual cultivation. We also need a fundamental commitment to understanding them, and our emotions and desires must be disciplined so that they do not distract us or lead us astray. Hence, the Buddha said we must renounce sensual desire, ill will, and cruelty. In this respect, he thought thinking and feeling, the mind and the heart, were closely connected.

The second part of the path concerns morality or ethics. Enlightenment requires moral as well as intellectual and emotional preparation. The Buddha spoke of morality at length, and he expected much more of members of the *Sangha* than of lay followers. But there are basic precepts that apply to all persons. These fall into three categories. Right speech requires that we speak in ways that are truthful, friendly, useful, and productive of harmony. Right action dictates that we do not kill any living beings (human or animal), nor steal, nor have illegitimate sexual relations. Right livelihood says we should not earn our living by harming others (for example, by selling arms). Violation of these precepts, the Buddha thought, would only reinforce self-centered desires and would hinder attainment of *Nibbāna*.

The third part of the path – concentration, or meditation – is the least familiar to persons in the West, but the most significant for the Buddha. Later we will need to consider the epistemological importance he assigned to meditation in understanding the Four Noble Truths. Though the Buddha taught many forms of meditation, the general aim of these mental disciplines is twofold: first, to purify the mind of disturbances so as to bring about a peaceful, concentrated, attentive and mindful mental state; and second, to know reality as it actually is by observing that all things in our ordinary experience are impermanent, involve suffering, and are empty of any self. The ultimate aim is not to escape from the world nor to acquire special powers: it is to attain *Nibbāna*.

SUGGESTED READING

The Four Noble Truths are explained in the *Saccavibhanga Sutta* ('The Exposition of the Truths'), M #141. The Buddha's first discourse is the

Dhammacakkappavattana Sutta ('Setting in Motion the Wheel of the *Dhamma*'), C II 1843–7. For the story of the wounded man and the unanswered questions, see the *Cūḷamālunkya Sutta* ('The Shorter Discourse to Mālunkyāputta'), M #63.

The Buddha's response to Mālunkyāputta's questions is interpreted in W.L. King (1983) and Organ (1954). For a scholarly discussion of the Four Noble Truths, see C.S. Anderson (1999). A translation and sympathetic commentary on the first *sutta* can be found in Dhamma (1997). For introductions to the teaching of the Buddha, see Gruzalski (2000), Jayatilleke (1974), Keown (1996), and Rahula (1974).

4

PRACTICAL DIMENSIONS
OF THE TEACHING

The Buddha's teaching appears sufficiently unusual to most stream-observers in the West that initially they find it natural to wonder how to characterize it. This query often takes the form of asking whether the Buddha taught a religion, a philosophy, or something else. The concepts of religion and philosophy are familiar to us, and most believe the Buddha's teaching must be one of these, if not both.[1] It is not a mistake to think in these terms: a reasonable, and to some extent inevitable, way to begin comprehending the beliefs and practices of other cultures is to relate them to our own ways of thinking. But there are also dangers in this approach. The most obvious is that the Buddha himself did not employ the concepts of religion and philosophy. These are our concepts, not his. Hence, to interpret his teaching as one or the other of these is to put it in a framework he would not have recognized. This need not mean the interpretation is simply wrong, but it may well be misleading or of limited value. We should always be on guard against misunderstandings that arise from the absence of common concepts.

Another danger is that philosophy and religion are contested concepts: there are significant disagreements about what they mean. It might be thought that we should first establish the correct definition of these terms, a set of conditions individually necessary and jointly sufficient for the proper application of each, and then we could determine whether the teaching of the Buddha meets the respective conditions. But this is not a helpful procedure. Any brief defense of such definitions would be inadequate given the complexities of the issues involved. As a result, any conclusions about the Buddha's teaching by reference to these definitions would appear arbitrary.

Nonetheless, if we proceed carefully, asking whether the Buddha taught a philosophy or a religion can be a valuable way to begin understanding his teaching. I will argue that in some respects, though not all, the Buddha taught what may reasonably be called a philosophy, and likewise for religion. This may seem an unremarkable contention, but both claims have been denied. In any case, the value of this approach comes from determining which respects are which, not being able to say at the end of the day that the Buddha's teaching is or is not a philosophy or a religion *tout court*.

This teaching is primarily practical in its purpose: the Buddha sought to show us how to overcome suffering by attaining *Nibbāna*. In this chapter, we will examine several aspects of the Buddha's message that pertain to its practical dimensions. But there is also a theory implicit in the practice, and in the next chapter we will consider the nature of the teaching with regard to its theoretical aspects. For the Buddha, theory and practice are closely related – this is not a distinction he stressed – and these chapters should be read as a complementary pair. Also, remember that our focus is the teaching of the Buddha and not the traditions of Buddhism that have developed since.

Since a central theme of this book is that what the Buddha taught may be fruitfully understood and evaluated as a philosophy, we need to see the senses in which this is true as well as the limitations of this claim. Nowadays, philosophy is primarily thought of as an academic discipline that involves university departments, professional societies, journals, conferences, and the like. Philosophy so understood looks rather remote from the Buddha's concerns: he did not intend to inaugurate a field of academic study, and contemporary philosophers typically do not regard their primary aim as anything so practical as overcoming suffering. But this is only one form philosophy can take, and there are other forms in the traditions of the West far more congenial to the Buddha's concerns.

The etymological meaning of 'philosophy' is love of wisdom. Socrates declared that the unexamined life is not worth living, that a good life requires the search for wisdom that philosophy undertakes. At the outset, Western philosophy was understood less as an academic discipline and more as an inquiry with the practical aim of living well. My suggestion is that one particular Western philosophical tradition directly inspired by Socrates – Hellenistic philosophy – bears some striking resemblances to the teaching of the Buddha. In this chapter, I will begin to explore this comparison. This will indicate some important respects in which the Buddha's teaching may be considered a philosophy and may engage the attention of students of Western philosophy. But I will also point out several aspects of the Buddha's practice that are very different from what the Hellenistic philosophers advocated and are much closer to features we usually think of as characteristic of religion.

1 The Buddha's teaching and Hellenistic philosophy

Hellenistic philosophy refers to the Epicurean, Stoic, and Skeptical schools that flourished mainly in Athens and later in Rome from the fourth century BCE to the second century CE. These schools developed in the wake not only of Socrates, but also of Plato and Aristotle. A brief mention of some major figures is sufficient to indicate the scope of Hellenistic thought: Epicureanism was founded by Epicurus and later developed by Lucretius; Stoicism was begun by Zeno of Citium, developed by Chrysippus, and later carried on by Seneca, Epictetus, and Marcus Aurelius; and Skepticism was established by Pyrrho of Elis, developed by Arcesilaus and Carneades, and most fully recorded by Sextus Empiricus. In many cases, we possess only fragments of the writings of these philosophers, and our knowledge of them often depends on others such as Cicero, Plutarch, and Diogenes Laertius. There are many important differences between the three schools as well as among figures within the schools. But for the purpose of this brief discussion, I will mainly emphasize common or typical themes in the whole of Hellenistic philosophy, especially moral philosophy, without regard for these differences (mostly these pertain to the Epicureans and Stoics; the Skeptics often elude otherwise sound generalizations about the Hellenistic thinkers, though the Skeptics are not without interest in the comparison with the Buddha).

There is no reason to think there is any influence one way or the other between the Buddha and the Hellenistic philosophers. (However, Pyrrho traveled with Alexander the Great to Western India and may have been influenced by skeptical *samanas* he encountered there.) My contention is only that there are interesting similarities between them. Throughout most of the history of Western philosophy, from late antiquity through medieval times, the renaissance and the modern period, many of the Hellenistic philosophers were well-known and often highly regarded (sometimes more so than Plato and Aristotle). In the twentieth century, the tendency was to believe that these philosophers were less important, but this century was an historical exception, and in recent decades there has been a substantial renewal of interest in them. To the extent that the teaching of the Buddha resembles Hellenistic philosophy we have prima facie reason to regard this teaching as a kind of philosophy familiar in the West.

The most important feature of Hellenistic philosophy is its orientation to practice. For these philosophers, philosophy was no mere academic study. Its aim was supremely practical: to enable human beings to achieve *eudaimonia*, commonly translated as happiness, flourishing, or well-being. Moreover, just as the Buddha's Four Noble Truths have the form of a medical diagnosis and course of treatment, all three Hellenistic schools explicitly employed a medical analogy to describe their understanding of philosophy. For them, even as medicine treats diseases of the body so philosophy treats diseases of the soul. Epicurus gives a representative expression of this idea:

> Empty are the words of that philosopher who offers therapy for no human suffering. For just as there is no use in medical expertise if it does not give therapy for bodily diseases, so too there is no use in philosophy if it does not expel the suffering of the soul.
>
> (Long and Sedley 1987: 155)

The Hellenistic philosophers began by offering a description of the ills of the soul. They said our lives are typically troubled, anxious, distressed, and fearful. In short, they are filled with various forms of actual or potential suffering. For example, we are constantly anxious to find and keep wealth, status, power and love. Throughout, the fear of death looms over us. As a result, we never really achieve the happiness we seek. Second, these philosophers gave an account of the cause of human suffering: it is rooted in our feelings and desires, and these in turn are dependent on false or unjustified beliefs. We are greedy for money because we think it will bring us happiness, but it does not. We think anger is a proper remedy for aggression, but it brings no relief. We think death is something to fear, but properly understood it is not. Third, the Hellenistic philosophers envisioned an alternative to our suffering, a state of health in which we are free from the diseases of the soul. This state, they variously said, would be one of happiness, joy, compassion, virtue, freedom from the contingencies of life, and, above all, tranquility. Finally, they prescribed a course of treatment that will bring us from the troubled state we find ourselves in to this state of ultimate well-being. Philosophy, by employing a variety of techniques of reason, moral discipline, imagination, and narration can free us from the false beliefs at the root of our suffering and thereby effect a radical transformation in our desires and feelings that will result in genuine happiness. As Martha Nussbaum has said, these philosophers practiced a 'therapy of desire' (Nussbaum 1994).

// We see here a close analogue to the Four Noble Truths of the Buddha: a description of human suffering, an account of its cause in terms of desire and ignorance, a portrayal of an alternative state of joy, compassion, and tranquility, and an assertion that there is a path available by which we may transform ourselves so as to achieve this state of health. Like the Buddha, the Hellenistic philosophers relied on an understanding of human nature to propose a radical alternative to beliefs and practices common in their societies. They argued that the ordinary pursuits most people think will lead to happiness in fact fail to do so. And they maintained that real happiness is achieved only by means of a fundamental reorientation of our typical ways of life. //

For the Epicureans, happiness is the absence of physical pain and mental anxiety. It is achieved by seeking to fulfill our natural and necessary desires, desires that are rather easily satisfied (for example, to relieve hunger), and by abandoning the large array of unnatural and unnecessary desires foisted on us by the false beliefs of society, desires the pursuit of which results only in frustration (for example, to gain wealth or status). The Stoics claimed that happiness consists only of being virtuous, the one thing each of us, as a rational being, controls. Hence, we should be indifferent to everything else, such as (again) wealth and status, things outside our control. The Pyrrhonian Skeptics said happiness is achieved by suspending all our beliefs, a result of the realization that none are justified, especially beliefs about what is really good and bad, or right and wrong. We should live without beliefs on the basis of 'appearances' such as our feelings and the customs of our society.

These brief summaries suggest real differences from the teaching of the Buddha, but they also show that the Hellenistic philosophers shared with

44

the Buddha the belief that genuine happiness requires a radical restructuring of our ordinary concerns. Moreover, despite the differences between them, all the Hellenistic schools agreed with the Buddha in depicting true happiness especially in terms of a deep tranquility (*ataraxia*) that is achieved by divesting ourselves of all or most of those aspirations that give rise to anxiety. Of the three, Stoic indifference to everything but one's own virtue comes closest to Buddhist non-attachment. In fact, because of the emphasis on tranquility, both the Buddha and the Hellenistic philosophers have been criticized for advocating a life of passivity.

Beyond this basic comparison, there are more specific similarities between the teachings of the Buddha and the Hellenistic philosophies. First, for both, **1** the diagnosis and treatment were presented as being applicable to, and hence valuable for, all human beings. In this sense, they were both universal in their outlook (for example, Epicurus was willing to teach his philosophy to women and slaves). Second, they were both individualistic in that the emphasis was **2** on achieving happiness by transforming individuals rather than by transforming the societies in which they lived. On the other hand, the Epicureans and Stoics shared the Buddha's belief in the importance of bringing about the transformation of individuals in a social context. Like the *Sangha*, Epicurus's 'garden' was not merely a school but a separate community. Third, both the **3** Buddha and the Hellenistic philosophers believed the virtue and happiness **(s)** of a person were closely linked. In contrast to much of modern Western philosophy, which tends to see the correspondence between these as questionable or at least indirect, the Buddha and the Hellenistic thinkers all supposed that they were directly connected: one cannot achieve real happiness in the absence of moral virtue (this and the remainder of the remarks in this paragraph do not apply to the Skeptics). Fourth, both emphasized the need **4** for vigilant self-examination as essential to achieve the basic transformation of personality advocated. Fifth, both the Buddha and the Hellenistic philoso- **5** phers stressed the value of knowledge for achieving happiness, but they discouraged the pursuit of philosophical questions judged to be irrelevant to achieving happiness. The value of knowledge was instrumental to this end **6** and was not an end in itself. Finally, they both understood the life of happiness as one in which positive value is always found in the present moment, undistracted by regrets about the past and anxieties about the future.

To sum up, with regard to these practical issues there are considerable affinities between the Buddha and the Hellenistic philosophers. This suggests that there are significant respects in which the Buddha's teaching might be regarded as a philosophy, at least as one important Western tradition understood that term. However, these affinities do not imply equivalence. Though they had some common concerns and proposed partly similar ways of life, the Buddha and the Hellenistic thinkers nonetheless differed from one another in many ways. For example, the shared emphasis on tranquility is striking, but the life advocated by the Buddha is by no means identical with that

7) medical analogy
8) dukka
9) deep tranquility

Religion? — Wittgenstein, Hicks, Lakoff

proposed by any of the three Hellenistic schools. In the next chapter, we will pursue this comparison further on several theoretical fronts. For now, we need to consider some aspects of the practice taught by the Buddha that go beyond anything proposed by the Hellenistic philosophers and take us into what looks like religion.

2 Some religious aspects

Three attributes, among others, are thought typically to characterize religious practice: communal institutions whose membership is determined primarily by acceptance of the importance and value of the religion's teaching; ritual actions, beyond strictly ethical actions, that are crucial to seriously living in accordance with this teaching; and persons, places, times, or objects that are regarded as sacred or in some manner worthy of special veneration or reverence. For example, for a given denomination in the Christian tradition, the Church is the central communal institution, Sunday worship is a fundamental ritual activity, and Jesus, Jerusalem, Easter, and the cross are respectively a sacred person, place, time, and object.

Renditions of these three attributes are also found in great profusion and diversity in the various traditions of Buddhism in the world today, and this is one reason why Buddhism is customarily thought of as a religion. Moreover, in the teaching of the Buddha himself, all three of these characteristic aspects of religion are sanctioned to some extent: he established the institution of the *Sangha*, he inaugurated ritual activities, and he identified four places worthy of special veneration (it is a large question, beyond our concern here, in what measure the practices of subsequent Buddhist traditions can find justification in this teaching). In all these respects, the practice taught by the Buddha exceeds that of the Hellenistic philosophers and all other Western philosophers except those who were explicitly religious figures – for example, Christian philosophers such as Augustine. To some extent, the community founded by Epicurus may have shared some of these attributes (there were ritual celebrations in his memory), but the extent is minimal. Here the similarities with the Hellenistic philosophers largely come to an end.

The Buddha thought the main way to achieve enlightenment was to join the *Sangha*. This was a community of men or women – the *bhikkhus* or *bhikkhunīs* – who had left behind the customary world of family and work in order to devote themselves full time to the Eightfold Path. In the ideal, they were highly disciplined, celibate, had no profession and very few possessions, lived on the charity of the supporting lay community, wore special yellow robes, and shaved their heads. The terms '*bhikkhus*' and '*bhikkhunīs*' are usually translated as 'monks' and 'nuns'. This is not inappropriate, though it may be misleading. Christian monks are popularly thought of as living in isolation from society (in fact, this is not always true). But the *bhikkhus* and *bhikkhunīs* were required to seek alms on a daily basis, and in turn to provide instruction and guidance to those who were interested. Hence, though they were separate from society, they were expected to interact with it regularly. Moreover, neither *bhikkhus* nor *bhikkhunīs* administered sacraments such as baptism, and in this respect terms such as 'priest' or 'minister' would also be misleading. On the other hand, the *bhikkhus* and *bhikkhunīs* were both expected to live a quite austere life for which the term 'monastic' is a fairly apt description if we discount its distinctive Christian connotations.

The Buddha prescribed life in the *Sangha* in great detail. The *Vinaya Piṭaka*, the first part of the *Tipiṭaka*, specifies more than 200 rules that govern the lives of individual members and the actions of the corporate community. The ten basic rules for novices gives a fair indication of its character: novices (as well as others) were to refrain from injuring anything alive, stealing, engaging in any sexual activity, lying, consuming intoxicants, eating beyond noon, viewing or participating in entertainments, wearing jewelry, perfume and the like, sleeping on luxurious beds, and handling money (the first five correspond to, but are not identical with, precepts that apply to all persons on the path). There were additional rules pertaining to such things as behavior with members of the opposite sex, permitted personal possessions, the nature of residences, comportment, and sanctions for violations of rules. The *Sangha* was meant to be a highly regulated community of persons seeking enlightenment about, and liberation from, the ills of human life. In many respects, it resembles other communities we customarily call religious.

In connection with the *Sangha*, the Buddha also prescribed a variety of ritual activities. For example, there was a minimal ceremony upon entry into the community, there were public confessions of transgressions of rules at the phases of the moon, and the daily round of begging for alms itself had a ritual quality. In addition, with respect to the sacred, the Buddha declared that his place of birth, enlightenment, first teaching, and death were to be places worthy of special reverence. According the Buddha, these places 'should arouse emotion in the faithful' and 'any who die while making the pilgrimage to these shrines with a devout heart will, at the breaking-up of the body after death, be reborn in a heavenly world' (L 263–4). To a large extent, the Buddha emphasized the importance of his teaching rather than himself. Just before his death, he left instructions to live 'with the *Dhamma* as your refuge, with no other refuge' (L 245). But of course the four sacred places do tend to draw attention to himself, and he also declared that he should be cremated in the fashion of a king: 'A stupa should be erected at the crossroads for the *Tathāgata*. And whoever lays wreaths or puts sweet perfumes and colours there with a devout heart, will reap benefit and happiness for a long time' (L 264). Such comments sowed the seeds for later worship of the Buddha.

There are thus several aspects of the practice taught by the Buddha that suggest it is a religious practice. However, there are also two factors that partly mitigate this suggestion. First, the heart of the practice is the Eightfold Path, and the path centrally features ethical rules for all followers (though the

Buddha clearly thought that joining the *Sangha* was the primary way to pursue this path). Moreover, the Eightfold Path does not emphasize either ritual practices or sacred places, persons, and the like. Hence, these last may reasonably be considered to have secondary importance. In addition, the not-self doctrine tends to undermine assigning special importance to the person of the Buddha over and above the importance assigned to what he taught.

Second, with respect to the rules of the *Sangha* and the ethical rules that apply to all followers, as well as the ritual practices, it is important to take into account comments the Buddha regularly made about what he called the 'fetters' (*saṁyojana*) to enlightenment. 'A well-taught noble disciple,' he declared about one of these fetters, 'does not abide with a mind obsessed and enslaved . . . by adherence to rules and observances' (M 538). This brings out an aspect of the practice taught by the Buddha that may appear paradoxical but is of the highest importance: we are not to be attached to the practice anymore than we are to be attached to anything else. Non-attachment applies to *everything*. On the one hand, the disciple of the Buddha was expected to live a highly disciplined life governed by rules and to some extent rituals. On the other hand, he or she was not to be 'obsessed and enslaved' by these. Since the goal of the discipline is non-attachment, we are successful in achieving this goal only insofar as we eventually come to follow the rules and rituals without being attached to them. Many religions warn against an obsession with rules and rituals, but the strong emphasis placed on non-attachment with respect to these and all else is a distinctive and fundamental feature of the Buddha's teaching.

SUGGESTED READING

The practical aspects of the Buddha's teaching are stressed in the *Mahā-Assapura Sutta* ('The Greater Discourse at Assapura'), M #39. See also the *Gaṇakamoggallāna Sutta* ('To Gaṇaka Moggallāna'), M #107.

A selection of texts in Hellenistic philosophy can be found in Long and Sedley (1987). For introductions to this tradition, see Long (1986) and Sharples (1996). For more detailed discussions, see Annas (1993), Hadot (1995 and 2002: part two), and Nussbaum (1994). Buddhism and aspects of Hellenistic philosophy are considered in Bouquet (1961), Flintoff (1980), and Garfield (2002: chapter 1). Socrates and the Buddha are compared in Dillon (2000). Accessible accounts of Buddhism and the Western philosophical tradition can be found in Batchelor (1994), and Revel and Ricard (1998). For discussion of the nature of religion, see Hick (1989: chapter 1) and Smart (1998: 10–22). Smart's seven dimensions of religion are applied to Buddhism in Keown (1996: chapter 1). Chatalian (1983) interprets Buddhism as a philosophy. Some religious and philosophical aspects of Buddhism are explained in Inada (1969) and R. Rajapakse (1986).

NOTE

1 The medical analogy implicit in the Four Noble Truths has also prompted comparisons with psychotherapy. Though hardly encouraged by Sigmund Freud, some have suggested that psychoanalysis and Buddhist meditation may be seen as processes of therapeutic change that are in part similar and in part complementary. Hence, it has been thought that these two approaches to personal development could learn from one another. For example, see Epstein (1995), Rubin (1996), and Wilber, Engler and Brown (1986). On a related topic, Buddhism is compared with cognitive psychology in Pickering (1997).

5

THEORETICAL DIMENSIONS OF THE TEACHING

The Buddha taught a practice that aimed to overcome suffering. In the last chapter, we saw that in some important respects this practical orientation is closely allied with that of the Hellenistic philosophers while in other respects it comes closer to features we often associate with religion. However, the practice taught by the Buddha also has significant theoretical dimensions. We now need to consider in what ways these dimensions may or may not resemble familiar understandings of philosophy as well as religion. This will allow us to see some additional avenues by which those in Western philosophical traditions might constructively engage the Buddha's teaching. It will be convenient to divide this examination into metaphysical and epistemological issues. At the end, we will return to the idea of non-attachment.

1 Metaphysics: human nature and the transcendent

The Buddha's teaching centered on human nature. In this regard, there are several doctrines put forward by the Buddha that are rejected by the Hellenistic philosophers. The most obvious is the not-self doctrine. In fact, the conception of the self briefly described in chapter 3 might be considered the standard view of the self in Western philosophy (namely, that each of us is an ontologically distinct being with identity through time that has the properties of thought, action, self-consciousness, and so on.). Surely, it might be said, in rejecting such a self, the Buddha was fundamentally in conflict with Western thought. However, there have been Western philosophers who have expressed skepticism about the self so conceived. David Hume's famous denial of the self has often been compared to the Buddha, both in substance and argument. More recently, Derek Parfit has suggested that his reductionist view of the self has affinities with the Buddha (see chapter 7, section 2). Moreover, there are other Western philosophers (for example, Benedict Spinoza, Immanuel Kant, Arthur Schopenhauer, Friedrich Nietzsche, William James, Jean-Paul Sartre, and Michel Foucault) who have expressed various forms of skepticism about this 'standard' view of the self. The existence and nature of the self is one of the central topics about which Western philosophers have debated. Though the Buddha's not-self doctrine is contrary to much Western thinking, in religion and philosophy both, it is not completely alien to all of it. The same may be said of the related doctrine that the world of ordinary experience is nothing more than a complex of mutually interdependent processes of change. This has not been the common view in the West, but a number of process philosophers from Heraclitus to Alfred North Whitehead have held comparable views.

On a related topic, none of the Hellenistic philosophers accepted the notion of a cycle of rebirths. In fact, they all rejected the idea of life both before and after our life here on earth. But, once again, this is not the sort of difference that puts the Buddha outside the realm of Western philosophy. After all, Plato famously accepted a doctrine of rebirth (along with some other ancient Greek philosophers), and many Western philosophers have believed in immortality, typically on account of the influence of Christianity. Cyclical rebirth has not been a commonly accepted idea in the West, but the example of Plato suggests that the idea of an existence before, as well as after, the life we know on earth has been considered a philosophical possibility. In the twentieth century, rebirth was defended by the philosophers C.J. Ducasse and J.M.E. McTaggart.

For the Buddha, rebirth is connected with the doctrine of *kamma*. If we take this doctrine to mean that the universe is ordered in such a way that our well-being varies as a function of the moral quality of our lives, then we need not look far in Western philosophy to find proponents of such a view. The Epicureans and Stoics thought real happiness could not be achieved without virtue. In a rather different example, Kant believed a person's happiness ought to be proportionate to his or her moral goodness, and he thought our moral convictions gave us reason to believe the universe is structured so as ultimately to ensure this outcome. Of course, Kant supposed we needed to postulate God to explain this coordination, and this marks a difference from the Buddha. But the general idea that the universe is ordered to proportion happiness to goodness is one the Buddha shares with many Western philosophers, and with major Western religious traditions as well.

None of this is to say that on these issues doctrines identical to those of the Buddha may be discerned among Western philosophers. Yet there are enough points of resemblance to encourage the belief that, in these respects at least, it may be fruitful for those in the West to inquire into the teaching of the Buddha as a philosophy. However, one central tenet of the Buddha's message, arguably the fundamental tenet, is the idea of *Nibbāna* understood as a state beyond not only this life but also the entire cycle of rebirth. So far as I know, there is no significant counterpart to this idea in Western philosophy – with the possible exception of Schopenhauer, the one major figure in this tradition who found, or thought he found, considerable affinity with Buddhism. Moreover, some stream-observers might think, if rebirth and *kamma* were not enough, surely when *Nibbāna* is taken into account we have ample

51

reason to suppose the teaching of the Buddha is much more a religion than a philosophy. What should we say about this contention?

It might be thought that religion should be defined as requiring belief in God, as in Judaism, Christianity, and Islam, where traditionally God has been understood as an omnipotent, omniscient, wholly good, personal being who created the universe. On this definition, the Buddha did not teach a religion: not only did he fail to say that God so-defined exists, but also much that he did say appears inconsistent with the existence of this God. For example, the Buddha rejected the idea that there is a creator of the universe, and the not-self doctrine seems incompatible with the understanding of God as a personal being.

However, nowadays religion is not commonly defined by reference to belief in God. One reason is that there is so much in the practices of Asian traditions – especially those that originated in India and China – that looks in many respects like religion but does not include belief in God, that it has seemed advisable to formulate an account of religion in broader terms. Sometimes these accounts are so broad as to make it difficult to prevent inclusion of paradigmatically secular worldviews such as Marxism. But those who aim to distinguish the religious from the secular (itself a Western distinction) usually claim that a characteristic, even if not essential, feature of religion is the idea that genuine well-being crucially depends on an ultimate reality that transcends the world of ordinary experience. For example, the philosopher of religion John Hick says:

> Most forms of religion have affirmed a salvific reality that transcends (whilst also usually being thought of as immanent within) human beings and the world, this reality being variously conceived as a personal God or non-personal Absolute, or as the cosmic structure or process or ground of the universe.
>
> (Hick 1989: 6)

It may be difficult to specify this general notion of transcendence with much precision, but it seems correct to say that religion broadly construed ordinarily involves some such a notion.

In this sense of religion, it might be said, the idea of *Nibbāna* shows that the Buddha taught a religion. According to Hick, both Christians and Buddhists 'speak of the transformation of our human situation from a state of alienation from the true [transcendent] structure of reality to a radically better state in harmony with reality' (Hick 1989: 10). *Nibbāna*, as a state beyond this life and the whole cycle of rebirth, is an ultimately real and unconditioned state in which there is perfect contentment and tranquility. The Buddha said that it is very difficult for the unenlightened to understand *Nibbāna* and that our language is inadequate to describe it. But he said enough to make it reasonable to depict *Nibbāna* as transcendent reality.

By way of objection, it is sometimes suggested that the Buddha's teaching contains nothing of the supernatural and is a form of naturalism. But this can be misleading. If the term 'supernatural' implies the existence of God, then the Buddha did not teach about the supernatural. But if, as is commonly the case, the term 'naturalism' implies that the only reality is that which is disclosed by the five senses (directly or by inference), then the Buddha did not teach naturalism either. The dichotomy between the conditioned world revealed by ordinary sense-experience and the unconditioned reality of *Nibbāna* revealed by meditation is fundamental to the Buddha's teaching. For this reason, it is correct to say that the Buddha taught a religion according to Hick's broad characterization.[1]

But does this mean the Buddha did *not* teach a philosophy? Only on an extremely narrow understanding of philosophy that is contrary to common usage. We do not suppose that figures such as René Descartes and Kant did (a) not teach a philosophy because God plays a central role in their theories. Likewise, we should not suppose that the Buddha did not teach a philosophy because the transcendent reality of *Nibbāna* is a central part of what he taught. In this respect, philosophers have as much to learn in the encounter with Asian traditions as students of religion: there are alternative understandings of transcendence, and such alternatives may engage the attention of Western philosophers as much as God has traditionally engaged these philosophers.

Moreover, we have seen enough to recognize that the teaching of the Buddha was put forward as a solution to a problem – how to achieve well-being – that was a primary problem in Hellenistic philosophy and has been a problem in much of the Western philosophical tradition overall. The Buddha offered a solution that, though similar at points to the ideas of some Western philosophers, differs on the whole from anything found in Western philosophy. Nonetheless, the fact that it is a different solution to a problem long recognized by Western philosophers suggests that it is worthy of investigation as a philosophy. Among philosophers and others, there is little agreement in the West about the nature of well-being and the means of its achievement. Perhaps there is something to be learned from another tradition.

In connection with the issue of transcendence, it should be observed that the Buddha's teaching also includes an extensive cosmology that elaborates the ideas of rebirth and *kamma*. Thus the universe is said to contain many worlds that expand and contract over long periods of time, are arranged in a hierarchy of thirty-one planes of existence, and are occupied by animals, ghosts, humans, gods, and so on according to the moral quality of their previous lives. Cosmologies such as this – that is, elaborate accounts of the nature and development of the universe that go well beyond what is evident to ordinary sense-experience – were not uncommon in the ancient era in which the Buddha lived (Plato's *Timaeus* is a prominent example), though they were also challenged by skeptics both East and West. Persons in the modern Western world might regard these cosmologies as myths, but the

Buddha's cosmology has been, and is, taken literally by many of his followers. Regardless of how it is interpreted, the cosmology often embodies other important aspects of the Buddha's teaching. Most importantly, the higher planes of existence correspond to levels of meditation, and hence of enlightenment, that we might achieve in this life. In any case, from a philosophical standpoint, what is crucial in the message of the Buddha in this regard are the basic ideas of rebirth and *kamma*. The cosmological details that fill out these ideas are of secondary importance.

2 Epistemology: reason, faith, and meditation

It might be thought that the differences between the Buddha and Western philosophy that most strongly call into question the claim that the Buddha taught a philosophy have less to do with metaphysics than they do with epistemology. The epistemological emphasis in Western philosophy is on reason broadly construed. Following the examples of Socrates, Plato, and Aristotle, most of the Hellenistic philosophers believed that reason is the distinctive characteristic of human beings and that by which happiness is achieved. The Stoic Seneca gave a typical statement of this conviction:

> What is best in man? Reason: with this he precedes the animals and
> follows the gods. Therefore perfect reason is man's peculiar good
> . . . . What is the peculiar characteristic of a man? Reason – which
> when right and perfect makes the full sum of human happiness . . . .
> This perfect reason is called virtue and is identical to rectitude.
>
> (Long and Sedley 1987: 395)

The Buddha did not deny that human beings are rational nor that reason has importance. But he did not think reason has the significance most Western philosophers have assigned to it, and he diminished our difference from animals by asserting that an animal could be reborn as a human being and vice versa. However, there have been many different voices on these issues in Western philosophical traditions. For example, the sixteenth-century philosopher Michel de Montaigne strongly contested the value of reason and stressed our similarities with animals. And there have been others, from the ancient skeptics to more recent philosophers such as the existentialists and postmodernists, who have sharply challenged the worth of human reason. Moreover, there have been yet other philosophers as diverse as Augustine, Hume, and Kant who have claimed that reason has value, but only within significant limits. Western philosophy may be predominantly rationalistic, but it is far from exclusively so.

The Buddha claimed to possess knowledge and to show us a path whereby we could acquire knowledge as well. At the time of his enlightenment, he is said to have gained knowledge of his past lives, the cycle of rebirth, and the

Four Noble Truths. He is also represented as possessing several 'supernormal powers' such as knowing what people are thinking or what they are saying in distant places. The *Theravāda* tradition has ascribed omniscience to the Buddha, though it is not clear he claimed this for himself. In any case, what is most important is the threefold knowledge of his enlightenment. It is this that is constantly emphasized in the *Sutta Piṭaka*, and of this, knowledge of the Four Noble Truths is the most significant. On what basis did the Buddha purport to have this knowledge and how did he think we might acquire it?

In an oft-quoted text, the Kālāmas in the town of Kesaputta told the Buddha that each *samaṇa* and brahmin claimed that he possessed the truth and that the others did not. As a result, the Kālāmas said, they were in doubt about who was speaking truly and who falsely. In response, the Buddha warned them not to be mislead by a variety of purported avenues of understanding such as oral tradition, logic or reasoning, and the apparent competence of a person. Instead, the Buddha urged the Kālāmas to 'know for yourselves' and live on the basis of that knowledge (N 65). The emphasis on knowing for oneself is an important part of the teaching of the Buddha. But he thought a person could achieve this knowledge not by flatly rejecting the aforementioned avenues, but by recognizing both their capacities and their limitations. Elsewhere, the Buddha identified five potential avenues of understanding: 'faith, approval, oral tradition, reasoned cogitation, and reflective acceptance of a view.' In each case, he said, something accepted on that basis may be false and something not so accepted may be true. Hence, each of these avenues is unreliable and insufficient for acquiring knowledge, and so none should be depended on to definitely conclude 'only this is true [*sacca*], anything else is wrong' (M 780). On the other hand, the Buddha thought these avenues have a role to play in gaining knowledge. We will see that he has much to say to render the Four Noble Truths rationally intelligible and compelling. But he believed that, by themselves, reason and the other avenues are not adequate for the highest understanding we can achieve. Something else is required. This additional avenue is concentration, what is usually called meditation in the West, and it is central. Yet much epistemic preparation is required for meditation to be effective. Hence, we can acquire knowledge for ourselves only by undertaking a long, complex, and difficult program of training that involves numerous epistemically important practices that culminate in meditation. The full description of this training is the Eightfold Path. For our present concerns, it is important to consider briefly several key features of this path.

The Buddha spoke a good deal about faith (the usual translation of '*saddhā*', though it might also be rendered as 'confidence'). The term is often placed at the beginning of lists that end with wisdom. For example, 'five factors of striving' are described as 'faith in the *Tathāgata's* enlightenment,' freedom from affliction and illness, honesty and sincerity, being energetic in ridding oneself of unwholesome states and acquiring wholesome ones, and possessing wisdom (M 707). The suggestion is that it would not make sense to begin a program of learning unless we had some confidence that our teacher could help us gain the requisite knowledge. The Buddha gave the example of going to a person to learn the skill of carrying an animal prod while riding an elephant. According to the Buddha, if the student 'had no faith, he could not achieve what can be achieved by one who has faith' (M 706). For the same reason, doubt is often described as one of the fetters that prevent enlightenment. If a student had substantial doubts about the knowledge of a teacher, the student would find it difficult to learn. Hence, the follower of the Buddha must have some initial faith that the Buddha is enlightened and can bring others to attain this enlightenment for themselves. He sometimes referred to the *bhikkhus* as those 'who have gone forth out of faith from the home life into homelessness under me' (M 566).

However, the Buddha emphasized two important features of the faith required. First, this initial faith must be supported by reasons. A person who turns to the Buddha should have not a blind faith, but a reasonable confidence or trust in the Buddha's enlightenment. The difficulty is that a person new to the Buddha's teaching has not yet attained enlightenment and cannot directly know if the Buddha is enlightened. In recognition of this, the Buddha urged the would-be follower to seek some signs of the Buddha's enlightenment before beginning the Eightfold Path. For example, he should hear a presentation of the teaching and make sure the Buddha is purified of any states of greed, hatred, or delusion: 'Then he places faith in him' (M 782). Only on the basis of such reasons should one have faith in the Buddha. In effect, the Buddha acknowledged the importance of guidelines to aid stream-observers in determining whether faith in the Buddha is warranted. Second, this faith is a temporary stage on the road to enlightenment. It is required at the beginning, but the goal is to directly know for oneself. Once a follower has become enlightened, faith in the Buddha is no longer necessary. Of course, since the road to enlightenment is long and difficult, for most persons faith may be necessary for an indefinite duration. Nonetheless, the Buddha rejected any role for faith as a dogmatic belief.

In some measure, the faith expected of a follower of the Buddha may resemble the faith of believers in major Western religious traditions. But it also resembles the faith found in mundane examples such as that of an athlete in his or her trainer, and it does not involve faith in God or acceptance of divine revelation out of faith.

The Buddha also urged his followers to think about his teachings in order to determine for themselves whether or not they make sense. Once a disciple has an initial faith in him, the Buddha said, he hears and memorizes the *Dhamma*. Then 'he examines the meaning of the teachings' and 'gains a reflective acceptance of those teachings.' After this, 'zeal springs up . . . he applies his will . . . he scrutinizes . . . he strives . . . [and] he realizes with the body the ultimate truth and sees it by penetrating it with wisdom' (M 782). The reference to examination, reflection, and scrutiny all suggest that the disciple is to critically assess the Buddha's teaching. This assessment partly involves reason. To a considerable extent, the Buddha shows great respect for the capacity and value of human reason. One hallmark of this respect is recognition of the importance of consistency and argument. Several *suttas* have the structure of Socratic dialogues in which the Buddha refutes the position of an interlocutor on the grounds that the person is inconsistent. In other places, he defends his own position against the charge of inconsistency. And there are many arguments, directly stated or implied, in favor of the Buddha's teaching. Often he makes explicit use of valid logical inferences. In short, part of the process leading to enlightenment is meant to involve rational reflection, and there is no indication that enlightenment requires going directly against reason.

On the other hand, the Buddha also thought the value of rational reflection is significantly limited. In a characteristic remark, he says the *Dhamma* is 'unattainable by mere reasoning' (M 260). Reason has a place, but it can take us only so far in the quest for full enlightenment/If we survey the entire *Sutta Piṭaka*, we do not find an emphasis on rational argumentation at all comparable to the Hellenistic philosophers/Nor is the emphasis on rational argumentation comparable to major figures in the Western philosophical traditions – philosophers such as Plato, Aristotle, Thomas Aquinas, Descartes, Hume, Kant, and so on. The *suttas* that focus on consistency and argument are much more the exception than the rule. In fact, at times, their purpose seems to be as much to show that the Buddha could successfully engage in rational argumentation against a worthy opponent as to employ such argumentation to actually demonstrate an aspect of his teaching. As a whole, the *Sutta Piṭaka* contains a broad assortment of instruments of instruction about the path to enlightenment: conversations, stories, similes, distinctions, classifications, lists, as well as inferences and arguments. Taken together, these are intended to present an intellectually compelling account. But there is more emphasis on what is the case and what ought to be done than on the structure of argument supporting these contentions. For example, the numerous similes (over 175 in the *Majjhima Nikāya* alone) often enable us to see what a claim means, but they do not establish that we should accept it as true.

It might be thought this shows that, in the end, the teaching of the Buddha is fundamentally dogmatic and unworthy of being considered a philosophy in any sense of the term that refers to the enterprise of Socrates and his successors. But this would be a mistaken – or, at any rate, premature – conclusion. If explicit and extensive rational argumentation were the only avenue to philosophical knowledge, then the Buddha's teaching would fall very short of this knowledge. However, this rationalist conception of philosophy has been accepted by only some Western philosophers and has been contested by others. In any case, we cannot easily depict the Buddha's position in terms of Western debates about rationality. A central contention of the Buddha is that the most important avenue to acquiring the knowledge he teaches is not reason but meditation, and Buddhist meditation has no significant correlate in Western epistemological discussions. Meditation is not rooted in subjective feelings or desires, nor is its aim a non-cognitive, dream-like condition. On the contrary, meditation is said to provide us with a form of objective knowledge of reality, the knowledge that enables us to overcome suffering. But the knowledge meditation gives us is not based on a rational grasp of self-evident truths, it is not the result of logical inferences, and it is not grounded in the ordinary experience of the five senses. Buddhist understanding as a whole may draw on all these epistemological sources. But meditation itself is *sui generis* and cannot be reduced to or understood in terms of any of them.

The Buddha taught two kinds of meditation: serenity meditation (*samatha-bhāvanā*) and insight meditation (*vipassanā-bhāvanā*). For both, to be effective, a good deal of intellectual, emotional, and moral preparation is required. The aim of serenity meditation is to purify the mind of various obstacles so that it may attain the highest degree of concentration. The Buddha thought our minds were typically in so much turmoil that, in the absence of radical modification, they had no hope of truly understanding reality. Serenity meditation involves extensive training in focusing our attention wholly and exclusively on a single object so as to end this turmoil and gain the ability to concentrate.

This provides a foundation for insight meditation. Here, the purpose is to directly know reality as it truly is. Insight meditation is a matter of heightened and attentive awareness rather than intellectual or theoretical thought. It involves detailed and mindful observation of all aspects of one's person through which one comes to realize the impermanence of things, the suffering associated with this, the absence of any self, and ultimately the Four Noble Truths. Insight meditation is a kind of experience, in a broad sense of the term, but experience that is quite different from, and beyond that ordinarily provided by, the five senses. The eventual outcome is the realization of *Nibbāna*, an immediate comprehension of the unconditioned realm beyond the ordinary world of sense experience, an understanding that cannot adequately be described in language, but that liberates us from attachment and enables us to live with compassion, joy, and tranquility.

The knowledge Buddhist meditation is supposed to provide purports to be objective in two senses of the word: it gives us knowledge of the way the universe really is, and this knowledge is something that anyone, with proper training, can acquire. The Buddha said: 'Let a wise man come, one who is honest and sincere, a man of rectitude. I instruct him, I teach him the *Dhamma* in such a way that by practicing as instructed he will soon know and see for himself' (M 664). Whether meditation actually results in objective knowledge is another question, but that it does is a central contention of the Buddha's teaching.

There is nothing similar to Buddhist meditation in the epistemologies of Western philosophy. Moreover, insofar as meditation culminates in the realization of *Nibbāna*, the objective knowledge it provides differs from the objective knowledge sought by many Western philosophers in that it grasps what is unconditioned and defies adequate linguistic description. We will see that the Buddha says a great deal intellectually to situate and show the value of the attainment of *Nibbāna*. But none of this diminishes the primacy he assigns to the epistemic value of this universally available but utterly unique transforming experience. Hence, though the Buddha shares with many Western philosophical traditions a concern for objective understanding, he challenges these traditions to consider the possibility of a form of objectivity they have not envisioned. We might be inclined to disregard this challenge on the grounds that we already know that no such knowledge is possible. But if we are truly fallibilists, both about what we know and how we know, we have reason to seriously consider the Buddha's proposal.

3 The teaching is for crossing over, not for grasping

It would be a mistake to conclude that the teaching of the Buddha is, or is not, a philosophy or a religion simply speaking. Given some typical Western understandings of these contested concepts, in some respects his teaching resembles each of these and in other respects it does not. Nonetheless, we have seen enough points of contiguity with Western philosophical traditions to suggest that it can be fruitful to understand and evaluate his teaching as a philosophy in some familiar senses of the term. In the end, our inquiry might lead us to revise our understanding of what philosophy is or can be. But there is enough in understandings already common in Western philosophy to provide a basis for beginning such an examination. Before we proceed, it will be helpful to close this discussion with a reminder concerning the purpose of the Buddha's teaching.

From first to last, the Buddha taught a practice whose goal was overcoming suffering. Though his teaching has significant theoretical dimensions, both metaphysical and epistemological, these are always subservient to the aim of the practice. The heart of the teaching involves the idea of non-clinging or non-attachment. In a well-known simile, the Buddha emphasized that ultimately we are not to be attached to anything, including the teaching itself. Suppose, he said, someone 'saw a great expanse of water, whose near shore was dangerous and fearful and whose further shore was safe and free from fear, but there was no ferryboat or bridge going to the far shore.' Suppose the man then built a raft and used it to arrive safely at the far shore. If he thought to himself, since this raft has been so helpful to me, I will 'hoist it on my head or load it on my shoulder, and then go wherever I want,' we would think he misunderstood the function of the raft. Its purpose was to bring him to safety. Now that that purpose has been achieved, he should 'haul it onto the dry land or set it adrift in the water.' The Buddha concludes: 'So I have shown you how the *Dhamma* is similar to a raft, being for the purpose of crossing over, not for the purpose of grasping' (M 228–9). In another version of the simile, the Buddha poses this question:

Bhikkhus, purified and bright as this view is, if you do not adhere to it, cherish it, treasure it, and treat it as a possession, would you then understand the *Dhamma* that has been taught as similar to a raft, being for the purpose of crossing over, not for the purpose of grasping?

(M 353)

The answer, of course, is 'Yes': the Buddha's teaching is not something to adhere to or cherish or possess. These are all forms of grasping or clinging, of attaching ourselves to the teaching. But the purpose of the teaching is to carry us from a life of suffering to *Nibbāna*, and to have arrived at *Nibbāna* is to be unattached to anything, including the teaching that brought us there. In attaining *Nibbāna* we are transformed and, so transformed, we have left the teaching aside and go wherever we want, liberated from suffering. We might say, to revert to the medical analogy, that the teaching is like a medicine: once it has cured us of suffering, we no longer need it. Having gained our health, we simply live our lives.

By applying non-attachment to his own teaching, the Buddha brought out the extraordinary nature of the state of health he envisioned. Once it is fully recognized that there is no self, that there is no real being to which the word 'I' refers, then it will be realized that 'I' cannot attach 'myself' to anything, and non-attachment will be the result. We need to consider carefully the meaning of non-attachment and whether our ultimate well-being requires it. The first step is to examine the not-self doctrine in detail.

SUGGESTED READING

Some epistemological dimensions of the Buddha's teaching are discussed in the *Cankī Sutta* ('With Cankī'), M #95. Also important in this connection is the *Sandaka Sutta* ('To Sandaka'), M #76 and 'To the Kālāmas,' N 64–7.

The nature of faith is analyzed in Sessions (1994), and the role of faith in the Buddha is considered in Hoffman (1987: chapter 5). For a classic but controversial discussion of Buddhist epistemology, see Jayatilleke (1963). More recent interpretations include Cruise (1983), Doore (1979), Hoffman (1982 and 1985), Holder (1996), Kalansuriya (1979), Montalvo (1999), Siderits (1979), and Swearer (1972). Buddhism and Schopenhauer are discussed in Conze (1963a), Magee (1997: chapter 15), and Nicholls (1999). Buddhism is interpreted as a form of naturalism in Inada (1970).

NOTE

1   Other broad accounts of religion, such as anthropologist Clifford Geertz's definition in terms of 'a system of symbols' would also include Buddhism as a religion
(see Geertz 1973: 90).

Part 2

THE NOT-SELF DOCTRINE

6

AN INTERPRETATION OF
THE NOT-SELF DOCTRINE

The teaching of the Buddha is primarily practical in aim. Its goal is to enable us to overcome suffering on the basis of the Four Noble Truths. But this practice rests squarely on a theoretical understanding of human nature. Both the not-self doctrine and the ideas of *kamma* and rebirth are central to the Buddha's message. Our purpose in this part of the book is to understand and evaluate the Buddha's teaching on these topics. This will put us in a position to examine the Four Noble Truths.

We will begin with the doctrine of not-self (*anattā*, the negation of *attā*, meaning 'self'). The contention that we are not selves (nor have selves) is probably the greatest theoretical obstacle in Buddhism for Western stream-observers. Yet acceptance of this contention appears fundamental to the Buddha's portrayal of the path from suffering to *Nibbāna*. Unfortunately, what the Buddha says concerning the absence of self seems to conflict with other things he says and is not obviously a cogent account of our experience. Partly as a result, the not-self doctrine has been interpreted in different ways. In this chapter, I will propose a resolution of these problems. First, I will survey some typical expressions of the not-self doctrine and discuss the main difficulties in interpreting them. Then I will draw a distinction between two conceptions of selves – substance-selves and process-selves – and I will suggest that the Buddha taught that substance-selves have no reality in any sense, while process-selves have no independent reality but do have a form of dependent reality. Specifically, the existence of a person's process-self depends on certain beliefs and attitudes the person has, but may and should abandon. In the absence of these, the process-self ceases to exist. This is what happens when *Nibbāna* is fully attained: the relevant beliefs and attitudes are given up, and so there is no longer a process-self. Since there never was a substance-self, there is no self at all. In light of the distinction between substance- and process-selves, the Buddha's teaching concerning the self may be rendered consistent with his overall teaching and, perhaps, intelligible as an interpretation of our lives.

Of course, whether it is correct is another matter. In chapters 7 and 8, we will explore the considerations the Buddha offered to bring us to the realization that there are no substance-selves and we will examine whether he could answer some important objections to his view that the only selves that exist are dependent process-selves. Finally, in chapter 9, we will turn to *kamma* and rebirth. To complete the argument of the present chapter, I will argue that these ideas are consistent with the Buddha's not-self teaching on the ground that the dependent existence of process-selves is sufficient to explain what he says concerning these ideas. Beyond this, we will need to consider why the Buddha believed in *kamma* and rebirth, and what may be said for and against our doing so.

1 Characteristic expressions of the not-self doctrine

The Buddha speaks of the absence of selves in numerous texts. In whatever manner these may be interpreted, there is no question that he taught some not-self doctrine. To see what this is, let us first examine some of the more important statements concerning the absence of self. The Buddha says he does 'not see any doctrine of self that would not arouse sorrow, lamentation, pain, grief, and despair in one who clings to it' (M 231). Since a doctrine of self results in sorrow and the like, and the central teaching of the Buddha is that all such forms of suffering can and should be overcome, there should be no clinging to any doctrine of self. It might be thought that the Buddha's objection is not to a doctrine of self per se, but merely to clinging to it: the Buddha thinks clinging is conducive to suffering and should be abandoned. Though this is true, it is also significant that the Buddha regularly singles out a doctrine of self as one view to which it is especially important not to cling. For example, he says that when he has achieved 'true knowledge,' a *bhikkhu* 'no longer clings to sensual pleasures, no longer clings to views, no longer clings to rules and observances, no longer clings to a doctrine of self.' When he does not cling in this way, the Buddha says, he is not agitated and 'personally attains *Nibbāna*' (M 163). Though all forms of clinging are problematic, clinging to a doctrine of self is especially problematic. (As we will see, this is because it is the source of all other forms of clinging.) Just as clinging to a doctrine of self results in suffering, no longer clinging to such a doctrine is instrumental to attaining *Nibbāna*.

Moreover, the problem is not simply clinging to a doctrine of self. It is also that any such doctrine is false. Just after the first passage above, the Buddha says:

> Since a self and what belongs to a self are not apprehended as true and established, then this standpoint for views, namely, 'The self and the world are the same; after death I shall be permanent, everlasting, eternal, not subject to change; I shall endure as long as eternity' – would it not be an utterly and completely foolish teaching?
>
> (M 232)

64

The answer to this rhetorical question is 'Yes.' Here the Buddha plainly says that a self is 'not apprehended as true and established.' Since there is no self, it is false both that the self and the world are the same and that the self exists eternally after death (these views refer to the emerging ideas of the *Upaniṣads*). In this connection, the Buddha elsewhere distinguishes three kinds of persons: those who 'describe an existing self that is unimpaired after death,' those who 'describe the annihilation, destruction, and extermination of an existing being (at death),' and those who 'assert *Nibbāna* here and now' (M 839). The Buddha's position is obviously the last of these. It is distinguished from the first two views – that the self exists after death and that it is destroyed at death – because these views both mistakenly assume there is a self that may or may not continue to exist beyond the time of death. For the Buddha, there is no such self.

Oftentimes the not-self doctrine is expressed by indicating the inappropriateness of the words 'I', 'my', and 'mine'. These words have no ultimate reference for a person who has attained *Nibbāna*. For example, the Buddha says a person who thinks '*I* am at peace, *I* have attained *Nibbāna*, *I* am without clinging' is actually still clinging (M 846). Liberation, he goes on to say, is 'through not clinging.' Once *Nibbāna* has been achieved, it will no longer make sense to have any thoughts involving the word 'I.' Such thoughts refer to a self and hence they are not free from the clinging that is associated with a self. Addressing his son, Rāhula, the Buddha says, 'develop meditation on the perception of impermanence,' for when you do this, 'the conceit "I am" will be abandoned' (M 531). About himself, he says, 'It is by knowing thus, seeing thus, friends, that in regard to this body with its consciousness and all external signs, I-making, mine-making, and the underlying tendency to conceit have been eradicated in me'(M 908). Once enlightenment has been achieved, there will no longer be occasion to think in terms of such self-referring concepts as 'I' and 'mine'.

The most frequent statements of the not-self doctrine occur in connection with the five aggregates: material form, feeling, perception, formations, and (∾) consciousness. We will consider these more closely in the next chapter. For now, the important point is that these are put forward as an exhaustive list of what we ordinarily think constitutes a person. Hence, if a person is or has a self, then this self must be found in connection with one or more of these aggregates. But the Buddha maintains that it is not: 'Material form is not self, feeling is not self, perception is not self, formations are not self, consciousness is not self . . . all things are not self' (M 324). In a frequent refrain, the Buddha says we should 'not regard material form as self, or self as possessed of material form, or material form as in self, or self as in material form,' and likewise for the other four aggregates (M 889). Just as often the Buddha says, 'One sees all material form as it actually is with proper wisdom thus: "This is not mine, this I am not, this is not my self",' and similarly for the remaining aggregates (M 890). Sometimes this point is expressed in the language of emptiness or voidness (*suññatā*). For example, with respect to different aspects of the aggregates, it is said of each aspect that it 'is empty of self and of what belongs to self' (C II 1164).

To sum up, according to the Buddha, 'It is impossible, it cannot happen that a person possessing right view could treat anything as self – there is no such possibility' (M 928).

2 Some interpretive problems

It is evident that the Buddha has much to say to the effect that there is no self. But there are different interpretations of the not-self doctrine, and some have argued that, despite the texts we have just reviewed, the Buddha actually maintains that there is a self in some significant sense. (In fact, this was held early on by some purported followers of the Buddha called the 'Personalists'.) There are several reasons why some interpreters of the Buddha have resisted the conclusion that he thinks there is no self in any sense. First, the absence of any self is a threatening idea to many. Much that we take to be valuable about human beings seems to center on the thought that we are selves: if this were wrong, our lives might seem meaningless or less worthy than we thought. Moreover, without a self, our understanding of individual moral responsibility might appear undermined: how can I be responsible for what I did yesterday if 'I' does not refer to a self? Second, it is often difficult to understand what the Buddha means by saying there are no selves. For example, it is hard to grasp what it means for the Buddha to have attained *Nibbāna*, but not be able to correctly think '*I* have attained *Nibbāna*.' Such concerns lead to the suspicion that there must be some sort of self he implicitly affirms. Third, it may be wondered whether the not-self view provides a cogent account of our lives. What are we, if we are not selves? If a strict not-self doctrine cannot make intelligible sense of our experience, then perhaps there is a tacit acceptance of some kind of self. Finally, there are things the Buddha says that seem to leave open the possibility that there is a self and even to deny the not-self doctrine, and there is much else that he says that appears to presuppose a self. Once again, this gives us reason to think he must accept a self in some sense.

The first two of these reasons for supposing there must be a doctrine of self in the Buddha's teaching are not very compelling, but the last two require serious consideration. That we find an idea of someone else threatening or difficult to understand may give us some basis for suspecting we have misunderstood it. But in the absence of other considerations, these grounds of suspicion cannot cast much doubt on what appears the evident interpretation. There is no reason to think that, in general, the ideas of other people in distant times and places are unlikely to be threatening or hard to grasp: it is misguided charity to insist on interpreting such ideas so that they conform more or less to what we already think. However, if the not-self doctrine does not provide five aggregates may not be exhaustive. (weak) obj.

THE NOT-SELF DOCTRINE

a cogent account of our lives, or if there are grounds in the teaching of the Buddha himself for thinking he believes there is a self or does not rule it out, then perhaps the not-self passages quoted in the last section should not be taken at face value. A number of reasons have been advanced for thinking the Buddha may have endorsed or not precluded a self. Let us begin by briefly examining these reasons. We can then consider what the best overall interpretation of the Buddha's teaching concerning the self might be in light of everything he says and the presumption that it could provide a coherent interpretation of our experience.

To start, the most prominent argument for the not-self doctrine, that no self is found with respect to each of the five aggregates, is consistent with the (a) existence of a self independent of these aggregates. Even if the self is not material form, feeling, perception, formations, and consciousness, it may be something else. Hence, this argument is consistent with the existence of a self. However, by itself, this contention provides no reason to think the Buddha believes there is a self. If he thinks this, it may be expected that he would talk about, or at least assume, such a self; and if he speaks in these ways, then the texts showing this would be the primary reason for discerning a doctrine of self in his teaching.

There is an important passage in which the wanderer Vacchagotta asks 'Is there a self?' and 'Is there no self?' The Buddha remains silent in response to both questions. But if he believes there is no self, it might seem he would not be silent: surely he would directly say there is no self. However, the continuation of the passage shows that the Buddha has no hesitation about the not-self doctrine. Queried by Ānanda about his perplexing response, the Buddha says he interprets Vacchagotta's questions as pertaining to the dispute between the eternalists and the annihilationists. The eternalists held that the self exists eternally after death, while the annihilationists held that it ceases to exist at death. Hence, both presupposed that there is a self; Silent their disagreement concerned the duration of this self. Since the Buddha Buddha believes there is no self, he rejects both positions, and he could not answer Vacchagotta's questions in a way that suggested he sided with either. He could not say 'there is a self' because this would contradict his position that 'all phenomena are nonself.' But neither could he say 'there is no self' because 'Vacchagotta, already confused, would have fallen into even greater confusion, thinking, "It seems that the self I formerly had does not exist now"' (C II 1393–4). To sum up, the Buddha is silent because Vacchagotta's questions falsely presuppose that there is a self that may or may not exist after death. Similarly, I might be at a loss what to say to someone who asks if I still surf when I never surfed in the first place: 'Yes' and 'No' are both misleading answers. Of course, we might wonder why the Buddha does not go on to offer his full teaching to Vacchagotta. But the fact that he does not implies no backing away from the not-self doctrine. He evidently thinks this is not the appropriate occasion for explaining that doctrine, that doing so would only further bewilder Vacchagotta, given his preoccupation with the eternalist–annihilationist debate.

A similar point may be made about another text in which the Buddha appears to reject the not-self teaching. Speaking about a person who is pre-occupied with his past, present, and future existence, the Buddha says, 'When he attends unwisely in this way, one of six views arises in him.' The first two of these views are described as follows: 'The view "self exists for me" arises in him as true and established; or the view "no self exists for me" arises in him as true and established.' All six views are said to be those of an 'untaught ordinary person' who is 'not freed from suffering' (M 92–3). The implication might seem to be that an enlightened person would think neither that the self exists for me nor that it does not. Hence, the Buddha appears to reject, or at least not accept, the not-self doctrine. However, if we take the view 'self exists for me' to mean the self exists eternally (eternalism) and the view 'no self exists for me' to mean the self is destroyed at death (annihilationism), then we may understand the text as stating that neither eternalism nor annihilationism should be accepted because they both falsely presuppose there is a self.[1] Moreover, the context makes it clear that the Buddha thinks these views are among those things that are 'unfit for attention.' One who 'attends wisely' does not concern himself with the dispute between eternalism and annihilationism. Rather, he focuses on the Four Noble Truths. When he does this, he is said to abandon three fetters, the first of which is 'personality view' (M 93).

More serious concerns are raised by the fact that in expressing his own outlook the Buddha often speaks as if there is a self. For example, he says that one of the 'seven qualities of the true man' is that he is a 'knower . . . of self' (L 502). Again, the Buddha speaks a great deal about self-cultivation and self-discipline. For instance, in *The Dhammapada* he says that 'with oneself fully controlled one gains a protector which is hard to gain' (Buddharakkhita translation: section 160). Moreover, he regularly employs personal pronouns such as 'I' and 'he' that appear to refer to a self. Thus, in describing a meditation exercise, the Buddha says, 'Breathing in long, he understands: "I breathe in long"; or breathing out long, he understands: "I breathe out long"' (M 531). What do words such as 'I' and 'he' refer to if not a self?

It may be that in these passages the Buddha is merely employing conventional modes of speech without intending to endorse their ordinary metaphysical implications. But what do these pronouns refer to in the absence of selves? In any case, the most troublesome philosophical difficulty is the fact that the doctrines of *kamma* and rebirth seem to presuppose the existence of selves. If there are no selves, then what can it mean to say that my morally wrong actions now will bring unhappiness to me in the future? Must there not be a self that both performs the action and bears the fruit of it? Again, if there are no selves, then what is reborn? Does not the cycle of rebirth require that my self existed in previous lives and will exist in future lives until *Nibbāna* is attained?

One possibility, of course, is that the Buddha does not have a consistent teaching concerning the self. However, we should accept this conclusion only after we have found deficient all attempts to reconcile his not-self teaching with comments that seem to presuppose a self and in particular the doctrines of *kamma* and rebirth. In my view, the Buddha does have a consistent doctrine of the self. In order to establish this, I will argue that the best interpretation of his teaching is that he implicitly accepts a distinction between substance-selves that have no reality and process-selves that have a dependent reality that ends with the attainment of *Nibbāna*. Let us now turn to this distinction.

3 Two conceptions of the self: substance and process

A view prominent at the time of the Buddha held that each person's true self was identical with the ultimate ground of reality (*brahman*). It might be $\overline{\text{India}}$ suspected that the Buddha's not-self doctrine is nothing more than a rejection of this distinctive understanding of the self. If this were the case, then Western stream-observers might have little or no disagreement with the Buddha's teaching about the absence of self (since they are unlikely to understand their selves as identical with the ground of reality). However, though the Buddha does deny views about the self that were prominent in his culture, his not-self doctrine has implications that go beyond the denial of these local views. In particular, he rejects a conception of the self that is probably accepted by many stream-observers and has been widely endorsed in the Western philosophical tradition. I will call this the substance conception of the self (it was briefly discussed in chapter 3, section 3). On the other hand, there is another conception of the self that the Buddha implicitly appears to affirm, albeit in a significantly qualified form. I will call this the process conception of the self. Let us first describe these two conceptions and then consider what the Buddha says about them.

According to the *substance conception*, a self is a single, unified substance (we might also say it is a being, entity, or thing). In this respect, a self is like other substances in the world such as ordinary physical objects. A substance is something that is *ontologically distinct* from other substances – that is, though a substance has properties, it is not itself the property of another substance. Moreover, though one substance may causally depend on other substances, each substance remains a distinct or separate entity. For example, the sun might cause a plant to live, but the sun is one thing and the plant is another. In addition, a substance is something that has *identity* – that is, in some respects it persists through time unchanged so long as it exists. A substance may change, but it cannot change in every respect and remain the substance it is. Hence, some properties of a substance may change over time. For instance, a planet might gradually change from bright red to reddish-brown. The color of a planet is an accidental property. But a substance also has essential properties, properties that cannot change without the substance

69

ceasing to be what it is. These properties are necessary to the identity of the substance. An essential property of planets is that they orbit a star such as the sun. If Pluto ceased to orbit the sun and moved unendingly away from it, it would no longer be a planet. Hence, as long as a particular planet exists, it has the property of orbiting a sun.

Planet

On this account, then, a self is a substance in the sense of being ontologically distinct from other substances and having a set of essential, unchanging properties that are necessary for its identity as a self. The properties that are distinctive of a self, in contrast to substances such as plants and planets, are that it has capacities that enable it to regularly experience, remember, imagine, feel, desire, think, decide, act, and so on. A self is a substance that has all or most of these attributes as essential properties (hence, we say a self is a subject who experiences and an agent who acts). In some cases, a self *undergoes* these things. For example, we might think of an experience or feeling as something that happens to us. But in other cases, a self *does* these things. For example, thinking, deciding, and acting are usually considered things a self does rather than undergoes. Sometimes, as in a daydream, it may be unclear whether an attribute of a self is something it undergoes or does. But that a self is a substance that undergoes some things and does others is essential to what it means to be a self. Moreover, a self *controls* those things it does in a sense that it does not control those things it undergoes. For example, I cannot change the fact that when I look at the book in front of me I have an experience of something rectangular, but I can determine whether or not to pick up the book. Finally, on this account, a self has a reflexive property: it is capable of being *aware of itself as a substance-self.* A self not only experiences and decides, it can be and often is aware of the fact that it is a self that experiences and decides. A self has the capacity for self-awareness or self-consciousness.

To sum up, according to the substance conception, a self is a substance-self, a substance that is ontologically distinct from other substances (*distinctness*) and has essential properties that do not change (*identity*); these properties include the regularly exercised capacities to experience, remember, imagine, feel, desire, think, decide, act, and the like (*attributes of undergoing and doing*); the substance-self controls those things it does (*self-control*); and it has the capacity to be aware of itself as a substance-self (*self-awareness*). This conception of the self is familiar in Western traditions. For example, Descartes appeared to have such a conception in mind when he declared that he was 'a thing that thinks' – that is, 'a thing that doubts, understands, affirms, denies, is willing, is unwilling, and also imagines and has sensory perceptions' (Descartes 1984: 19). Each aspect of the substance conception of the self may invite controversy and would require a more detailed formulation to be fully adequate. But this account should be sufficient for our present purpose. It is important to recognize that this description is neutral with respect to several important philosophical controversies concerning the self. For instance, it does not specify whether or not the self is immortal, is distinct from the

70

body, is found in human beings but not other animals, or possesses a free will. (Descartes affirmed all of these points, but they are not part of the substance conception of the self as defined here.) Nonetheless, for many persons, an essential part of the reason human beings have the value they have – for example, that they are worthy of love or respect – is the fact that they are substance-selves.

Let us now turn to the *process conception* of the self. On this account, there are no substance-selves. Rather, the phenomena the previous account described as substances-selves are in fact process-selves. The key difference between the two accounts is that the process conception rejects what the substance conception regards as fundamental: that the world is made up of substances that are ontologically distinct and have identity through time. Instead, according to the process conception, the world should be understood as consisting solely of processes. Whereas the substance conception takes (apparently) discrete and stable objects such as moons and monoliths as its paradigms of what is real, the process conception suggests that the proper paradigms are occurrences such as whirlpools and wind storms that are (w obviously interdependent on their environment and ever-changing. On this account, a process is not a thing, entity, or being, but an event, activity, or becoming: it is a specific movement within the world, interconnected with other movements and in constant change in every respect. A particular process is not a thing that has necessary properties and is distinct from other things. It is an aspect of the overall movement that constitutes the world. As a movement, a process has an important temporal character: it involves a continuous passage of becoming from past to present to future. But ordinarily a process is not random: it manifests an ordered, lawful causal development. Moreover, on account of interconnection, processes involve other processes: a given process typically contains smaller-scale processes and is contained within larger-scale processes.

Now, according to the process conception, a self is not a substance, but an integrated set of processes. Specifically, a process-self is a structured nexus of continuous, interacting processes that are not ontologically distinct from other processes and that are in constant change in every respect. The specific processes that constitute the process-self are typically the aforementioned undergoings and doings of the self. But instead of describing these as necessary properties of a substance, the process conception says a self is nothing but a nexus of processes such as experiencing, remembering, imagining, feeling, desiring, thinking, acting, and so on. Moreover, since a process-self is not ontologically distinct from other processes, both what it does and what it undergoes are conditioned by other processes. (However, a distinction between doing and undergoing is still affirmed.) Finally, a process-self has false self-awareness: it mistakenly believes it is aware of itself as a substance-self (this feature may distinguish this account of the self from other process accounts; we will see momentarily why it is an important aspect of the Buddha's position).

71

In short, according to the process conception, a self is a process-self, a nexus of processes such as experiencing, acting and the like that is not ontologically distinct from other processes, that is in constant change in every respect, that is conditioned in what it does as well as what it undergoes, and that falsely believes it is aware of itself as a substance-self. On this account, a self is not a distinct substance with identity through time. Rather, it is an integrated set of ever-changing processes enmeshed in a world of other processes. Process understandings of reality are not predominant in Western philosophical traditions, but they have been accepted by a minority of philosophers from Heraclitus in the sixth century BCE to Whitehead in the twentieth century. Among persons in the West, the substance conception of the person is probably closer to the 'common sense' view than the process conception is, but it is a large question as to which conception is philosophically more adequate. As we will see in chapter 8, each account has its share of perplexities.

4 A coherent interpretation of the Buddha

We may now return to the teaching of the Buddha. A problem of interpretation arises because the Buddha speaks a great deal about the absence of any self and yet sometimes seems to refer to or presuppose a self. In my view, the resolution of this problem – the best overall interpretation of his teaching – is that he believed that substance-selves have no reality and that process-selves have no independent reality but do have a form of dependent reality. There are no substance-selves because reality does not consist of substances. When the Buddha speaks of the absence of any self he should be understood as meaning (in part) the absence of any substance-self. On the other hand, when he appears to presuppose selves in the doctrines of *kamma* and rebirth, and more generally when he seems to refer to selves, he should be understood as referring to the dependent reality of process-selves. However, process-selves have no independent reality. Hence, in independent reality there are no selves at all. This is the Buddha's not-self doctrine.

In order to understand this interpretation, we need to consider the distinction between dependent and independent reality. The reality or existence of some things directly depends on mental states such as beliefs, desires, or attitudes (understood here as processes). For example, the value of a monetary currency such as the dollar directly depends on the belief that it has value. If people stopped believing this (as tends to happen in times of severe inflation), then the dollar would lose its value. In one sense, the value of the dollar is obviously a real feature of the world. People make important decisions in their lives based on this assumption. But in another sense it is not real. For example, ordinarily we suppose that the existence of the moon does not directly depend on mental states such as what we think about it. In this sense, the moon has independent reality. The value of the dollar, by contrast, does not have independent reality the way the moon does.

Let us say that something has *dependent* reality if its reality directly depends on mental states, and that something has *independent reality* if its reality does not directly depend on mental states. According to the Buddha's teaching of dependent origination, ultimately everything is interdependent and thus nothing is completely independent. Nonetheless, only some things are directly dependent on mental states. By comparison, other things may be said to be independent, meaning not directly dependent on mental states. Hence, the distinction between dependent and independent reality as defined here is consistent with dependent origination.[2]

The distinctive idea of the Buddha is that the dependent reality of process-selves is the only reality of selves there is. Substance-selves have no reality. On the other hand, process-selves have no independent reality, but they do have dependent reality: they exist only insofar as there are certain beliefs, desires, feelings, attitudes, and so on. Specifically, a person's process-self exists only insofar as the person falsely believes it is a substance-self and hence is attached to its desires and feelings as properties of its substance-self, as features of the world it regards as 'mine.' The delusion that I am a substance-self maintains the dependent reality of my being a process-self. As long as this delusion and the consequent attachments to desires and feelings continues, the process-self referred to by 'me' will continue to exist (and suffer and be reborn and suffer again, and so on). But once the belief that I am a substance-self ceases along with the attachments to specific desires and feelings as 'mine,' the process-self that was me ceases – and *Nibbāna* is attained. Like the value of a monetary currency, a process-self exists because of what is believed. However, there is an important disanalogy in this comparison. Belief in the value of the dollar need not involve a mistake on our part (we might be correct in thinking it is worth a certain amount), but the belief that one is a substance-self is a mistake for the Buddha. In fact, it is the most fundamental error we make: it is what preserves the existence of process-selves and brings about suffering.

It is important to remember that the not-self doctrine is only part of the Buddha's teaching about the nature of human persons. His full teaching may be summarized as follows.

(1) We are not substance-selves in any sense.
(2) We are process-selves in a dependent sense and hence have better or worse, but always unsatisfactory, rebirths in accord with the morality of our actions.
(3) We are that which has the opportunity to escape the cycle of rebirth and attain *Nibbāna*.

We are dependently process-selves because we mistakenly think we are substance-selves. As a result, we suffer through repeated rebirths. Completely liberated from this delusion, we attain *Nibbāna*, the highest form of happiness, provisionally during life and fully after death. Our most fundamental reality gives us a genuine hope of this attainment; if not in this lifetime, then in lives to come. Emphasis on (1) and (2) alone may seem a depressing prospect. But this misses (3), and (3) is what really matters from the Buddha's standpoint. Our highest fulfillment is found in literally living selflessly.

The idea of *Nibbāna* raises its own perplexities (these will be discussed in chapters 12 and 13). For now, we need to consider the validity of (1) and (2) as an interpretation of the Buddha's not-self doctrine. An interpretation of this doctrine should strive to make consistent sense of everything the Buddha says or assumes concerning both the absence of self and the presence of self, and it should try to show how the doctrine could be thought to provide a cogent account of our lives. In the chapters to come, we will see to what extent the interpretation offered here achieves these goals. A key issue will be whether or not the ideas of *kamma* and rebirth can be understood solely in terms of the dependent reality of process-selves. Does it make sense to say, with reference to a process-self, that its morally good (bad) actions cause its future happiness (unhappiness) and that it has existed before this life and may exist again after this life? We will discuss this issue in chapter 9. Our immediate concern is to evaluate the rationale for the not-self teaching. What considerations did the Buddha put forward for believing substance-selves have no reality? Can the full not-self doctrine – that substance-selves have no reality and that process-selves have only dependent reality – withstand objections rooted in our ordinary beliefs concerning the self? We will discuss these questions in chapters 7 and 8.

SUGGESTED READING

Some standard expressions of the not-self doctrine are found in the *Mahāpuṇṇama Sutta* ('The Greater Discourse on the Full-moon Night'), M #109. See also the *Chachakka Sutta* ('The Six Sets of Six'), M #148. Additionally, see the suggestions in chapters 7 and 8.

The best works on the Buddha's not-self teaching are Collins (1982) and Harvey (1995a). Collins (1994) and Matilal (1989) are also valuable. Challenges to the interpretation defended here may be found in Conze (1967) and especially Pérez-Remón (1980). Hamilton (2000) tries to shift the emphasis away from the question of selfhood and toward how the person works in light of dependent origination. The philosophical idea of the self is examined in G. Strawson (1999). For interpretations of Buddhism as a process philosophy, see Hartshorne (1960), Inada (1975 and 1979) and Malalasekera (1964). A classic work in process philosophy is Whitehead (1929); a more introductory work is Whitehead (1925). For an accessible introduction to process philosophy, see Rescher (1996).

NOTES

1   This is the interpretation offered in the note to the text (M, number 39 on page 1170). However, it must be admitted that the text itself does not explicitly support this interpretation. On the other hand, since neither 'self exists for me' nor 'no self exists for me' are affirmed, the passage cannot be taken to show that the Buddha accepted some doctrine of the self.

2   Some later Buddhist traditions, such as the *Yogācāra* school, did move in an idealist direction, but this was not the teaching of the Buddha in the *Sutta Piṭaka*.

7

THE RATIONALE FOR
THINKING THERE ARE NO
SUBSTANCE-SELVES

The Buddha's not-self doctrine, as I understand it, is the view that there are no substance-selves and that process-selves have only dependent reality. The purpose of this chapter is to consider the rationale the Buddha offers for accepting the first part of this doctrine: that persons are not ontologically distinct substances with identity through time. After some preliminary remarks, we will focus on the three main ideas on which the Buddha relies to challenge the belief that we are substance-selves: impermanence, a conception of causality, and suffering. These ideas take us to the heart of the metaphysics the Buddha employs in articulating the practical concerns of the Four Noble Truths.

1 Some preliminaries

Stream-observers typically believe they are selves, and after some philosophical reflection they may think the best articulation of this belief is that they are substance-selves. That we are substance-selves certainly appears to be a common view. An underlying reason for this view may be the thought of many persons that, though there is much about me that may change (my body, experiences, opinions, feelings, and so on) there is something – the essence of *me* – that is always the same throughout these changes and is distinct from everything else in the universe. This essence, it may be supposed, is the substance that is my self. Perhaps some stream-observers do not think they are substance-selves. If so, they may not disagree with the Buddha's not-self teaching (though the Buddha thinks unenlightened persons ordinarily have some false beliefs concerning the self). But those who do think they are substance-selves might first reflect on *why* they think this before considering the Buddha's arguments to the contrary. Is it obvious that we are substance-selves?

One lesson the natural sciences have taught us is that much that may seem obvious about the world is not true. For example, it appears obvious that the desk in front of me is a single, distinct, solid, and unmoving object. But physics tells us this is not really so. In fact, the desk consists of a huge number

76

of incredibly minute atoms consisting of a nucleus of protons and neutrons (themselves consisting of up and down quarks) surrounded by orbiting electrons. Moreover, contemporary 'string theory,' a theory that promises to unify general relativity and quantum mechanics into a 'theory of everything,' says that even these particles are not the most basic features of nature. According to physicist Brian Greene: 'The elementary ingredients of the universe are *not* point particles. Rather, they are tiny, one-dimensional filaments somewhat like infinitely thin rubber bands, vibrating to and fro' (Greene 2000: 136). I am not sure whether the oscillating loops of 'string' that string theory postulates as the ultimate material of the universe are more like substances or processes (perhaps neither is an accurate model). But it is clear that the world as understood by modern physics is utterly different from the world of our ordinary experience. And if a desk is completely different from what we usually take it to be, then perhaps the same is true of what we call our selves.

It might be said that, irrespective of physics, just as it is pragmatically (a) convenient to speak of desks and other substances in ordinary life, so it is useful to refer to substance-selves in ordinary human interactions: in routine circumstances, we assume that we can clearly distinguish one person from another and that a person at ages twenty, thirty, and forty is in some significant sense the same person throughout. Whatever the truth of the ultimate nature of the universe, it might be said, these assumptions are 'correct' for the purpose of everyday living. However, it may be that the idea of process-selves is sufficient to account for our ordinary interactions with one another (we will consider this in the next chapter). Moreover, if the idea of substance-selves is accepted as pragmatically useful without supposing it to correspond to anything real (according to the correct scientific account), then the Buddha has an important response: from the perspective of overcoming suffering, it would be even more useful to give up the idea of substance-selves.

Those who believe they are substance-selves usually take this fact to be central to the value they ascribe to themselves and other human beings: it is because we are substance-selves, people often think, that we are thought worthy of the special love, concern, and respect that is appropriate for human beings in contrast to what may be owed to animals, plants, and inanimate objects. Many people probably agree with Kant when he says: 'The fact that man is aware of an ego-concept raises him infinitely above all other creatures living on earth' (Kant 1978: 9). This suggests that our belief that we are substance-selves is intimately tied to our moral and religious values. But is this belief forced upon us by an unyielding reality that we ignore at our peril (as we might say about the force of gravity)? Or is it an interpretation of reality about which reasonable persons in different times and places have disagreed? According to Geertz, 'Some conception of what a human individual is, as opposed to a rock, an animal, a rainstorm, or a god, is, so far as I can see, universal.' But he adds that 'the actual conceptions involved vary from one group to the next, and often quite sharply' (Geertz 1983: 59).

If Geertz is right, the idea that we are substance-selves may not be part of the universal 'common sense' of human beings. It may be that it is a controversial interpretation of human beings that requires some justification.

None of these considerations shows that we are not substance-selves, much less that the Buddha's not-self teaching is correct. But they do suggest that it may not be as obvious as we thought that we are substance-selves. With this awareness in mind, we may now turn to the rationale presented by the Buddha for supposing we are not. Three preliminary observations should be made about this rationale. First, the Buddha puts forward numerous pertinent considerations, but they all involve a single group of ideas: the rationale consists of a set of interconnected lines of reasoning. Second, though we can articulate an intellectual account of this rationale, for the Buddha full comprehension of it requires meditation. Third, the rationale is closely linked to the practical concern to overcome suffering. We will distinguish two metaphysical arguments based on impermanence and dependent origination respectively. But the Buddha never separates these from the practical context stressed in the last argument focusing on suffering.

2 Impermanence: the five aggregates

The Buddha regularly speaks of 'the perception of non-self in all things without exception' (N 177). Crucial to this claim is the contention that all things we experience in the world are impermanent (*anicca*). The connection between impermanence and the absence of substance-selves is as follows. If everything is impermanent, is in a constant process of change, then there are no substances and hence no substance-selves. On a substance account, there is a certain kind of stability in the world. It consists of substances that have identity through time: though they may change in some respects, in other respects they persist unchanged (so long as they exist). According to the Buddha, the world is not stable in this way. There are no things with identity. Everything is in a constant process of change in every respect.

It may be objected that there are features of the world that are permanent. For example, perhaps the scientific laws that govern the physical world, such as the law of gravity, are permanent. The Buddha does not deny that there are unchanging laws that govern changes in the world. In fact, the doctrine of *kamma* affirms such a law. But a law is not a substance; it is a regularity in the processes of change in the world. The stability of laws is not the stability of things. Hence, the fact that there are unchanging laws does not mean there are substances with identity.

It might also be said that God is unchanging. The Buddha denies that there is a god who is an unchanging and eternal substance. This is a fundamental difference between the Buddha's teaching and orthodox forms of monotheism. On the other hand, the Buddha's claim is that nothing in the world of ordinary experience is unchanging. *Nibbāna* is portrayed as beyond the impermanence of this world. Though *Nibbāna* is not a substance, it is outside the realm of change. It may be suggested that the descriptions of God by theists and those of *Nibbāna* by Buddhists are efforts to understand the same transcendent reality (see chapter 13, section 1). Perhaps this is so. But orthodox accounts of God and *Nibbāna* are prima facie incompatible because God is ordinarily taken to be a self and *Nibbāna* is not.

In any case, what is directly relevant here is whether there are some permanent features of the world that could plausibly be considered our selves. Usually the argument from impermanence to the absence of selves is made by reference to the five aggregates (material form, feelings, perceptions, formations, and consciousness). The assumption is that anything that could be reasonably thought to be a self would have to be found in connection with one or more of these aggregates. Since everything associated with the aggregates is impermanent, no such self may be found. Here is a representative dialogue:

> '*Bhikkhus*, what do you think? Is material form permanent or impermanent?'
> 'Impermanent, venerable sir.'
> 'Is what is impermanent suffering or happiness?'
> 'Suffering, venerable sir.'
> 'Is what is impermanent, suffering, and subject to change, fit to be regarded thus: "This is mine, this I am, this is my self"?'
> 'No venerable sir.'

The same exchange occurs concerning the other four aggregates. The Buddha continues:

> Therefore, *bhikkhus*, any kind of material form whatever, whether past, future, or present, internal or external, gross or subtle, inferior or superior, far or near, all material form should be seen as it actually is with proper wisdom thus: 'This is not mine, this I am not, this is not my self.'
>
> (M 232)[1]

As before, the same point is made regarding the other aggregates. The Buddha goes on to say that realization of this leads to disenchantment with the aggregates, and this in turn leads to enlightenment.

There is much involved in this passage. Its three principal elements – impermanence, suffering, and not-self – are described by the Buddha as the three conditions of existence in the world of everyday experience (see N 77). We will return to the role of suffering in this argument (see section 4 and chapter 11). What is important now is that the Buddha thinks enlightenment involves the recognition of impermanence and hence of not-self with respect to each of the aggregates.

In order to evaluate this argument, we first need to consider what the Buddha means by the aggregates (*khandhas*). These are intended to be an exhaustive account of everything we typically take to be involved in a person and hence to be candidates for what could be considered a self. Though the five aggregates are distinguished, it is clear that they interact with one another. Material form (*rūpa*) concerns our physical nature. It refers to our entire body and in particular those aspects of it that make possible the five senses. The remaining aggregates are all mental in nature. Feelings (*vedanā*) have to do with our sensations, whether originating from the mind or the body, and their quality as pleasant, unpleasant, or indifferent. Perceptions (*saññā*) go beyond sensations and involve judgments about the world (for example, that there is a red book in front of me). Formations (*sankhāra*) refer to anything that moves us to act – desires, wishes, volitions, and so on. They are classified as being ethically good, bad, or neutral (and thus are related to *kamma*). Finally, consciousness (*viññāna*) concerns the general fact that we are aware, either of the world, or of 'ourselves' as having the other aggregates.

In part, the doctrine of the aggregates is an attempt to classify the various undergoings and doings of the self discussed in the last chapter. As such, it refers to familiar features of persons. For our present purpose, what matters is not so much whether this doctrine is exactly right, but whether it leaves out anything we might associate with a person that is permanent and hence could be a substance-self. If there were such an unchanging aspect, then there would be a flaw in the Buddha's argument. According to the Buddha, every aspect of what we ordinarily regard as a person is encompassed by one or more of the five aggregates, and each of these aggregates is impermanent. Whether we consider the body or aspects of the mind such as feelings, perceptions, volitions and the like, all we ever find is something that changes: this sensation, that desire, this judgment, that feeling, and so on. Each of these particular elements changes constantly and there is nothing to be found that does not change.

It has often been observed that this argument resembles Hume's well-known argument for the conclusion that what we call the self is 'nothing but a bundle or collection of different perceptions.' According to Hume:

> When I enter most intimately into what I call *myself*, I always stumble on some particular perception or other, of heat or cold, light or shade, love or hatred, pain or pleasure. I never can catch *myself* at any time without a perception, and never can observe any thing but the perception.
>
> (Hume 1967: 252)[2]

Though there is a striking similarity here, there are also important differences: the most important is that Hume's argument is a corollary of an epistemological theory, with no practical implications anticipated, whereas the Buddha's argument is one element in a large program aimed at overcoming suffering and attaining *Nibbāna*. More recently, Parfit has defended a reductionist view of the person he claims is quite similar to the Buddha's (see Parfit 1984: 273). Moreover, Parfit believes his view of the self has significant ethical implications, a feature of his position that, in comparison with Hume, brings him closer to the Buddha. Nonetheless, it can hardly be said that Parfit embraces the Buddha's overall outlook.

To return to the Buddha, he maintains that, if we carefully observe what we call 'ourselves,' we will realize that all we ever actually observe are particular impermanent aggregates such as a red sensation. We do not observe an unchanging 'I,' a substance-self, that has this sensation. Here it may be objected, in the spirit of Descartes's famous line, 'I am thinking, therefore I exist' (Descartes 1985: 127), that, though we do not observe a substance-self, *we necessarily presuppose it* – that is, we cannot make sense of a red sensation unless we assume there is an 'I' having this sensation. Hence, we may infer that there is a substance-self even if we cannot directly observe it.

How might the Buddha respond? A later text explicitly denies the inference: 'There is suffering, but none who suffers; doing exists although there is no doer' (Buddhaghosa 1999: 521). On the face of it, this seems perverse. However, that sensations imply an 'I' who has the sensations is a ground for substance-selves only if this 'I' must be a substance-self. If this were true, then the 'I' that has a red sensation now is the same 'I' that had a blue sensation ten minutes or ten years ago (on account of identity), and this is a less obvious point. The Buddha could allow that in our ordinary experience sensations are thought to imply an 'I,' but insist that in fact there is nothing more to this 'I' than a process-self having only dependent reality. In this way, the Cartesian argument could be partly accepted. But it would also be partly rejected since in independent reality there are no substance-selves: in this respect, 'there is suffering, but none who suffers.'

For this response to be plausible, the Buddha needs to explain why we often suppose there is identity. For example, we usually think it makes sense to say that smoking in my youth caused me to have cancer in later life or that the man who is now president of the USA went to Yale several decades ago. Moreover, the doctrine of *kamma* presupposes that these may be reasonable things to say: it claims that my present state of happiness is the fruit of the moral quality of my past actions. If I am nothing more than an ever-changing process-self, there is no common element between me now and me earlier. So what sense is there in these statements? We will address this question in chapters 8 and 9. To anticipate, the answer is that there is no identity through time, but there is continuity. Just as a hundred-foot rope may consist only of overlapping strands none of which is longer than ten feet, so a process-self may consist of overlapping and ever-changing aggregates. In each case, there is no common element at the beginning and the end. But there is enough continuity to make identity statements intelligible. In the case of the rope, it makes

81

sense to say that you are pulling on one end and I am pulling on the other, even though there is no strand that we are both grasping. Something similar may be said about the aforementioned statements about persons. In another later text, *The Questions of King Milinda*, it is said that a child who becomes an adult is 'neither the same nor another' (Mendis 1993: 39). There is neither identity nor complete discontinuity.

Another objection to the Buddha is as follows. What is essential to selves is not particular sensations per se, but the capacity to have them (and similarly for other aggregates); though we do not directly observe this capacity, its existence is a reasonable inference from what we do observe; and, while particular sensations change frequently, the capacity to have them is an enduring property that presupposes a substance-self.

The Buddha might respond by denying the inference to capacities. However, this is a perilous move. It is hard to deny that we have a capacity to perceive that cannot be reduced to a set of sensations. A more plausible approach would be to explain the capacity in terms of the nexus of processes that constitutes the process-self. It is obvious that some capacities, such as the abilities to reason or remember, develop and decline over time. A process approach would understand all human capacities not as unchanging properties of substance-selves, but as ever-changing yet continuous features of process-selves.

There is a different kind of response to these objections. The observation that reveals the aggregates to be impermanent and hence to involve no substance-self is not the everyday observation of introspective experience (as in Hume's argument), but the highly disciplined observation of insight meditation. In his advice to Rāhula, the Buddha says, 'Develop meditation on the perception of impermanence; for when you [do so] the conceit "I am" will be abandoned' (M 531). Ordinary observation is likely to be adversely influenced by our belief that we are substance-selves and the array of attachments to which this belief gives rise. Thus, we may be mislead into thinking sensations necessarily imply a substance-self. The Buddha might regard the objections just considered as primary examples of the way the belief that we are substance-selves distorts our interpretation of the world. The aim of meditation is to purify the mind of these distorting elements so that we will see things as they really are. The key contention of the Buddha is that the observation of meditation reveals each of the aggregates to be impermanent and hence empty of self:

> *Bhikkhus,* suppose that this river Ganges was carrying along a great lump of foam. A man with good sight would inspect it, ponder it, and carefully investigate it, and it would appear to him to be void, hollow, insubstantial. For what substance could there be in a lump of foam? So too, *bhikkhus,* whatever kind of form there is, whether past, future, or present, internal or external, gross or subtle, inferior or superior,

far or near: a *bhikkhu* inspects it, ponders it, and carefully investi-
gates it, and it would appear to him to be void, hollow, insubstantial.
For what substance could there be in form?

(C I 951)

The same point is made with respect to the other aggregates: with the
proper inspection and investigation of meditation, no substance-self is found
in connection with any of the aggregates. The force of this argument – and
others in this chapter – obviously depends on the capacity of insight meditation to see things as they really are (see chapter 16). At this stage, we may
regard this argument as presenting us with a challenge: is there anything about
a person that is truly unchanging and could plausibly be regarded as having
the identity required of a substance-self? If there is, this constitutes a significant objection to the Buddha's teaching. If not, in this respect the Buddha
appears correct.

3 Causality: dependent origination

Though the Buddha thinks everything is impermanent, he does not think
change is chaotic or random: there are unchanging causal laws that govern
all change. Hence, there is a kind of stability in the world. It is the stability
not of substances, but of law-governed processes. On this account, the basic
ontological category is not a substance but a process. Processes are always
in change in every respect, but these changes are governed by causal laws
according to which the state of each process is dependent on, or conditioned
by, other processes. The Buddha appears to think the processes that make up
the world are often interdependent: they condition one another.

The basic expression of causality is the doctrine of dependent origination
(*paṭicca samuppāda*). Sāriputta says understanding this doctrine is equivalent
to understanding the Buddha's teaching as a whole. In brief and abstract form,
it says: 'When this exists, that comes to be; with the arising of this, that arises.
When this does not exist, that does not come to be; with the cessation of this,
that ceases' (M 655; cf. 927). A process is always in a state of becoming: from
not existing it arises into existence, then ceases back into non-existence.
Dependent origination says that, for whatever state a process is in, that state
is conditioned by other processes. Hence, the state of every process has a
causal explanation.

Though dependent origination has general application to all processes in
the world, in this context the Buddha is interested in applying it to persons.
Once again, the understanding of persons as process-selves comes to the
fore: what we call the self is not a substance-self, but a nexus of interconnected processes referred to by the five aggregates. Moreover, in accord with
dependent origination, the state of each process-self – or of each aspect of it
– is conditioned by other processes (whether these originate in what we

customarily distinguish as the person, other persons, or nature). For example, 'each feeling arises in dependence upon its corresponding condition, and with the cessation of its corresponding condition, the feeling ceases' (M 1122).

Since process-selves are part of the ever-changing, interdependent network of processes in the world, they are not ontologically distinct in the sense of being distinct substances. Hence, there are no substance-selves both because nothing is permanent and because nothing is truly distinct. On the substance account, substances are separate from one another: here is one substance, here is another, here is a third and so on – as coins or chessmen appear to be. That substances are fundamentally distinct or separate entities is the primary ontological fact; the causal relationships among these substances is secondary. On a process account, by contrast, causal relationships are the primary ontological fact, and we cannot understand a particular process without understanding its place in the overall causal network of the world (think of drops of food colors in a bowl of water). Hence, there are no substances – and, in particular, no substances-selves – that are distinct. There are only interdependent process-selves.

This is not to say that process-selves are properties of other substances and thus are dependent on them in the way that, according to a substance account, properties are dependent upon their substances. For example, this might seem natural when speaking of my blue jacket: its property of blueness depends on the substance that is my jacket; if there were no jacket, then that particular blueness would no longer exist. On the process view, since there are no substances, the question as to whether something is a property of a substance does not arise. Process-selves lack ontological distinctness not because they are properties of substances, but because they are nothing more than causally interrelated processes.

It might be objected that we ordinarily have no trouble distinguishing one person from another, and also that it is typically clear that this sensation is mine and that one is yours. What makes me one process-self and you another, and this my sensation and that yours, if we are each a nexus of processes that is part of the network of processes in the world?

This is perhaps the most difficult question the Buddha's account must answer, and we will return to it in the next chapter. By way of a preliminary, it is clear that the particular aggregates that constitute each of us must be unified in some fashion so that we can observe that this is me and that is you, and that this is my sensation and that is yours. The unifying factor cannot be a substance. It must be a feature of the processes themselves. An analogy may help us understand this. We distinguish two neighboring sandbars by supposing that each is a unified nexus of processes that is part of the overall network of processes. It is not necessary to suppose they are distinct substances. Perhaps a person is just a more complex integration of processes. As already noted, for the Buddha the source of the unification of process-selves is the *belief* of each unenlightened person, manifested in multiple attachments, that I am a substance-self (remember that a belief is understood as a process). Like a magnet, an 'I conceit' (*asmi māna*) brings a set of particular aggregates together as 'mine,' and likewise for you. Hence, our respective process-selves may each say, 'This is my sensation,' despite the fact that we are both part of the network of interdependent processes in the world. We are not distinct in the sense of being distinct substances, but we are not identical either.

Dependent origination in persons is often elaborated via a twelvefold formula of conditioning links. In a representative passage, Ānanda asks how a *bhikkhu* can 'be called skilled in dependent origination.' The Buddha responds:

> With ignorance [*avijjā*] as condition [*paccaya*], formations [*sankhāra*] (comes to be); with formations as condition, consciousness [*viññāna*]; with consciousness as condition, mentality-materiality [*nāmarūpa*]; with mentality-materiality as condition, the sixfold base [*saḷāyatana*] (the senses and the mind); with the sixfold-base as condition, contact [*phassa*]; with contact as condition, feeling [*vedanā*]; with feeling as condition, craving [*taṇhā*]; with craving as condition, clinging [*upādāna*]; with clinging as condition, being [*bhava*]; with being as condition, birth [*jāti*]; with birth as condition, aging and death [*jarāmaraṇa*], sorrow, lamentation, pain, grief, and despair come to be. Such is the origin of this whole mass of suffering.
>
> (M 927; cf. 353–4)

Though the twelvefold formula is usually emphasized, other formulae with greater or fewer elements are sometimes given. The general idea is clear enough: ignorance conditions formations, these condition consciousness, and so on until we reach suffering. The origin of suffering is ignorance mediated by factors such as craving and clinging.

Sometimes the elements of the formula are presented in terms of cessations in order to show us how to end suffering. The passage just quoted continues (leaving out the middle steps): 'But with the remainderless fading away and cessation of ignorance comes cessation of formations . . . with the cessation of birth, aging and death, sorrow, lamentation, pain, grief, and despair cease. Such is the cessation of this whole mass of suffering' (M 927–8). These two versions of the twelvefold formula, in terms of conditions and cessations, are obviously elaborations of the account of the origin and cessation of suffering in the second and third of the Four Noble Truths. Regarding such formulae, the Buddha says: 'It is through not understanding, not penetrating this doctrine that this generation has . . . [been] unable to pass beyond states of woe, the ill destiny, ruin and the round of birth-and-death' (L 223).

The twelvefold formula has been understood in different ways (see chapter 11, section 3). If we take it at face value, as a pair of linear sequences, we need an interpretation of the causal conditioning between the parts. To simplify discussion, let us reduce it to three key elements: ignorance, craving, and suffering. It is obvious that these elements should be understood as processes rather than substances. Now, on the one hand, it seems that each element is a necessary condition of the element that follows. Thus, ignorance is a necessary condition of craving (if there is craving, then there is ignorance), and craving is a necessary condition of suffering (if there is suffering, then there is craving). Because this is so, the cessation of suffering can be achieved through the cessation of ignorance, craving, and the like – as stated in the cessation version. On the other hand, it does not seem that every element could be a sufficient condition of the element that follows (for example, that ignorance makes craving inevitable). If every element were a sufficient condition, then we could not bring about the cessation of suffering. Since unenlightened persons always find themselves already in ignorance, with craving, and so on, suffering would be inevitable if these were all sufficient conditions. Moreover, a fully enlightened person, an *arahant* who is still alive, has some of these elements (for example, mentality-materiality, a feature of any living person), but this would be impossible if each element was sufficient for the subsequent one. Hence, at least some of the elements must not be sufficient conditions of subsequent ones. Those that are not sufficient conditions still create a very strong propensity for the next element, such that the element ordinarily occurs, but this propensity can be overcome through the efforts involved in the Eightfold Path. That we can overcome the propensities that result in suffering is an important part of the Buddha's fundamental teaching

In this connection, we might wonder where the Buddha stands in the debate concerning free will and determinism. Insofar as this debate presupposes substance-selves whose actions may be free or determined, he obviously has no position. Even with respect to process-selves, it cannot be said that the Buddha recognizes and seeks to resolve a problem of free will and determinism. Nonetheless, in the Buddha's own terms there is an issue here, and up to a point it is possible to discern his position concerning it. Dependent origination, the twelvefold sequence of causal conditioning, and the doctrine of *kamma* all imply a conception of persons as enmeshed in causal relations. This might be thought to involve a form of causal determinism that precludes 'free choices' – that is, choices that are not strictly determined by antecedent states of affairs. However, the Buddha rejects this suggestion. As just seen, at least in some respects, causal conditioning brings about strong propensities where it remains up to us to decide how to act with respect to these propensities. The *Sutta Piṭaka* contains a tremendous amount of exhortation that appears to presuppose that it is not already determined whether or not we will attain *Nibbāna* (and more generally will have greater or lesser future happiness) and that present and future choices in some sense within our power are instrumental to achieving this. For example, my current character traits may be more or less conducive to attaining *Nibbāna* and these are the result of my past choices. But my character traits do not strictly determine my present and future choices. Whatever my character, I am always free to choose to act in ways that will improve or worsen my future well-being. Similar points may be made about the ways in which other persons or the world as a whole may have conditioned my life (see the critique of the fatalism of the Ājīvikas at 94–5 and M 513– L 14).

The heart of the Buddha's position is that causal conditioning in the sense of creating powerful inclinations is consistent with choices and actions contrary to those inclinations. The Buddha does not articulate a defense of this position. He appears to rely on an assumption many of us make to the effect that, with respect to much human behavior, conditioning may be real without fully determining our actions or precluding free choices. For example, we often suppose that a person whose short temper is conditioned by his or her upbringing or genetic endowment is nonetheless able to learn to control that temper. We acknowledge that the conditioning factors are quite real. But ordinarily we do not think they are so overpowering that the person cannot learn to diminish the propensity to anger. With respect to a broad range of behavior, we usually suppose that human beings have a capacity to freely direct their lives despite the fact that they are conditioned in these familiar ways. In similar fashion, the Buddha thinks our ability to heed his exhortations to follow the Eightfold Path is compatible with the doctrine of dependent origination. In both cases, philosophical perplexities may be on the horizon. But it is not evident that they are more problematic for the Buddha than they are for us.

It might be objected that, in comparison with a process account, a substance account can make better sense of free choices because it regards substance-selves as ontologically distinct. However, in a substance account, distinctness per se does not guarantee freedom. If it did, chairs would be free. Moreover, though substances are distinct, they remain part of the causal structure of the universe. If we think substance-selves can make free choices, we have to show that this capacity is compatible with their place in the causal structure. Perhaps this can be established, but more needs to be said than that substances are distinct. Of course, on the other side, the Buddha's process account needs to reconcile causal conditioning and freedom without recourse to distinctness in this sense.

4 Suffering: the practical context

The contention that all things are impermanent and causally conditioned is central to the rationale for supposing there are no substance-selves. But the Buddha is not interested in these metaphysical considerations for their own sake, and he presents them only in the context of the practical concern to overcome suffering. We now need to return to that context. In the dialogue quoted on page 79, the Buddha argues as follows. Each aggregate is impermanent.

What is impermanent is suffering. Therefore, each aggregate is 'not fit to be regarded thus: "This is mine, I am this, this is my self."' This argument may strike us as curious. Why suppose impermanence involves suffering? And why think that something that suffers cannot be a self?

With respect to the second question, it may seem obvious to Western stream-observers that a self can suffer. However, this aspect of the Buddha's argument is addressed to those in his culture who held that our true self is identical with the ultimate ground of reality (*brahman*). As such, the self was thought to be both permanent and beyond suffering. According to this view, expressed in the *Upaniṣads*, what appears to be our self may suffer, but our true self cannot suffer. By showing that each of the aggregates is imperma-nent, and hence suffers, the Buddha thinks he establishes that this alleged true self cannot be found in connection with any of the aggregates. Since Western stream observers are not likely to think their true self is beyond suffering, this feature of the Buddha's argument need not concern them. But the purported connection between impermanence and suffering is another matter. It plays a central role in the contentions concerning the origin and cessation of suffering in the Four Noble Truths.

Apropos these contentions, the Buddha makes two important claims about the connection between suffering and the belief that one is a substance-self. First, if persons accept this belief, then they have a strong propensity to suffer. Second, if persons truly give up believing they are substance-selves, then suffering will be overcome and *Nibbāna* achieved: 'One who perceives non-self achieves the elimination of the conceit "I am" and attains *Nibbāna* in this very life' (N 229).

We will explore these claims in Part 3. For now, recall that the Buddha thinks the belief that one is a substance-self distinct from others is the source of an orientation to the world in terms of what is 'mine' and what is 'not mine,' and that this orientation gives rise to anger, hatred, greed, desire for power and fame, and so on. He thinks these states naturally issue in forms of suffering. Again, the Buddha supposes that belief that one is a substance-self with identity through time is the origin of an unhealthy preoccupation with regrets about the past and worries about the future. These anxieties are forms of suffering. Throughout, the Buddha maintains, the belief that one is a substance-self gives rise to attachment to one's desires as 'mine,' and in an impermanent and conditioned world, such attachment will only result in frustration. We see in these claims aspects of the connection between imper-manence and suffering.

On the other hand, if a person fully gives up the belief that he or she is a substance-self, the person will no longer be a self in any sense. This will elim-inate the separation from others that is the source of negative states such as anger, and this in turn will liberate the person's capacity for universal compas-sion. Moreover, without the belief in being a self with identity, the person will no longer be obsessed with his or her own past and future. This will free the person to focus on, and find goodness in, each present moment. Hence, the capacity for joy will be released. Liberated in these ways from attachment to desires as 'mine,' the person will achieve the state of ultimate tranquility the Buddha calls *Nibbāna*. These purported psychological truths stand at the heart of the Buddha's practical teaching.

The Buddha's overall rationale for denying that there are substance-selves may be summarized as follows. Since in the world of ordinary experience everything is impermanent and causally conditioned, there is no reason to think – and in fact every reason to deny – that there are substances-selves understood as distinct substances with identity. From a theoretical standpoint, the belief in substances-selves is thereby undermined. When we observe persons closely, all we find are process-selves. Thus, any good reason to think there are substance-selves would have to come from the practical standpoint, from our concern to achieve happiness via our moral and religious values. But when we turn to this concern, we find that this reason for believing there are substance-selves is also undermined. Belief that one is a substance-self promotes suffering, and abandoning this belief brings about *Nibbāna*, the ultimate form of happiness. Therefore, whether we consider the matter from a theoretical or a practical perspective, we have compelling reasons to give up the belief that we are substance-selves.

SUGGESTED READING

Important discussions of the not-self teaching are found in the *Alagaddūpama Sutta* ('The Simile of the Snake'), M #22. On the aggregates, see the *Khandhasaṃyutta* ('Connected Discourses on the Aggregates'), C I 853–983.

The five aggregates are discussed in Gethin (1986) and Hamilton (1996). Free will in Buddhism is examined in Gómez (1975), Mitchell (1975), and Siderits (1987). Hume's critique of the self can be found in Hume (1967: 251–63). For interpretations of Hume and the Buddha, see Bastow (1986), Conze (1963b), Giles (1993 and 1997: chapter 5), B. Gupta (1978), Jacobson (1969), Lesser (1979), Mathur (1978), and Richards (1978). Parfit's major work is 1984; briefer presentations of his conception of the person can be found in 1987 and 1995. Parfit and the Buddha are compared in Bastow (1986), Basu (1997), Collins (1985 and 1997), and Stone (1988). For primary and secondary sources on causality, see chapter 11.

NOTES

1   A similar passage can be found in what is purported to be the second *sutta* of the Buddha. See C I 902–3.

2   In supposing that there is no direct perception of the self as something with identity through time, Kant agrees with Hume (for example, see Kant 1997: A381–2, B413, and B420). But it is mainly Hume who has attracted comparisons with the Buddha.

8

SOME PHILOSOPHICAL ISSUES:
ARE WE SUBSTANCE-SELVES
OR PROCESS-SELVES?

According to the Buddha, there are no substance-selves, but there are process-selves – at least as long as there are beliefs about being substance-selves and related attachments to desires as 'mine.' That is, though none of us is a substance-self, all of us – short of attaining *Nibbāna* – are process-selves. Despite the arguments of the last chapter, this teaching is likely to meet with considerable resistance among Western stream-observers. For many such persons, it may seem an obvious and overwhelming fact of everyday experience that we are substance-selves. In the face of this experience, the Buddha's teaching can appear perverse.

The Buddha acknowledges that we experience one another as substance-selves. But he thinks this experience is a delusion. Moreover, he has an explanation of this delusion: our everyday experience is so permeated by our attachments that we perceive everything in terms of what is 'mine' and 'not mine,' and hence we do not see the world as it really is. Only meditation can fully overcome the distortions caused by our attachments and reveal the true nature of things. The difficulty for stream-observers is that they do not have the direct experience of meditation. They only have the ordinary experience the Buddha regards as misleading. However, the Buddha does have something important to say about our everyday experience of one another as selves. His implicit claim is that we can make sense of this experience by supposing we are process-selves rather than substance-selves. Meditation is required to completely comprehend this claim, but preliminary understanding is possible for those who have not yet undertaken the Eightfold Path. Hence, stream observers are encouraged to consider whether the substance view or the process view of the self is more plausible in light of their ordinary experience.

Recent philosophical debates about personal identity have much to say about this topic. They suggest that it is not obvious that the idea of substance-selves makes coherent sense of our ordinary experience. But they also raise fundamental problems for the idea of process-selves. Each view has its own perplexities. Let us first consider some difficulties for the substance view.

1 Problems for the substance view

A substance-self is an ontologically distinct entity with some essential properties that constitute its identity. These properties are necessarily present as
long as the self exists. They are usually thought to involve regularly exercised
capacities such as the capacity to experience, think, remember, desire, act,
and so on. Are human beings selves in this sense? Is there something that
constitutes our identity that is always with us? Let us consider some different
approaches to these questions.

The content approach

We often suppose that a person's identity is constituted by some qualitative
features that are distinctive of the person. For example, I am the specific
person I am in virtue of the particular beliefs, memories, desires, hopes, and
so on that I have, and likewise for you. It is by reference to such features that
we are likely to determine whether someone physically unrecognizable who
claims to be a long-lost childhood friend really is 'the same person.' This
suggests that we think of a person's identity as constituted by the specific
psychological qualities – the content – that are characteristic of his or her self.
The relevant content might be specified in different ways, and it might be
understood in mental terms, as features of the mind, or in physical terms,
perhaps as features of the brain (or some combination of the two). However
it is understood, the content approach has perplexing consequences.

It seems logically possible that a Self Recorder could transfer the content
that makes up a self from one place to another (just as a VCR can transfer a
movie from one tape to another). That is, all the particular thoughts, memories, desires, and so on that constitute myself on the content approach could
be copied from my mind or brain to another one. Now, suppose the content of
myself was transferred to another 'blank mind' and then my original mind was
destroyed. Does myself still exist? According to the content approach it does,
and we might be tempted to agree. After all, the second mind has *exactly* the
thoughts, memories, desires, and so on that I had. But now suppose this was
done twice. That is, the content of myself was transferred to one blank mind,
then to another, and then the original was destroyed. Now there are two minds
whose qualitative content is identical to what mine was. Does myself still
exist? If so, which mind is it? The content approach suggests that myself is
both new minds. But this is hard to accept. Myself would then consist of two
distinct entities, and a substance-self is thought to be a single distinct entity.
Yet it seems arbitrary to say that myself is one of the two new minds, but not
both, since there is as much reason to say myself is one as the other. On the
other hand, it does not seem correct to say that myself no longer exists,
since each mind has the exact same qualitative content as myself before the
procedure (hence, the temptation to agree that myself still exists in the first

scenario). Therefore, none of the possible answers to the question of whether myself still exists appear altogether convincing.

The bare particular approach

At this point, we might begin to doubt that the identity of the self should be understood in terms of qualitative content. The content approach suggests that reproducing a self is similar to reproducing a video in the following sense. If I make an exact copy of *Gone with the Wind*, and my original video is destroyed, I still have *Gone with the Wind*. In this respect, though the original and the copy were numerically distinct, nothing important has been lost. Likewise, according to the content approach, if an exact copy of a self is made, and the original is destroyed, the self still exists. Once again, though the original and the copy were numerically distinct, nothing important has been lost.

Many people think this comparison shows that the content approach is deeply mistaken. On their view, the copy of myself would not be myself. Something important would be lost. We might put this by saying that the copy would lack something essential to myself – namely, it would not be *me*. Hence, another self could have precisely the same qualitative content as I have (the same thoughts, memories, desires, and so on), but it still would not be me. It would be another self whose content is just like mine. In this case, numerical difference makes all the difference. The idea that the self cannot be reproduced in this way may seem to capture something correct and important about persons: each individual is valuable for being the distinct person he or she is, in contrast to any other actual or possible person in the world, no matter how similar.

But what does it mean to 'be me' here? And why is it important? If myself is not my psychological content, then it seems it must be something else that has or underlies this content, something that is itself without content and hence uncopiable. A consequence of this view – the bare particular approach (so-called because it says the self is a particular thing bare of content) – is that a person's self is radically divorced from the qualitative content emphasized in the first approach. Thus, I would still be myself even if I were to have entirely different content, and likewise (as was just suggested) all my content could be transferred to another mind without that mind becoming me. The difficulty is that we typically identify and value people for being their particular selves precisely because of their specific features. But on the bare particular approach, however much we value these features, we value particular selves for something else that is independent of these features. For example, suppose that all of a man's psychological attributes changed for the worse and that, at the moment before, all the wonderful attributes he used to have were transferred to another mind (associated with a body just like his, we may imagine). According to the bare particular approach, if his wife loved the now wretched man for his self, then in an important respect she would still have as much reason to love him as before, no matter how terrible he had become, and she would not have any reason to love the other self who now has all the outstanding attributes her husband used to have (for example, *he* never forgets 'their' anniversary).

Intuitions differ about what to say regarding this scenario. The French religious thinker Blaise Pascal writes: 'Would we love the substance of a person's soul, in the abstract, whatever qualities might be in it? That is not possible, and it would be wrong. Therefore we never love anyone, but only qualities' (Pascal 1966: section 688). By contrast, McTaggart says: 'Love is for the person, and not for his qualities, nor is it for him in respect of his qualities. It is for him' (McTaggart 1927: 154). If we agree with Pascal, then it would seem that the bare particular approach is mistaken – for it implies that we value a self independent of his or her qualities. But it might seem that this misses something captured by McTaggart – for it is common to think that I am I and you are you, and that however similar we may be, this distinction remains crucially important. The problem with McTaggart's view, and the bare particular view, is that it does not capture the very large extent to which we think the qualities of a person do matter both to whom that person specifically is and to that person's particular value.

The fusion approach

If neither the content approach nor the bare particular approach is right, taken by itself, then perhaps the correct account would combine the two. On this view, both qualitative content and being one specific individual are essential to being a self. Myself is a particular – *me* – that has some psychological content as necessary properties. The properties, we might say, are fused into the particular that is me. As a result, myself would not continue to exist if I were destroyed and my necessary psychological content were copied elsewhere (if this were possible, that would create another self). Moreover, it would not make sense to suppose this content could be replaced with completely different content (since my properties are fused into me, such replacement is not possible). It seems that a plausible substance view of the self will need to say something like this.

But what psychological content is essential to me, is a necessary part of my identity? It would have to be something that is necessarily present as long as myself exits, presumably at least from the day I was born until the day I die. Nothing that I now think, intend, hope for, and so on was a feature of me when I was born. So nothing of this sort could be part of my identity. This is the Buddhist objection: these things constantly change. However, as we saw in the last chapter, a more plausible approach is to suppose that my identity consists of a set of capacities: not specific thoughts, but the capacity to think; not particular intentions, but the capacity to intend, and so on (where these capacities are common to well-formed human beings, but may take somewhat varied forms in different individuals). On this view, though my thoughts and intentions may change, my capacities to think and intend persist throughout my life: they are necessary features of myself.

The difficulty is that the Buddhist objection can also be applied to this view. At birth, none of us had the capacities to think and intend, and as we become old and approach death we typically lose such capacities (sometimes radically, as in the case of those who have Alzheimer's disease). In general, all our capacities undergo constant developments of maturation and decline. Therefore, we possess no capacities that are the same throughout our lives and hence could be an essential part of our identity. The grid of identity, of sameness through time, cannot be made to fit an ever-changing world precisely any more than a circle can be made to circumscribe a square exactly.

To respond to this objection, a proponent of the substance view needs to identify something that is the same throughout these changes. One approach would be to say that we are selves only during a part of our lives – roughly speaking, between the time our capacities become fully mature and the time they begin to decline. But it is not obvious that our capacities are unchanging even through the middle portion of our lives. Moreover, it seems arbitrary to define selfhood in this way, and we do not ordinarily accept this limitation. For example, we typically think children have selves that develop, not that they develop from selfless beings into selved ones. Again, we resist the idea that a person in the advanced stages of Alzheimer's disease has no self at all.

These considerations suggest that a more plausible approach would be to say that there is a sense in which our capacities are present in the same form throughout our lives from birth to death. Thus, we might say that as an infant a self has a latent capacity to think, as an adult it has an actual capacity to think, and as a victim of Alzheimer's disease it has a damaged capacity to think – but throughout it has the very same underlying capacity (perhaps corresponding to a portion of the person's genetic code).

The Buddhist is committed to objecting that, if we observe carefully (through meditation), we will realize that even what purports to be this 'same underlying capacity' changes through time and hence cannot be part of the identity of a substance-self. For example, perhaps the apparent stability at the level represented by our genetic code conceals a deeper level of impermanence in the way that the apparent stability of a desk conceals change at the quantum level. In any case, we have followed this dialectic far enough to grasp the nature of the difficulty the Buddhist sees. We begin with some confidence that we know what it means to be a substance-self. As we attempt to elucidate this notion by locating something that has identity and distinctness, we formulate conceptions of the self that turn out to be distorted versions of what we ordinarily take a self to be. On the current view, something could be a self but have neither thoughts nor an actual capacity to think. In the search for identity, we have come a long way from Descartes's claim to be 'a thing that thinks.' The Buddha believes this search is futile: we will never find identity and distinctness in a world of impermanence and interdependence. Worse, he believes, the need to find something that is the substance-self betrays an attachment to 'what is mine' that prevents us from seeing the world as it really is and results in suffering in our lives.

2 Problems for the process view

Let us now consider some difficulties for the process view. On my interpretation, the Buddha denies that we are substance-selves, but thinks we are process-selves until we attain *Nibbāna*. Hence, he is committed to the position that the process conception of the self can make sense of our ordinary experience of one another as selves (and of *kamma* and rebirth). But can it? According to the process view, the self is a structured nexus of continuous, interacting processes, both mental and physical, that are in constant change in every respect and are not ontologically distinct from other processes in the world. The processes that constitute the self are our beliefs, experiences, desires, hopes, and so on (what the Buddha calls the aggregates), and prominent among these is the false belief that this nexus is aware of itself as a substance-self. These processes are not properties of a substance that is the self. Rather, the self is nothing more than these processes unified in a certain way.

The process view avoids the aforementioned problems for the substance view because the process view does not suppose there must be an unequivocal answer to the question 'Is this the same self as that?' If selves are distinct substances with identity, then the answer to this question must be either 'Yes' or 'No.' But if selves are processes, then the answer may be 'To some extent.' For example, if we ask whether someone who has Alzheimer's disease is the same person as the person who wrote a book twenty years ago, the answer may be 'In some respects yes, and in some respects no.' Strictly speaking, on the process view, a person over a period of time is always partly similar and partly dissimilar. Since there is no respect in which a process-self is immune to change, the extent to which a person is similar or dissimilar is just a matter of degree. Likewise, if we ask whether identical twins have the same self or whether a person with multiple personalities has more than one self, the answer on the process view may be 'Partly yes, and partly no.'

The main problem for the process view is to make sense of the fact that *ordinarily* it is obvious that there is one self or more than one – for example, that I am the same person as the person who married my wife several years ago and am not the same person as my neighbor. If selves are constantly changing processes and are not ontologically distinct from other processes in the world, how do we account for these everyday observations? The Buddha recognized that typically we regard the aggregates as unified into particular persons. In a well-known passage, it is said: 'Just as, with an assemblage of parts, the word "chariot" is used, so, when the aggregates exist, there is the

SOME PHILOSOPHICAL ISSUES

convention "a being"' (C I 230). The parts of a chariot must be unified in a certain way for the chariot to exist. Only then can we say that this is the same chariot as the one we used last year, and that this chariot is going south and that one north. Likewise, the aggregates must be unified in a certain way for a being – that is, a process-self – to exist. Only then can we speak of my being the person who married my wife some time ago and of my being a different person than my next-door neighbor. We saw earlier that the Buddha thought the aggregates making up a particular process-self are unified, not by a substance-self, but by an 'I conceit' – the belief that I am a substance-self, as manifested in various attachments – that brings a particular set of aggregates together as 'mine' (and likewise for other process-selves). The main challenge for the process view is to show that this account of unity is coherent and sufficient to explain our everyday experience of one another as selves.

If the unity problem were solved, then several standard objections to the process view could be answered. First, it is said that the use of proper names and personal pronouns presupposes that there are distinct selves with identity over time. But the selves presupposed by our language need not be sub-stances-selves if process-selves have sufficient unity to allow us ordinarily to speak of ourselves in these ways. Second, it is objected that, if a self is nothing but a nexus of processes, then if any one of my processes had been different (for example, if I had woken up at 8:35 rather than 8:30 this morning), I would have been a different person. However, the process view rejects the idea that I either am or am not the same person. All such statements are matters of degree, and in this case I would have been a different person only to a very slight extent. Third, it is claimed that the process view cannot account for our belief that some attributes are essential to who a particular person is, while others are not. But the process view rejects this belief: no single attribute is essential to being a particular self. Of course, some attributes are correctly thought to be especially important. When these change, we may speak of someone becoming a 'different person' (or hardly being a person at all). What this means, on the process view, is that there is a striking dissimilarity among other similarities.

The central objection to the process view is that a process-self does not have enough unity, or the right kind of unity, to make coherent sense of our experience of one another as selves. There are two aspects to this problem, both anticipated in the last chapter. They concern the *appearance* of identity and distinctness: we ordinarily think that the same person may exist over a long period of time and that one person may clearly be distinguished from another person. Not just any conception of unity can account for what is needed here. For example, it is not sufficient to say that my various processes are unified by membership in a set because there are many sets of processes that do not constitute selves (for example, the set of beliefs of left-handed persons). If we say that my processes are unified by membership in the set 'processes of Chris Gowans,' then we need to know what makes *tornado*

something a member of this set. On the process view, it cannot be the fact that the processes are properties of the substance Chris Gowans. So how are these processes unified?

In one respect, it is not difficult to envision an answer. We can imagine examples that are clearly more process-like than substance- or thing-like, such as a tornado, where a pure process can give the semblance but not the reality of identity and distinctness. Though a tornado is fully interdependent with its meteorological environment, it has enough internal integration and unity of processes relative to this environment for us to speak as if it were one thing that may be distinguished from other things. Likewise, though a tornado lacks strict identity, through time there may be enough causal continuity of processes, and consequent similarities, to make it intelligible to say that the tornado that touched down here is the same one that touched down earlier over there. The Buddhist account of persons as process-selves bears some resemblance to this example, with the qualification that persons have more stability than tornadoes. Thus, the aggregates that constitute a person, though interdependent with their environment, have a high degree of internal integration and unity. Moreover, though they are in constant change, there are relations of causal continuity and consequent similarity through these changes. In this way, persons ordinarily appear to have identity and distinctness, though strictly speaking they do not.

On the Buddha's account, the relevant causal relationships are understood in terms of the ideas of dependent origination and, more specifically, *kamma*. The account need not deny that there are enduring features of persons such as capacities and character traits. But it understands these as continuously developing processes rather than as properties of substances with identity. It might be objected that capacities and character traits presuppose a substance that has them as properties. However, a tornado may have swirling wind as an enduring feature without our supposing this is a property of a substance. It might also be objected that there are some elements of sameness over an entire person's life – for example, it has always been true of me that I was born on a certain date. But according to the process account, the 'I' in this statement does not refer to something that is unchanging. Hence, all that can be said, properly speaking, is that this process-self ('me now') and that similar process-self ('me then') are causally related to one another in certain respects, and that both originated on the same date.

There is a further dimension to these issues that arises from the fact that we have an inner or subjective life. For example, I may feel warm or remember seeing someone last week. An important feature of these inner episodes is that they are felt as our own. Another person may have an experience or memory that is qualitatively similar to mine. But no one else can have my actual experiences and memories. Related to this, our subjective life seems to presuppose a distinction between experiences and the subject who has the experiences (and likewise for memories and other inner episodes). Hence, it is hard to see how the self could be a bundle of inner episodes with no subject that has these episodes. Together these features of our subjective life are commonly thought to require a substance-self: a distinct entity with identity that has its own inner episodes. The process account needs to provide an alternative picture of the apparent unity of these subjective phenomena.

Since the Buddha denies that there are substance-selves, he cannot say that experience presupposes a subject that is a substance-self. But at the level of ordinary understanding, we take it as obvious that an experience requires a subject who has it and, relatedly, that there is distinction between one's own experiences and those of other persons. The process view needs to make sense of this understanding. On the other hand, it is important to remember that the Buddha considers this sense of an inner episode being 'one's own' to be problematic. Regarding something as one's own is a form of clinging or attachment that results in suffering. In order to overcome suffering, attachment must and can be eliminated/This is achieved by correcting the mistake presupposed by attachment – namely, the belief that we are substance-selves./ What is required, then, is an account of the ownership-feel of subjective experience that shows it to be ordinarily experientially real and yet ultimately eliminable because it is rooted in a corrgible mistake. This takes us to the heart of the Buddha's philosophy.

In order to sketch such an account, let us imagine how the thought of being a substance-self might naturally but mistakenly emerge from a collection of processes. As an entrée, think first of a highly coordinated collection of organic beings such as an ant colony. Each ant has primitive correlates of forms of consciousness we call experience, memory, desire, and intentional action. But there is such a high degree of integration among the members of the colony that it becomes intelligible to speak of these primitive forms of consciousness in collective terms. For example, there is a rudimentary sense in which the colony as a whole experiences a source of food, remembers this, desires the food, and intentionally acts to bring it into the colony.

Next imagine a similar scenario, but with a much greater and more complex level of physical and psychic integration. Here too the parts have forms of these same elements of consciousness, but now the degree of coordination and unification is so high that the conscious aspects of the parts overflow into one another. Some parts begin to directly share the experience, memory, and so on of the other parts. A sense of a unified field of consciousness begins to emerge. At this stage, it becomes far more plausible to think that the entire collection of parts experiences, remembers, desires, and acts as one being. Perhaps in some cases an individual animal is just such a unified collection of organic processes.

Now we come to the crucial stage. Whatever may be said about other animals, those animals that are human beings consist of organic processes that are unified to an exceptionally high degree. Here a subjective unity of consciousness becomes quite apparent. In these beings, the belief naturally but mistakenly arises that more is involved than being a tightly integrated collection of organic processes. It is supposed that for each human being there is a single entity, a substance-self, that possesses these processes, or their subjective manifestations, but cannot be reduced to them. The processes themselves are ever-changing and interdependent with their environment. But when highly unified with one another, a sense of 'I' emerges that is thought to refer to a distinct substance with identity. With this conviction, the belief that these are 'my' experiences and that there must be a subject – the substance-self 'me' – who has these experiences becomes inescapable. The process-self now exists. The ownership-feel of subjective experiences feels very real, even though it involves a mistake.

The Buddha has little to say about the origin of this mistake except that it is deeply ingrained within us. However, he has a great deal to say about its unfortunate consequences and how to overcome them. Belief in the substance-self dominates the activities of the entire collection of processes that makes up the human being: virtually everything is centered on protecting and promoting this supposed substance-self. It can hardly be denied that this self is closely connected with the processes actually constituting the person. After all, it is thought to possess these processes or their manifestations. Yet the processes undergo constant changes as they interact with the larger environment. The friction between these two creates the unsatisfactory nature of human life: the impermanence and interdependence of the processes inevitably destabilize whatever adjustments the substance-self seeks in protecting and promoting what it takes to be its essential features. For example, it may regard memories of certain events as essential to itself and suffer when these events begin to elude its best efforts at recall. On the other hand, in the fully enlightened person during this lifetime, the processes continue in many respects as before, but there is no longer a sense of ownership or attachment by a substance-self. In the absence of this, the friction disappears and suffering is overcome. Old age, disease, and impending death remain, as they did for the Buddha. This is the nature of the processes that constitute a person. But they are no longer regarded as a threat to 'myself.'

This is a rather speculative account and it is not the full story of the Buddha's teaching (kamma, rebirth, and Nibbāna need to be brought into the picture). But it may be enough to suggest what the Buddha might say about the ownership objection to the process account of the self. On this point, there is some parallel between the Buddha's position and Kant's claim that from the unity of consciousness we naturally but mistakenly infer a single, unified substance. According to Kant, 'The unity of a thought consisting of many representations ... can be related to the collective unity of the substances cooperating in it (as the movement of a body is the composite movement of all its parts) just as easily as to the absolute unity of the subject' (Kant 1997: A353). Nonetheless, in addition to having a radically dissimilar philosophical framework, the Buddha differed from Kant in thinking that this mistake is the source of suffering and its rectification enables us to overcome suffering. Kant's concerns here are primarily theoretical and only shadow the existential dimensions of the Buddha's teaching. Moreover, in his moral philosophy Kant affirms a substantial conception of the self at odds with the Buddha's not-doctrine self (see chapter 15, section 3).

Many questions could be raised concerning this process account of the self. Does it provide an adequate explanation of our ordinary understanding of one another as selves? In particular, does it render intelligible what we find natural to say about the identity and distinctness of selves? Also, is the account coherent? For example, does it make sense to say that the ownership-feel of subjective experience and the belief that experience requires a subject involve an illusion? These important questions are not easy to answer. However, it must be admitted that, though they have concerned some Buddhist philosophers, they did not much exercise the Buddha himself. To the extent that there are answers, they would have to be drawn from the doctrine of dependent origination and the depiction of the twelvefold series of conditioning links (see chapter 7, section 3 and chapter 11, section 3). But the discussion of these ideas primarily concerns the details of what maintains us as process-selves and how we can bring these selves to an end. This practical perspective is primary, and further philosophical reflection is discouraged. We might also ask how the illusion of a substance-self arose and why it is so deeply ingrained within us. Here little is said beyond a cosmological account of the cycles of the world (see L 409 ff.).

3 Buddhist approaches to debates about the self

The purpose of this chapter has been to probe the Buddha's teaching concerning the self by exploring some philosophical issues involved in the claims that we are respectively substance-selves or process-selves. Each view has its own difficulties and these suggest that, whatever our view, our understanding of one another as selves is more involved and problematic than we might have thought. The Buddha thinks we are not substance-selves and are only provisionally process-selves. Hence, with respect to the issues raised in this chapter, he is committed to believing that the process view makes better overall sense of our ordinary experience than the substance view. Yet we do not find a detailed, theoretical defense of this position in the Buddha. Why not? Three answers may be given: each is partly correct, and together they tell us something about the complexity of the Buddha's teaching and the diverse ways it might be developed.

First, it may be observed that the Buddha accepted significant philosophical theses. He believed that the fact that all things are impermanent and causally conditioned undermines the substance view and supports the process view. Moreover, he did not see anything problematic about the process view. Hence, the implication of his position is that the debate just outlined can be resolved in favor of the process view. However, since this debate reflects the perspectives of contemporary philosophers of personal identity, it cannot be expected that the Buddha himself would have directly addressed this debate in these terms. Nonetheless, defending the Buddha's position vis-à-vis this debate remains an important task for contemporary Buddhist philosophers, a task rooted in the Buddha's own commitments.

This interpretation correctly emphasizes the Buddha's philosophical beliefs, but it might be regarded as misleading in suggesting that the Buddha thought abstract, philosophical reflection was needed to achieve enlightenment. A *second* answer stresses the importance of meditation in coming to a proper understanding of the Buddha's not-self teaching. The Buddha clearly thought meditation was essential to achieving enlightenment and overcoming suffering. Moreover, though meditation requires intellectual and moral preparation, in its highest forms it takes us beyond intellectual activity. However, there are two ways of understanding the relationship between meditation and intellectual inquiry. One is that, though intellectual reflection by itself is insufficient and must be complemented by meditation, the reality revealed by meditation cannot contradict our rational understanding. Hence, the understanding of the absence of self achieved by meditation must be coherent even if it cannot be fully grasped intellectually. The second way is that the reality revealed by meditation is not coherent from the standpoint of intellectual comprehension. Hence, intellectual reflection can be harmful and must be transcended. The first reading leaves an important place for intellectual thought, while the second discourages this. Each reading has found followers in Buddhist traditions that have developed since the time of the Buddha. The first, represented in much of the *Theravāda* tradition and elsewhere, finds support in the fact that there is a great deal of intellectual articulation in the teaching of the Buddha. The second, followed especially by Chinese Ch'an and Japanese Zen Buddhists, finds a basis in some depictions of the enlightenment experience produced by meditation. These approaches pursue two rather different strands implicit in the teaching of the Buddha.

A *final* response emphasizes the practical orientation of the Buddha's teaching. His primary aim was to teach us how to overcome suffering, not to provide a philosophical theory. This was the point of the story of the man wounded by the poison arrow: his main interest should be in healing the wound, not figuring out who shot the arrow or why (see chapter 3, section 2). In view of this, it might be said that our focus should not be on resolving metaphysical perplexities about the self, but on attaining *Nibbāna*. However, if this means that what matters is that we accept the not-self doctrine in order to overcome suffering *irrespective of the truth of this doctrine*, then this is a misunderstanding of the Buddha. He plainly understands enlightenment as an understanding of reality that enables us to attain *Nibbāna*. Though he leaves questions about some philosophical issues unanswered, the not-self doctrine ·is not one of them. Hence, the Buddha's practical orientation does not permit us to be indifferent to whether or not there really are substance-selves. By whatever means, he thinks we can come to recognize the truth of the not-self teaching.

However, in view of the perplexities concerning both the substance view and the process view, the Buddha's practical orientation might lead a follower of the Buddha to propose the following *revision* of his thought. On philosophical grounds there is currently no resolution of the dispute between these views. On account of this, it is reasonable to set aside the theoretical debate and resolve the dispute on practical grounds. In particular, we are entitled to decide which view to accept by considering the practical consequences of holding each view, specifically with respect to suffering. When we do this, we will discover that the belief that we are substance-selves only leads to more suffering, whereas the belief that we are not substance-selves and are process-selves only insofar as we believe we are substance-selves enables us to overcome suffering. Hence, on these pragmatic grounds, we should abandon the belief that we are substance-selves and accept the belief that we are (dependent) process-selves.

This is not the Buddha's position because he did not think the dispute between the substance and process views was theoretically unresolved. But a contemporary Buddhist with an understanding of current philosophical issues might accept this revision. If she did so, she would be departing from the Buddha in one respect, by asserting theoretical uncertainty, but she would be following the spirit of the Buddha in another respect – for the Buddha was not interested in pursuing theoretical questions as such, and he warned against the dangers of becoming preoccupied with them. Instead, he was primarily concerned with the practical issues regarding suffering. Hence, the effect of this revision would be to emphasize the practical context that was always the Buddha's center of attention.

SUGGESTED READING

A dialogue on the not-self teaching can be found in the *Cūḷasaccaka Sutta* ('The Shorter Discourse to Saccaka'), M #35.

For some classic discussions of personal identity, see Perry (1975) and Rorty (1976). For examples of defenses of substance accounts of the self, see Chisholm (1976: chapter 1), Lowe (1991), and P.F. Strawson (1963: chapter 3). Under the label of the bundle theory, the process view of the person is defended by Brennan (1994) and critiqued by S.L. Anderson (1978). Recent personal identity debates are related to Buddhism in Kapstein (2001: part 1), Kupperman (1984) and Siderits (1997). Critiques of Buddhist views of the self may be found in Nozick (1989: chapter 13) and Yandell (1999: chapters 12 and 13).

- Conventional objections to ~~no~~ kamma, rebirth
- Lacks immaginative interpretations
- Cosmic Justice ← Evaluate

9

KAMMA, REBIRTH, AND THE
NOT-SELF DOCTRINE

We now need to consider two additional features of the Buddha's understanding of human nature: *kamma* and rebirth. After reviewing the essentials of these ideas, we will evaluate two questions. Are *kamma* and rebirth consistent with the not-self doctrine? And what may be said in support of these ideas, both from the Buddha's perspective and from our own? Finally, we will discuss two qualifications of the Buddha's theory of human nature, and we will survey some critical responses to his teaching that may appeal to stream-observers at this stage of our inquiry.

1 The nature of *kamma* and rebirth

A central teaching of the Buddha is that each person lives a series of lives extending indefinitely into both the past and the future (until *Nibbāna* is attained), and that the moral quality of a particular life of a person causally influences the happiness of the lives of that person that follow. These are the basic notions of rebirth and *kamma* respectively. In a representative statement, the Buddha says: 'It is by reason of conduct not in accordance with the *Dhamma*, by reason of unrighteous conduct that some beings here, on the dissolution of the body, after death, reappear in states of deprivation, in an unhappy destination, in perdition, even in hell.' On the other hand, 'it is by reason of conduct in accordance with the *Dhamma*, by reason of righteous conduct that some beings here, on the dissolution of the body, after death, reappear in a happy destination, even in the heavenly world' (M 380). As examples of the kinds of unrighteous conduct that will lead to an unhappy destination, the Buddha refers to killing living beings, stealing, engaging in sexual misconduct, speaking falsely, maliciously, harshly, and uselessly, being covetous, and having wrong views. Forms of conduct contrary to these are righteous and lead to a happy destination. In general, the roots of unrighteous conduct are 'greed, hatred, and delusion,' while the roots of righteous conduct are the opposite of these (N 49).

The importance of *kamma* and rebirth is indicated by the fact that they are said to be an essential part of the three forms of knowledge the Buddha

104

attained at the time of his enlightenment. The last was the Four Noble Truths. The first two were 'knowledge of the recollection of past lives' and 'knowledge of the passing away and reappearance of beings' in which those who were ill-conducted 'have reappeared in a state of deprivation' while those who were well-conducted 'have reappeared in a good destination' (M 105–6).

The doctrine of *kamma* concerns the effects of our actions (the word '*kamma*' means action). At first glance, the idea is straightforward conceptually: insofar as a person's actions are morally wholesome (*kusala*) they will improve the person's well-being in the future, and insofar as a person's actions are morally unwholesome (*akusala*) they will diminish the person's well-being in the future. The future effects of our actions may be in this life or in future lives. The most important factor in determining the moral quality of actions is the person's intention. For example, it is intentional honesty that brings about happiness and intentional theft that results in unhappiness. It is tempting to see this idea as a form of the common belief that morally good persons deserve to be happy while morally bad persons deserve to be unhappy – with the important addition that the universe is causally constructed to ensure that desert is always correctly allocated. However, the Buddha does not present *kamma* as a doctrine of desert per se, much less as a theory of cosmic reward and punishment. Rather, *kamma* is a central instance of dependent origination: it is understood as a law of nature, similar to the principle of gravity, that dictates the causal effects produced by morally good and bad actions. Sometimes the moral quality of an action is compared to a seed that will naturally grow in a happy or unhappy direction. *Kamma* is not administered by an agent such as God. It is an impersonal feature of the causal relationships in the world, and there is no prospect of deviation from the causal effects of *kamma* on the ground of mercy.

Kamma is not a form of determinism about actions. Though a person's current state of well-being is always a causal function of his or her past actions, what a person does at a given time is not determined by past actions. As we have seen, the Buddha thinks we are always free to choose the morally better or worse course. Since these choices affect our future well-being, it is always in our power to improve or diminish our future happiness, and to achieve ultimate happiness through enlightenment. To some extent our character may be determined by past actions, but our character never fully determines our actions.

The cycle of rebirth is described by the Buddha in vast cosmological terms. The universe is said to be arranged in a hierarchy of thirty-one planes of existence, understood to involve higher and lower degrees of well-being. The human level is found among eleven planes of the sense-sphere realm. Below us stand the progressively worse levels of titans, ghosts, animals, and hell; above us are the six levels of the lower gods (*devas*). Above the sense-sphere realm are the sixteen planes of the form realm in which the higher gods dwell, and above these are the four planes of the formless realm: infinite

105

space, infinite consciousness, nothingness, and neither-perception-nor-non-perception. Hence, each human being may be reborn at a lower level (for example, as an animal) or at a higher level (for example, as a god). Animals, humans, and gods belong to a single cosmic framework of rebirth. Depending on the moral quality of our lives, each of us may be reborn above or below our current human level, or at the human level in better or worse circumstances. But no rebirth is a final destination. We are all involved in an ongoing process of rebirth called *saṁsāra* ('perpetual wondering'). This process extends indefinitely into the past and will extend indefinitely into the future until one escapes the cycle of rebirth altogether and attains *Nibbāna* (understood as a state beyond the thirty-one planes from which no return is possible).

No account of the ultimate purpose of this cosmic scheme is offered, but it is obviously intended to show that our well-being will be improved as we move to higher levels of existence and ultimately attain *Nibbāna*. For our purpose, the details of this cosmology are not important. We are interested in the basic rationale for the ideas of *kamma* and rebirth.

2 The consistency objection

Among the oldest quandaries in the teaching of the Buddha is the question of whether or not the notions of *kamma* and rebirth are consistent with the not-self doctrine. If I am not a self, then in what sense can my morally good actions now increase my happiness later? And if there are no selves, then what does it mean to say we will be reborn? On my interpretation, the basic answer to these questions is that the dependent reality of process-selves is sufficient to render the ideas of *kamma* and rebirth intelligible. In fact, one of the main reasons for accepting this interpretation – that the Buddha denies any reality to substance-selves, but grants dependent reality to process-selves – is that it reconciles these ideas and his not-self teaching.

A process-self is a unified nexus of continuous, interacting processes (the aggregates) that are in constant change in every respect and are not ontologically distinct from other processes in the world. We saw in the last chapter that, in order to account for our ordinary understanding of one another as selves, the process view needs to be able to explain the appearance of identity and distinctness: that I am the same person as the person who married my wife several years ago, and that I am a distinct person from my neighbor. The heart of the solution is that this appearance may be explained in terms of the causal continuity and consequent similarity of the processes constituting the person over time, and the internal integration of these processes at a given time. Let us suppose for the sake of argument that this solution is adequate. If it is, then it is relatively unproblematic for the process view also to make sense of *kamma* and rebirth.

Consider *kamma* first. The issue here may be understood by thinking about a single life in which I perform a morally good action now and this results in greater happiness for me next year. The objection is that this makes sense only if I am a substance-self, a distinct entity with identity that both performs the action now and gains the benefit later. The response is that this also makes sense if I am a process-self. As long as there is sufficient causal continuity and similarity between my process-self now and my process-self later, the idea of *kamma* is coherent. If we restrict ourselves to a single life, the notion of *kamma* raises no issue beyond the problems raised in the last chapter. If the process view can make sense of ordinary cases in which we speak of identity over time, then it can also make sense of *kamma*. Of course, it is another question whether *kamma* is true.

A related objection is that process-selves are not adequate to explain our beliefs concerning moral responsibility – for example, that we hold persons accountable, and praise and blame them, for what they have done. We should remember that *kamma* is not put forth as a doctrine of moral responsibility. It is an account of the causal relationships between the moral quality of our actions and our subsequent well-being, and it does not refer to our practices of holding people accountable. Nonetheless, we might reasonably think that, in order to be adequate, the process view should be able to make sense of these practices. According to the process view, it does make sense of them. Once again, all we need is causal continuity and similarity, not identity. As long as my process-self now stands in the right causal relationships to my process-self in the past, it is reasonable to hold my current process-self accountable for the actions of my past process-self.

Let us now consider the consistency of the idea of rebirth and the not-self doctrine. The objection is that I could be reborn only if the substance-self that is now me were to exist in a later life. The response is that rebirth would also make sense if I were a process-self and not a substance-self. A dialogue with the *bhikkhu* Sāti suggests that the Buddha accepted this view. Sāti wonders whether 'it is this same consciousness that runs and wanders through the round of rebirths, not another.' The Buddha replies: 'Misguided man, to whom have you ever known me to teach the *Dhamma* in that way? Misguided man, in many discourses have I not stated consciousness to be dependently arisen, since without a condition there is no origination of consciousness?' (M 350). The Buddha rejects the claim that 'this same consciousness' is reborn. That is a version of the substance view. Instead, the Buddha says we should think of consciousness in terms of dependent origination. This refers to the process view, and it suggests that rebirth should be understood in terms of a causal continuity between a process-self in one life and in another life that is its rebirth.

There is an obvious complication here. Suppose I die and am reborn as a person in a subsequent life. There is no *physical* continuity between me and this later person. At death my body disintegrates, and there is no evident causal connection between that disintegrating body and the physical beginning of the life of the later person. But on this account there has to be some causal continuity between me and the later person if he or she is to be the rebirth of me. Hence, the causal continuity must concern my *mental* attributes, and this mental continuity must be understood as not depending on physical continuity. In short, the Buddha thought that in rebirth my mental process-self now stands in a relationship of causal continuity, and presumably consequent similarity, with the later mental process-self that is my rebirth (this would obviously have to be the case if I were reborn as a god). He assigned consciousness (*viññāṇa*) the role of conveying this continuity (see L 226). In this way, the process view can make sense of rebirth. Moreover, as long as there is mental continuity, the effects of the morality of my actions in this life can be felt in the experiences of a successor life. Hence, both *kamma* and rebirth may be reconciled with the not-self doctrine.

This reconciliation presupposes that the physical world is not the whole of reality. But it is obvious for many reasons that the Buddha accepted this presupposition. The distinction between mentality (*nāma*) and materiality (*rūpa*) is pervasive. Moreover, any account of rebirth would need to accept it as well, since it is difficult to render rebirth intelligible in a strictly physical framework (given what we know of the physical world). Hence, this presupposition is not problematic in showing the consistency of the idea of rebirth and the not-self teaching. Of course, it is a further question as to whether this idea is correct.

A final word about the consistency objection is in order. Early in the history of Buddhism a distinction was drawn between 'ultimate truth' (*paramattha sacca*) and 'conventional truth' (*sammuti sacca*). It is sometimes said that this distinction may be employed to answer the consistency objection as follows. When the Buddha says there are no selves, he should be understood as expressing ultimate truth, and when he speaks as if there are selves, as in the doctrines of *kamma* and rebirth, he should be interpreted as referring to conventional truth. The distinction between ultimate and conventional truth is not explicitly drawn in the *Sutta Piṭaka*, but it has such a long history that it is commonly regarded as an implicit feature of the Buddha's teaching.[1] However, despite its long lineage, the use of the distinction in the response to the consistency objection is misleading. The problem is not merely that the Buddha speaks as if there are selves. It is that the ideas of *kamma* and rebirth require that there be some intelligible notion of a self that has some kind of reality. Hence, the consistency problem can be resolved only by supposing there are process-selves that have dependent reality (or selves in some sense). We might express this by saying that, though in ultimate truth there are no selves in any sense, in conventional truth there are process-selves. However, this is misleading at least insofar as the English phrase 'conventional truth' implies conventions people have agreed to for the sake of convenience, such as the division of the week into seven days. The reality of process-selves is more fundamental and stubborn than a mere convention; though it does depend on what we believe, it is deeply rooted in our entire way of living, and it can be overcome only by the rigorous program of the Eightfold Path.

3 Why believe in *kamma* and rebirth?

Western stream-observers are likely to approach the ideas of *kamma* and rebirth with skepticism. These notions are foreign to the mainstream of our culture and probably appear to many of us to defy our common sense. Moreover, as we will see, their rationale in the Buddha's teaching is likely to disappoint. In any case, our present task is to consider what may be said for and against these ideas.

It might be thought that the Buddha was simply following the customary beliefs of his culture in accepting *kamma* and rebirth. However, though many in his society did accept similar ideas, there were others such as the materialists and the skeptics who rejected such notions. Hence, the Buddha was aware of alternative positions, and he thought he had a sound basis for accepting the ideas of *kamma* and rebirth outlined on pages 104–6. In fact, in several texts, the Buddha or one of his followers engages critics of these ideas, and it will be helpful to consider three of these.

On one occasion, Prince Pāyāsi declares that 'there is no other world, there are no spontaneously born beings, there is no fruit or result of good or evil deeds' (L 351). Pāyāsi offers several reasons for these denials, and to each Kumāra-Kassapa, a disciple of the Buddha, gives what is supposed to be a convincing reply. For example, Pāyāsi says he asked persons to report back to him if they discovered some form of existence after death, but he has received no such message from those who have died. To this Kassapa responds that, if these persons had gone to a 'place of woe' they would not have been allowed to return with such a message, and if they had gone to a 'happy state' they would not have wanted to return. In a different argument, Pāyāsi says there is no evidence that a soul departs the body at death (for example, no soul is seen departing, and the body weighs no less after death than before). To this Kassapa declares that Pāyāsi is 'looking foolishly, senselessly and unreasonably for another world' (L 361). He points out that we should not assume that something does not exist because we are unaware of it, and he refers Pāyāsi to those in meditative states who 'see both this world and the next' (L 356). We will see the importance of this advice shortly. For now, whatever might be said about this exchange, it clearly does not provide us with a reason for believing in *kamma* and rebirth. At most, it puts into question reasons for disbelieving.

Something similar may be said about the Buddha's response to the objection that sometimes morally good lives appear to result in unhappiness and morally bad lives seem to result in happiness. For example, suppose someone 'kills living beings ... and holds wrong view,' but 'after death, reappears in a happy destination.' According to the Buddha, 'Either earlier he did a good action to be felt as pleasant, or later he did a good action to be felt as pleasant, or at the time of death he acquired and undertook right view.' On the other hand, since he has killed living beings and held wrong view, 'he will experience the result of that either here and now, or in his next rebirth, or in some subsequent existence' (M 1064). In short, any apparent mismatch between morality and happiness may be explained by reference to a broader perspective: if there has been moral wrongdoing, then at some point – later in this life, or in the next, or in a subsequent life – unhappiness will result; and if there is now happiness, then at some previous point there must have been some morally correct action. This shows how *kamma* could still be true in the face of recalcitrant experience. But unless we can directly observe the broader perspective, the series of lives, we cannot verify or falsify that *kamma* is correct. Here we have only the word of the Buddha that direct observation in meditation substantiates his position. Without corroboration of his observation, the doctrine is in danger of being consistent with any experience we might have – always a ground for epistemological suspicion.

Finally, the Buddha gives an argument, somewhat similar to Pascal's 'wager argument' (Pascal 1966: section. 418), for believing in *kamma* and rebirth. We are given a choice between:

(1) being an immoral person who rejects *kamma* and rebirth, and
(2) being a moral person who accepts *kamma* and rebirth.

The Buddha argues that, whether or not *kamma* and rebirth are true, (2) is a better choice than (1). Suppose someone chooses (1). If there is no other world, 'this good person is here and now censured by the wise as an immoral person, one of wrong view.' If there is another world, then the person 'is censured by the wise here and now, and . . . on the dissolution of the body, after death, he will reappear in a state of deprivation' (M 508). On the other hand, suppose the person chooses (2). If there is no other world, 'this person is here and now praised by the wise as a virtuous person, one with right view.' If there is another world, then the person 'is praised by the wise here and now, and . . . on the dissolution of the body, after death, he will reappear in a happy destination' (M 509).

We might wonder why we have to choose between (1) and (2). Obviously there are other choices. In any case, it is easy to see why (2) is a better choice than (1) if *kamma* and rebirth are true. But if they are not true, then (2) is the better choice only because 'the wise' censure one who chooses (1) and praise one who chooses (2). If this is to give us a reason for choosing (2), we must already have reason to think 'the wise' really are wise in their allocation of praise and censure. However, surely they are wise in the relevant respect only if *kamma* and rebirth are true. Since the point of the argument is to convince us of this, we are no better off knowing that such persons would praise and censure us in this way. We still need to know why this should matter to us. In the end, the argument appears to rest on an appeal to authority.

The three texts we have considered may show that the Buddha was not simply dogmatic with respect to *kamma* and rebirth, but they do not give a skeptical stream-observer any reason to accept these ideas. On the other hand, this may not be their main purpose. They are probably meant to assuage the doubts of persons already inclined to follow the Buddha who have heard criticisms of his views. In general, on this topic the Buddha does not give evidence or arguments that are intended to convince an outright skeptic. He believed in *kamma* and rebirth as the basis of his enlightenment experience and not mainly, if at all, because of ordinary empirical observation or philosophical argument.

To a large extent, *kamma* is implausible without rebirth. As the Buddha recognized, in this lifetime sometimes good persons suffer and immoral persons prosper. This would be a decisive refutation of *kamma* in the absence of rebirth. Some other objections to *kamma* also depend on the rejection of rebirth. For example, it is sometimes said that *kamma* is cruel because it requires us to believe that a young child suffering from cancer deserves his or her fate. But we probably would not think this cruel if the child was the rebirth of Joseph Stalin. It might be said that it is still cruel since we do not know this. However, aside from saying we could know, the Buddha may have responses to this. First, the *kamma* teaching is not a doctrine of desert at all. Second, its emphasis is less retrospective, seeing people as having brought about their current status, and more prospective, seeing people as having an opportunity to gain future happiness. We might think of it as a form of individual empowerment. *Kamma* could be used as an excuse for cruelty, but this would run contrary to the Buddha's stress on compassion (see page 167). In any case, evidence for rebirth is a crucial issue. *Kamma* could be true only if there was rebirth (or some life after death).

Suppose, in fact, the Buddha did learn in meditation that *kamma* and rebirth – especially rebirth – were real. What evidential value could this have for contemporary stream-observers? How would *we* know he had this knowledge? The Buddha claimed that, in principle, each of us could gain this knowledge for ourselves. But on his own view we can do this only with great difficulty. The situation is not at all comparable to the way each of us could verify that a famous restaurant across town, or for that matter in Singapore, has reopened under a new name. Moreover, if the Buddha were correct, it would seem that among the millions of his followers there would be many persons who have acquired such knowledge. Indeed, it is sometimes claimed there are such persons. But do they provide the quantity and quality of evidence that would properly provide a skeptical stream-observer with reason to accept *kamma* and rebirth?

If I claimed I found your long-lost brother living in Alaska, I might be able to provide enough evidence to convince you that the person I met in Alaska is in fact your brother. Do we have comparable evidence for instances of rebirth? Given that rebirth is said to be pervasive (everyone has been reborn many times), it would seem that there ought to be many cases in which it can convincingly be shown that, for example, this person here is a rebirth of

111

John F. Kennedy or writer Jack Kerouac. It may be said in response that there are various difficulties in showing this. However, if this is the extent of the response, then we may have reason to think rebirth could be true, but we have not been given a reason to think it actually is true. In short, an obvious objection to the Buddha's claims concerning *kamma* and rebirth is that there is inadequate confirmation.

Another objection is that it is unclear how these claims relate to what we know about the world from the sciences. Can rebirth be reconciled with the contention of evolution that human beings have gradually evolved rather recently from nonhuman species? Is it consistent with the fact that the human population has grown immensely during recorded history? Is it compatible with what genetics tells us about heredity? Can it be squared with the apparent fact that our mental life depends upon a properly functioning brain? Regarding *kamma*, how is the causal relationship between morality and happiness coordinated with known scientific laws of the universe? An adequate defense of *kamma* and rebirth would need to confront these questions.

Finally, it may be objected that it is unclear exactly what rebirth would mean. The basic claim is that one person is the rebirth of another if there are sufficient causal continuities and consequent similarities between the two persons. For example, if this person here is the rebirth of musician John Coltrane, then there must be some continuities in the mental attributes of the two persons. But which continuities? Dispositions and memories are the most likely candidates. Does this mean Coltrane's successor would play the sax or remember appearing at the Vanguard? Again, it is said to be possible that a person will be reborn as an animal such as a llama or a skunk. But what would it mean to say, for example, that this skunk is the rebirth of Richard Nixon? What would the particular continuities and similarities be? As before, responses to these objections may be given. But if they are to convince a skeptical stream-observer, they would have to show more than the possibility that *kamma* and rebirth could be true. They would need to provide some plausible evidence that they are true.

These objections are enough to suggest the intellectual obstacles that face someone considering whether there is reason to believe in *kamma* and rebirth. These ideas have received some attention in the West in recent years, and we may conclude by briefly looking at two prominent arguments thought to support them. The first is a *moral* argument: justice requires that a person's happiness be proportionate to his or her moral goodness; plainly this does not happen in this life; hence, there must be other lives in which this proportion is brought about overall. For this argument to be sound, an additional premise is required stating that what happens in the world is just. Without this, there would be no basis for the inference to other lives. The Buddha may have accepted something close to this premise, and in fact he hints at this argument without actually endorsing it (see M 1053–7). In any case, the question is why we should suppose that the universe actually is just in this way. That it is was said to be apparent to the Buddha in meditation. But if this argument were to provide an independent ground for accepting *kamma* and rebirth, there would have to be another reason for accepting this premise. Also, even if the universe were just, it would have to be shown that rebirth is a superior explanation to other forms of life beyond this life. Moreover, it seems that for justice to prevail it would have to be established that everyone begins the cycle of rebirth in a position of equality.

The second argument is an *empirical* one. It has been claimed that there is scientific evidence establishing that some children can remember the details of the lives of persons who existed in the past (for a recent example, see Stevenson 1987). If this were true, it would provide some grounds for rebirth (though not necessarily for *kamma*), and this kind of argument has gained the support of some Buddhists (see V.F. Gunaratna 1980). However, various objections have been raised concerning this research. First, it is contended that there was often contact between the families of the child and the deceased person that could explain the apparent memories without rebirth. Second, questions have been raised about the techniques employed to gather evidence about the memories – for example, whether leading questions were asked. Third, most of these cases are from a culture (India) in which belief in rebirth is widespread; hence it is possible that this belief helped to construct these apparent memories. Finally, in some cases the children or their families had something to gain from their purported memories, since they recalled the life of a person of a higher caste; hence, there may be reason to suspect fraud in these cases. If rebirth were the pervasive phenomenon the Buddha takes it to be, and if it rendered the recollection of past lives likely, then it would seem that it ought to be possible to find cases in which objections such as these could not be raised. The question is whether the amount and quality of the evidence concerning the recall of past lives provides any real basis for rebirth.

4 Two qualifications

The doctrines of not-self, *kamma*, and rebirth are central themes in the Buddha's teaching about human nature (an additional theme, our capacity to attain *Nibbāna*, is still to come). We may conclude by recalling two important qualifications of this teaching.

First, the Buddha did not claim to give a complete account of human nature. As we saw earlier (chapter 3, section 5), he refused to make a declaration about the truth of the following ten propositions: 'the world is eternal,' 'the world is not eternal,' 'the world is finite,' 'the world is infinite,' 'the soul [*jīva*] is the same as the body,' 'the soul is one thing and the body another,' 'after death a *Tathāgata* exists,' 'after death a *Tathāgata* does not exist,' 'after death a *Tathāgata* both exists and does not exist,' and 'after death a *Tathāgata* neither exists nor does not exist' (M 533). These are often referred to as the 'undetermined questions.' The last six plainly concern human nature. Two reasons are commonly given to explain the Buddha's silence concerning these propositions. First, knowing whether they are true or false does not enable us to overcome suffering: this is the explicit point of the simile of the man wounded by the arrow (see chapter 3, section 2). Second, the last six propositions contain a false presupposition – namely, that a substance-self or soul now exists that stands in some relationship to the body and that, once enlightened, either will or will not exist after death. Just as a yes-or-no answer to the question 'Are you still married?' would be misleading if you had never married, so such a declaration concerning these propositions would be misleading given the not-self teaching. We will discuss the propositions concerning the fate of the *Tathāgata* when we consider *Nibbāna*-after-death in chapter 13, section 2. Here we may wonder why the Buddha does not speak about the propositions regarding soul and body. Though on his view they contain a false presupposition as they stand, these propositions nonetheless point to a topic about which the Buddha plainly has commitments: the doctrine of rebirth shows that he does not think the process-self is entirely a physical entity. In this respect, the Buddha does have a view about the mind–body problem, as it is usually called in Western philosophy, despite his silence concerning these propositions. Moreover, coming to a correct understanding of this topic would appear to be important to the enlightenment needed to overcoming suffering.

Second, though the Buddha often stresses the importance of holding right views and rejecting wrong views, he also warns of the danger of attachment to any view, right or wrong. The message of the simile of the raft is that enlightenment involves non-attachment to all views, including the Buddha's own teaching about not-self, *kamma*, and rebirth (see chapter 5, section 3). What could this mean? We are all familiar with persons who are primarily interested in being praised for their superior knowledge or who continue to hold views in the face of contrary evidence because they regard the presentation of the evidence as a threat to themselves. Persons such as these are less concerned about knowing the truth than protecting their own self-esteem. Their attachment to views is a form of self-assertion that presupposes a self that is to be compared with other selves. The Buddha's teaching is that we should accept the truth, but not be attached to it in the sense of regarding it as a personal possession that enhances our comparative worth. Hence, in seeking, holding, or speaking of the truth, I should not be attached to any views as 'mine.'

5 Preliminary responses to the Buddha: where do we go from here?

We are now ready to focus on what the Buddha considers most important: his practical teaching about overcoming suffering and attaining *Nibbāna*. By now stream-observers may be formulating some preliminary conclusions about the Buddha's teaching, and it might be helpful to survey the more obvious options. Some persons may be inclined to provisionally accept what the Buddha teaches (on his own view, full understanding would require a long-term commitment to the Eightfold Path and ultimately enlightenment). But I suspect few Western stream-observers are prepared to take such a step at this point. At the opposite extreme, some persons may believe the doctrines of not-self, *kamma*, and rebirth are so wrongheaded that there is no point in looking further. For example, those committed to a scientific and secular worldview might regard the idea of rebirth as absurd, while theists such as Christians, Jews, and Muslims might find the not-self teaching disturbing. It might be thought that any practical teaching based on these bizarre doctrines could have no value. However, it is possible that skeptical stream-observers will revise their assessment of the Buddha's teaching once its full practical dimensions have been explored.

Many stream-observers may find themselves between these two extremes. They may suspect that there could be some truth in the teaching of the Buddha, but be hesitant to fully endorse it. This response might take different forms. First, some persons may be attracted to some aspects of the Buddha's teaching, but feel troubled by the problems raised earlier concerning the doctrines of not-self, *kamma*, or rebirth. As a result, they may set out to resolve these problems by philosophical reflection, empirical research, Buddhist meditation, or some combination of approaches.

Second, some stream-observers may be drawn to some features of the Buddha's teaching, but believe the aforementioned problems arise from mistakenly taking these doctrines literally. If they were understood figuratively or symbolically, they could be seen as embodying some important truths about human nature, morality, and happiness. For example, perhaps the not-self doctrine should not be understood as a literal denial of the self, but merely as a prescription for living selflessly. As an interpretation of what the Buddha intended, this would be a mistake. But it might be acceptable as an expression of something valuable that could be distilled from the Buddha irrespective of what he intended.

Finally, some persons may think that some, but not all, aspects of the Buddha's teaching are correct taken literally. Little that is distinctive in his teaching would survive complete rejection of the not-self doctrine. Any affirmation of the Buddha must accept this in some form. But perhaps modified versions of Buddhism are possible that reject *kamma* and rebirth as he understands them. *Kamma* expresses the conviction that there is moral order in the universe. However, there are weaker conceptions of this order than the Buddha's. For example, Aristotle says that 'activities in accord with virtue control happiness, and the contrary activities control its contrary' (Aristotle 1999: 1100b10–11). He adds that a person's happiness may also be affected by fortune. But his basic point is that, in this life, living virtuously tends to make a person more happy. This might be accepted as a less striking, but more plausible, understanding of the moral order the Buddha thought he discovered – an order that has more to do with psychology and sociology than cosmology. Another more defensible revision would regard *kamma* in collective rather than individual terms: perhaps the morality of persons as a whole promotes the happiness of persons as a whole. (By rejecting the distinctness of selves, the not-self teaching might encourage a move in this direction.) With respect to rebirth, unless interpreted non-literally (for instance, as expressing hope that enlightenment is always possible), it is not obvious what a weaker but more defensible version would be. However, perhaps substantial truth could be found in the Buddha's teaching without the idea of rebirth – for example, in its guidelines for achieving happiness in this life. This would be a serious modification of his teaching. But for some stream-observers his teaching so modified may be the only truth to be discerned in the Buddha.

SUGGESTED READING

Rebirth is discussed in the *Mahātaṇhāsankhaya Sutta* ('The Greater Discourse on the Destruction of Craving'), M #38. *Kamma* is explained in the *Cūḷakammavibhanga Sutta* ('The Shorter Exposition of Action'), M #135. See also the *Kukkuravatika Sutta* ('The Dog-duty Ascetic'), M #57 and the *Mahākammavibhanga Sutta* ('The Greater Exposition of Action'), M#136.

For discussions on rebirth, see Gunaratna (1980), Inada (1970), W.L. King (1994), and Siderits (2001). *Kamma* is examined in Griffiths (1982 and 1984), Smart (1984), Varma (1963), and White (1983). On the relation between the mental and the physical in the Buddha, see Griffiths (1986) and Harvey (1993). Stevenson (1987) gives an empirical defense of rebirth. For critical evaluations of rebirth, see Edwards (1996) and Hick (1994: chapters 18–19). Edwards (1997) is an anthology of writings on life after death.

NOTE

1   The distinction is thought to be implied by a passage in which the Buddha, after speaking of the self, says 'These are merely names, expressions, turns of speech, designations in common use in the world, which the *Tathāgata* uses without misapprehending them' (L 169; see also C I 230). For discussion of this distinction, see Jayatilleke 1963: 361–8.

Part 3

THE NATURE, ORIGIN, AND CESSATION OF SUFFERING

10

THE NATURE AND EXTENT
OF SUFFERING

The heart of the Buddha's practical teaching is summarized in the Four Noble Truths. These concern the nature and extent of suffering, its origin, its cessation, and the path leading to its cessation. The importance of the Four Noble Truths is indicated by the fact that the last of the three kinds of knowledge the Buddha acquired at his enlightenment was knowledge of these truths. The Buddha says he declared these truths because they lead 'to peace, to direct knowledge, to enlightenment, to *Nibbāna*'(M 536). A person who has understood the Four Noble Truths is portrayed as 'one of right view' who 'has arrived at this true *Dhamma*' (M 134). In a capsule summary, the Buddha says, 'Both formerly and now what I teach is suffering and the cessation of suffering' (M 234).

We are now ready to examine the Four Noble Truths in detail. The first three truths will be considered in this part of the book and the fourth, the Eightfold Path, in Part 4. The subject of this chapter is the first truth. The Four Noble Truths were offered on the model of a medical diagnosis and program of treatment: they describe a disease, analyze its cause, depict the nature of liberation from the disease, and prescribe a treatment to cure the disease and thereby achieve this state of health. Hence, the Buddha is referred to as a 'physician' or 'surgeon' who cures the disease of human suffering. For those he hopes to cure, the first step is to recognize that there is a disease requiring treatment. This recognition was the motivation of the Buddha's first disciples. In a conversation with the *bhikkhus* he asks rhetorically, did you not follow me 'after considering thus: "I am a victim of birth, aging and death, of sorrow, lamentation, pain, grief, and despair; I am a victim of suffering, a prey to suffering. Surely an ending of this whole mass of suffering can be known?"' (M 567). Without some such realization and plea for help, the practical teaching of the Buddha will appear to have little relevance.

In the first *sutta*, the First Noble Truth is stated as follows:

> Now this, *bhikkhus*, is the noble truth of suffering: birth is suffering, aging is suffering, illness is suffering, death is suffering; union with what is displeasing is suffering; separation from what is pleasing is

suffering; not to get what one wants is suffering; in brief, the five aggregates subject to clinging are suffering.

(C II 1844)

At first glance, this statement is partly obvious and partly perplexing. No one would deny that aging, illness, and death typically involve suffering. But it is not evident that 'union with what is displeasing is suffering,' and it is not clear why 'the five aggregates subject to clinging are suffering.' Part of the problem is that the translation of the term '*dukkha*' as suffering is misleading. More important is the fact that this statement offers a progressive understanding of the nature of human suffering, beginning with a common sense description and explanation, and ending with an allusion to a complex philosophical analysis. We will start by discussing the meaning of '*dukkha*,' and we will then consider these two levels of understanding. Finally we will examine whether or not the First Truth embodies a pessimistic interpretation of the human condition.

Remember that for the Buddha full knowledge of the First Noble Truth comes only with the enlightenment that is the final goal of the Eightfold Path. This degree of insight cannot be attained by stream-observers. On the other hand, unless some preliminary understanding of the First Noble Truth were possible, no one would ever have reason to undertake the Eightfold Path in the first place. The Buddha obviously believed such preliminary knowledge is possible, and this is what we seek to gain here. Also, keep in mind the holistic nature of the Buddha's teaching. A follower of the Buddha declared that 'one who sees suffering also sees the origin of suffering, also sees the cessation of suffering, also sees the way leading to the cessation of suffering' (C II 1857). We can fully grasp the first truth only if we comprehend the other three. But we have to start somewhere, and we now have enough understanding of the Buddha's overall teaching to keep the context of the first truth in view.

1 The translation of '*dukkha*'

The translation of '*dukkha*' into English presents a fundamental problem to which there is no entirely adequate solution. Nowadays, the most common translation is 'suffering.' But everyone recognizes that this is problematic, and other alternatives have been suggested. 'Unsatisfactoriness' might well be the best translation were it not so multisyllabic. '*Dukkha*' certainly does include suffering as well as related states such as physical pain, mental anguish, misery, and so on. However, as employed by the Buddha, '*dukkha*' also has a set of connotations that are not properly conveyed by these terms. For example, it sometimes implies such things as disappointment, frustration, anxiety, discontentment, dissatisfaction, lack of fulfillment, falling short of perfection, and the absence of ease. In addition, the meaning of '*dukkha*' is broad enough that it might be interpreted as encompassing what in specific Western cultural contexts have been called a sense of finitude, melancholy, alienation, and *angst*. All this is too much for a single English word to bear, and 'suffering' is misleading in some of these respects. The problem is that '*dukkha*' refers to a wide range of unsatisfactory states of being, much more than 'suffering' suggests, and the Buddha connects these with a distinctive philosophical analysis of our condition.

Dukkha, to forego translation for a moment, is perhaps most usefully thought of as the failure to fully achieve an ideal of happiness we all implicitly seek ('*sukha*' means happiness or pleasure). For the Buddha, this ideal is *Nibbāna*. At one point, he lists several standard aspects of *dukkha* – birth, aging, sickness, death, sorrow, and defilement – and speaks of understanding the 'danger' in each of these and the need to seek the unborn, unaging, unailing, deathless, sorrowless, and undefiled 'supreme security from bondage, *Nibbāna*' (M 259–60). The basic contrast with *Nibbāna* is always present in descriptions of *dukkha*. Since *Nibbāna* is the supreme form of happiness, anything that falls short of this ideal is *dukkha*. For this reason, the Buddha regularly refers to states of being that are ordinarily called happy or pleasurable as *dukkha*. They are *dukkha* because they are less than the ideal. Moreover, the Buddha also gives *dukkha* metaphysical connotations: it is closely linked with impermanence, dependent origination, and the not-self doctrine.

In these respects, 'suffering' either misleads or fails to convey the full meaning of '*dukkha*.' However, it is not entirely wrong, and it is the common English translation in contemporary discussions. Hence, we may reluctantly employ it, with awareness of the aforementioned limitations.

2 The common sense analysis

The First Noble Truth begins with these words: 'Birth is suffering, aging is suffering, illness is suffering, death is suffering.' It may seem surprising that birth is the first item on this list. We usually think of the birth of a child as a time of joy, though by outward appearances the moment is surely a difficult one for the child. In any case, the significance of birth for the Buddha has less to do with the quality of the moment than with the fact that it is the beginning of a new life, another round in the cycle of rebirth. The twelvefold series of conditioning links concludes: 'With birth as condition, aging and death, sorrow, lamentation, pain, grief, and despair come to be. Such is the origin of this whole mass of suffering' (M 927). Birth is the precondition for all our suffering.

The reference to aging, illness, and death recalls the threefold discovery that prompted the Buddha's own search for enlightenment. There is a sense in which everyone becomes aware of these facts rather early in life. But it often takes longer to recognize the ways in which these features of the human condition impose strong feelings of limitation, imperfection, and outright pain

121

on our lives. Fear of our own death and sorrow in the face of the death of those we love, the inevitable decline of our mental and physical capabilities as we age, sickness and injury – these are universal features of human life that are the sources of much of the suffering we undergo. A full existential realization of the extent to which these concerns pervade our entire life was the Buddha's motivation for seeking to understand and overcome human suffering. He suggests that it also ought to motivate us to take his teaching seriously.

After the introductory passage, some versions of the First Noble Truth include these words: 'Sorrow, lamentation, pain, grief, and despair are suffering' (M 1098). With this the Buddha broadens his analysis. Though much suffering has its source in the aging, illness, and death of ourselves and others, there are many other sources, especially those involving forms of anguish. In an explanation of this list, the Buddha says grief is 'mental pain, mental discomfort, painful, uncomfortable feeling,' and despair is 'the tribulation and desperation, of one who has encountered some misfortune or is affected by some painful state' (M 1099). There are innumerable sources of disappointment, frustration, and despair that are common features of human lives. For example, the person you hoped to marry goes off with someone else, the career I sought is unattainable due to limitations in my talents or injustices in the world, the life we imagined living fails to materialize, and so on.

Next, the Buddha gives a general analysis of these sources: 'Union with what is displeasing is suffering; separation from what is pleasing is suffering; not to get what one wants is suffering.' On the one hand, we strive to escape many circumstances we regard as 'displeasing' and we are afflicted with them anyway. On the other hand, we seek a variety of conditions we judge to be 'pleasing' and yet we fail to achieve them. We struggle to avoid poverty, but then we can no longer find a job. We hope to have children, but we find that we cannot. In all these cases, the Buddha says in his most general statement, 'not to get what one wants is suffering' (where 'what one wants' includes both the pleasing conditions we seek and the displeasing ones we try to avoid).

In these ways, the First Noble Truth points out features that anyone with a moderate amount of experience and reflection can see render our lives imperfect and far from the ideal of happiness we all envision. That these defects pervade our lives, the Buddha thinks, is largely a matter of common sense.

3 The philosophical analysis

The final statement in the First Noble Truth says 'in brief, the five aggregates subject to clinging are suffering.' This takes us beyond ordinary experience and reflection to the Buddha's distinctive philosophical perspective. However, the philosophical analysis does not identify sources of suffering beyond those already mentioned. Rather, it provides an understanding of the nature of these various forms of suffering. Though this analysis is not explained in the first *sutta*, our knowledge of the rationale for the not-self teaching will enable us to grasp what the Buddha intends. Recall that the five aggregates are put forward as an account of the different aspects of a person: they are material form (the physical body), feelings (sensations), perceptions (judgments), formations (desires and volitions), and consciousness. What is most important at this juncture is that each of the aggregates is impermanent. Moreover, everything in the world as we ordinarily experience it is also impermanent. Both we ourselves and the world we live in are in constant change. And the Buddha thinks, 'what is impermanent is suffering' (C II 1133).

According to the Buddha, we ordinarily think of ourselves as substance-selves, as beings that have some permanent element, and we seek happiness by trying to connect this self to things in the world we consider pleasing and to disconnect it from things we consider displeasing – in both cases, on a permanent basis. But all these things are impermanent and so no enduring happiness is found. The Buddha does not deny that we have pleasant experiences and that many temporary forms of happiness may be attained. For example, he says that 'a layperson who enjoys sensual pleasures' may achieve 'four kinds of happiness,' that of wealth, enjoyment, debtlessness, and blamelessness (N 99). But none of these lasts forever: we do not find 'any possession that is permanent, everlasting, eternal, not subject to change, and that might endure as long as eternity' (M 231). Hence, our lives consist of a constant struggle to possess what we believe is positive and avoid what we think is negative. It is to this that the 'aggregates subject to clinging' refer: each of these aspects of our person is involved in this struggle. Often we fail to possess what is positive and avoid what is negative, and we are unhappy for this reason. But even to the extent that we succeed in possessing the positive and eluding the negative we are still not really happy because everything is in a process of change. The good things we now possess will eventually be gone, and the bad things we now avoid will eventually find us. For example:

> If property comes to the clansman while he works and strives and makes an effort thus, he experiences pain and grief in protecting it. ... as he guards and protects his property, kings or thieves make off with it, or fire burns it, or water sweeps it away, or hateful heirs make off with it. And he sorrows, grieves, and laments, he weeps beating his breast and becomes distraught, crying: 'What I had I have no longer!'
>
> (M 181)

With respect to everything good we have gained, and everything bad we have escaped, no matter how vigilant we are, our effort to maintain this state of well-being is ultimately futile. It is as if we are trying to swim upstream in a strong current: sooner or later, the impermanence of all things

123

will overcome us. '(Life in) any world is unstable, it is swept away: this is the first summary of the *Dhamma*' (M 686). Our attempts to achieve happiness on these terms are doomed to frustration. No matter how good our life may seem, we are always anxious about what the future holds. This is the basic philosophical reason the Buddha thinks suffering is pervasive in our lives. It is not that there are no positive aspects at any given time. Rather, because of the impermanence of all things, no enduring happiness is to be found in seeking to establish a permanent relationship respectively of connection and disconnection between the substance-selves we think we are and the good and bad things of the world.

At this point, an objection may be raised about the consistency of the Buddha's position. According to the doctrine of *kamma*, a person's morally good actions bring about happiness for that person, and it is always possible for a person to perform morally good actions. Hence, a person ultimately controls his or her happiness. This being the case, it would seem that on the Buddha's own view, our happiness need not be impermanent: as long as we live a moral life, our happiness will be secure.

One response to this objection is that morally good actions only bring temporary and lesser forms of happiness, not the enduring, true happiness that is attained in *Nibbāna*. The effects of good actions only last so long, and the happiness they bring is not fully satisfying. Aging and death remain inescapable features of any life. Moreover, additional good actions are always needed to generate more positive effects. Since the unenlightened are oriented towards the promotion of (what they take to be) their own substance-selves, they do not find it easy to perform such actions. As a result, so long as persons remain within the cycle of rebirth, their happiness is at best short-lived, imperfect, and difficult to achieve. Thus, suffering in a broad sense is a feature of every human life within this cycle.

This response may seem only partly convincing insofar as the account of suffering above emphasized the fact that happiness is not simply impermanent but *beyond our control*. However, the Buddha's main point is that, in the absence of understanding his teaching, happiness does appear beyond our control, and this lack of understanding thereby contributes to our suffering. We are anxious because we do not seem in control of our happiness. In this respect, we may think of his teaching as enabling us to overcome suffering and thus achieve happiness at two levels. First, we can partly overcome suffering insofar as we discover that morally good actions produce temporary and lower levels of happiness. Second, we can fully overcome suffering insofar as we discover that the Eightfold Path brings the permanent and ultimate happiness associated with enlightenment and the attainment of *Nibbāna*. These two levels are connected: enlightenment both requires and produces morally good actions. But it involves much more than this. Among other things, enlightenment informs us that, contrary to what is typically believed, true happiness does not consist of possessing the impermanent things we judge to be good and avoiding the impermanent things we believe to be bad. Rather, real happiness is achieved by freedom from clinging or attachment to desires to gain or escape these ever-changing things.

4 The pessimism objection *Nice fourfold reply.*

A common objection to the First Noble Truth is that it expresses a pessimistic outlook by emphasizing what is bad and failing to recognize what is good in our lives. There are several responses to this objection. The most obvious *1* is that the First Noble Truth is only the first of four truths. The ultimate aim of the Buddha's teaching is to show us how to *overcome* suffering. Hence, he denies that suffering is an inevitable feature of human life that we are power-less to alleviate. He teaches the road the *Nibbāna*, the polar opposite of suffering, a life of joy, compassion, and tranquility. Nonetheless, he thinks, if we are to follow this road, we must first recognize where we are now. For most persons this means acknowledging the suffering in their lives.

Second, the Buddha thinks the First Noble Truth presents an objective *2* assessment of human lives that is neither optimistic nor pessimistic, but real-istic. He does not deny that there are many aspects of our lives that involve pleasure or happiness. But he thinks these positive aspects are temporary, only partly fulfilling, and hard to attain. Moreover, sickness, injury, aging, and death are features of every human life (unless the first two bring about death before we have the opportunity to age). In addition, who can deny the sources of frustration and despair mentioned above? Surely poverty, oppression, unre-quited love, failed careers, disappointed expectations, and so on are very common features of human lives.

Third, the observation of suffering is hardly unique to the Buddha. It is *3* found in many traditions throughout the world. For example, consider these words from *Ecclesiastes*: 'It is an unhappy business that God has given to the sons of men to be busy with. I have seen everything that is done under the sun; and behold, all is vanity and a striving after wind' (*Ecclesiastes* 1: 13–14, Revised Standard Version). Though religious traditions differ in their understanding of suffering and the remedies they offer for it, they often agree about the fact of suffering in human life. In this context, the Buddha does not stand out as unduly pessimistic.

Finally, the First Noble Truth may appear pessimistic because it disrupts *4* our self-deceptive efforts to disguise the real nature of our lives. In this respect, the Buddha might appeal to an analysis of Pascal, who argued that many people try to avoid confronting the true difficulties of the human situation by diverting themselves through a variety of entertainments, amuse-ments, recreations, and the like: 'The only thing that consoles us for our miseries is diversion. And yet it is the greatest of our miseries. For it is that above all which prevents us thinking about ourselves and leads us impercep-tibly to destruction' (Pascal 1966: section 414). Similarly, the Buddha might argue, some persons may resist the First Noble Truth because, through diversion, they live as if it were not true, they prevent themselves from moving from a nominal acknowledgement of suffering to a full, personal realization of its significance.

Buddha agrees? →

It might be said in response that, regardless of how much suffering there is in life, it is a good idea not to dwell on it. But this response may mean two things. If it means refusing to confront suffering so that we might learn to overcome it, the Buddha thinks it is a bad idea. Like a tumor growing inside us, sooner or later the suffering will be painfully evident whether or not we confront it now. On the other hand, if this response means we should not be attached to the sources of suffering, and in this way should not be overwhelmed by them, it might be taken as a step in the direction of the Buddha. His central teaching is that non-attachment is the key to overcoming suffering.

Without some acceptance of the First Noble Truth, a stream-observer has little reason to follow the Buddha further. If I think a doctor has misdiagnosed me, I will probably not be interested in his or her subsequent advice. No doubt, in the more pleasant moments and moods of life, this truth may seem a distant horizon at the periphery of our concerns. Its recognition may require a long accumulation of experience or some existential crisis such as the Buddha himself apparently underwent – perhaps a dark night of the soul, or a sudden surge of alienation from the world. But if the Buddha is correct, eventually all of us will come to know and feel that this is a basic truth about our lives.

SUGGESTED READING

Some themes in the First Noble Truth are discussed in the *Mahādukkhakkhandha Sutta* ('The Greater Discourse on the Mass of Suffering'), M #13.

The first truth is not the focus of many discussions, but it is touched on in Herman (1996), Inada (1969), Kalupahana (1992: chapter 8), and Smart (1984).

tanhā

11

THE ORIGIN OF SUFFERING

The First Noble Truth is intended to describe the 'disease' that afflicts us and to motivate us to seek a cure. The Second Noble Truth provides the first step in understanding this cure by giving an analysis of the origin or cause of suffering. In the first *sutta*, this truth is stated as follows:

> Now this, *bhikkhus*, is the noble truth of the origin of suffering: it is this craving which leads to renewed existence, accompanied by delight and lust, seeking delight here and there; that is, craving for sensual pleasures, craving for existence, craving for extermination.
>
> (C II 1844)

The central contention is that craving is the origin of suffering. We need to examine the meaning the term 'craving' translates – *taṇhā* – as well as the three spheres of craving here described: sensual pleasures, existence, and extermination. Moreover, as stated in this passage, the Second Noble Truth is an abbreviated description of a more complex account. As we have already seen (chapter 7, section 3), the twelvefold formula of conditioning links that elaborates the idea of dependent origination depicts the origin of suffering in terms of a chain of conditions that begins with ignorance, includes craving, and culminates with birth and suffering. In order to comprehend the Second Noble Truth, we need to consider the twelvefold series further. At the end, we will reflect on whether or not the Second Noble Truth is in fact true.

It is important to remember that the Second and Third Noble Truths complement one another: the second says the origin of suffering is craving, while the third says the cessation of suffering consists of 'the giving up and relinquishing of' craving. To identify the cause of suffering is to point to the cure: if the cause is craving, then the cure is giving up craving. We will explore what giving up craving might mean in the next chapter, but this complementary idea should be kept in mind throughout this chapter.

1 The meaning of '*taṇhā*'

The term featured in the Second Noble Truth is '*taṇhā*.' Its literal meaning is 'thirst', and it is intended to connote not simply desire, but a powerful, incessant desire that can never be permanently or fully satisfied. 'Craving' is thus an appropriate translation of the term. The Buddha also employs other terms such as '*rāga*' (lust), '*lobha*' (greed), and '*dosa*' (hatred or anger) to capture aspects of the same general idea: lust, greed, hatred, and anger are forms our craving commonly takes. Moreover, in the twelvefold series, craving is said to condition *upādāna*, ordinarily translated as 'clinging,' 'grasping,' or 'attaching.' As a first approximation, we may say that the origin of suffering is in strong, unrelenting, unfulfillable desires that lead us to try to attach ourselves to things in the world.

In a well-known passage, the Buddha suggests that craving is like a fire that inflames every facet of our being:

Fire Analogy

> *Bhikkhus*, all is burning. And what, *bhikkhus*, is the all that is burning? The eye is burning, forms are burning, eye-consciousness is burning, eye-contact is burning, and whatever feeling arises with eye-contact as condition – whether pleasant or painful or neither-painful-nor-pleasant – that too is burning. Burning with what? Burning with the fire of lust, with the fire of hatred, with the fire of delusion; burning with birth, aging and death; with sorrow, lamentation, pain, displeasure, and despair, I say.
>
> (C II 1143)

Likewise, the ear, nose, tongue, body, and mind are said to be burning. The image of fire connotes all-consuming movement, something hot, dangerous, destructive, and potentially out of control. The implication is that craving in the form of lust and hatred is a fire that inflames every aspect of a person – all the aggregates – and thus brings suffering in its wake. (We will see the importance of delusion on pages 132–3.) We have powerful desires to grasp or maintain what appears pleasant, and to avoid or eliminate what appears painful. Often we are not successful, but even when we are, our success is impermanent and provides no ultimate satisfaction: eventually the pleasure disappears and another pain reappears. Our desires return and seek new satisfactions, but with the same unfulfilling result. Suffering is the outcome of this frustrating state of affairs.

2 Three forms of craving

The Second Noble Truth depicts three objects of craving. First, we crave for sensual pleasures. Elsewhere the Buddha says: 'Wherever in the world there is anything agreeable or pleasurable, there this craving arises and establishes itself' (L 346). This statement is followed by reference to the eye, ear, nose, tongue, body, and mind, as in the burning simile. Thus, 'pondering on sights, sounds, smells, tastes, tangibles and mind-objects in the world is agreeable and pleasurable, and there this craving arises and establishes itself' (L 347). For the most part, this list suggests that craving concerns desires and appetites of the body. We try to experience those sights, sounds, smells, and so on that appear pleasurable and we try to escape those that appear painful. Physical desire in all its forms – especially sexual desire – is a central instance of craving for the Buddha, and the fact that these desires are at most temporarily fulfilled and so constantly seek new satisfactions informs his entire discussion. In this regard, his account resonates with a dominant tradition in Western philosophy, beginning with Plato, that sees bodily desires as disruptive, a source of unhappiness, and so in need of regulation. But the Buddha differs from this tradition in significant respects. He does not understand regulation primarily on the model of reason regulating physical desires. More importantly, he does not contrast craving rooted in physical desires with other forms of craving that are unproblematic because they are rooted in other desires that are higher (for example, by being mental or spiritual). For the Buddha, there is a provisional sense in which some desires are higher than others, but craving is always problematic and always involves suffering, whatever kind of desire it is rooted in, whatever its form and object (including craving for *Nibbāna*). Craving for sensual pleasures is a paradigm case, but craving as such is the source of suffering.

This leads us to the second two objects of craving: we crave for existence and for extermination. It is less obvious what these mean. At first sight, it is clear that we crave for existence in the sense that we desire self-preservation, and the Buddha does have this in mind. But what are we to make of craving for extermination? People desire to end their lives only exceptionally; suicidal tendencies are not on a par with the instinct for self-preservation. This passage is traditionally interpreted narrowly as referring to the doctrines of eternalism and annihilationism. On this view, we crave continued existence not only in the sense of a long life, but also in the form of rebirth in a future life or an eternal life. Such a life is what eternalism promises. But what does annihilationism promise? It declares that our life on earth is our only life, that there is no sense in which we survive the death of the body. This may strike us as more of a threat than a promise. But annihilation may appear more attractive in comparison with a subsequent life of unhappiness in consequence of our immoral actions in this life, or more generally with an unending cycle of lives constituted by suffering. In any case, the overall teaching of the Buddha suggests the need to read this passage more broadly.

In general, we crave for the new or continued existence of those things we judge to be pleasant, agreeable, positive, or in some way good. The objects of these cravings might be anything. Thus, we may crave for health, wealth, power, status, success, a spouse, children, friends, and so on. Since we think we will continue to have these things only insofar as we continue to exist, we do crave for the continued existence of ourselves (hence, the desire for life after death). But presumably no one desires unending life irrespective of its quality. We only desire this life insofar as it is understood to include possession of those things we believe to be positive. In this respect, the most general category is craving to acquire and forever maintain those things we take to be positive.

On the other hand, with respect to those things we regard as painful, disagreeable, negative, or in some fashion bad, we crave for their non-existence (perhaps a better translation of '*vibhava*' than 'extermination'). For things we judge in this manner, we crave to get rid of those we now possess and to avoid those we do not possess. Once again, the objects of these cravings might be anything. Thus, we might crave to eliminate or avoid disease, poverty, disgrace, prejudice, loneliness, and so on. In extreme moments, when these things appear utterly unavoidable, we may seek to end our life. But we do not seek non-existence as such: ordinarily we would prefer continued existence in the absence of these things.

In short, the Second Noble Truth says the origin of suffering is found in the general fact of craving, irrespective of its object. We crave to permanently possess or avoid things that are by nature impermanent, and the result is suffering. With respect to those things we crave to possess because we believe they are good, we suffer because we do not now possess them or fear that we will lose them in the future. With respect to those things we crave to avoid because we believe they are bad, we suffer because we have not avoided them or fear that we will not in the future.

However, this is not the whole story. Though *Nibbāna* as ultimate reality is a state beyond change, we are not to crave attainment of it either. The problem with craving is not simply that its objects are impermanent (though this is almost always true), but that the supposed subject of craving, the self, is also impermanent – indeed, ultimately unreal. In craving, we presuppose that we are substance-selves, things with identity through time, to which positive features are to be permanently attached and negative features are to be permanently separated. Since there is no such self, all craving, even for *Nibbāna*, brings about suffering. Trying to attach oneself to *Nibbāna* will only result in frustration because there is no self to which *Nibbāna* can be attached. *Nibbāna* is attained only through the realization that there is no self, and this realization undermines craving.

3 The twelvefold formula

The Second Noble Truth appears to state that craving is the one and only cause of suffering. However, though the Buddha thinks craving has central importance, he does not think it is the only cause of suffering. First of all, he tends not to think in terms of a single cause of an event. He depicts the world of experience as one in which typically processes causally interact with one another in complex ways: for a given effect, there are multiple causes, and for a given cause, there are multiple effects. In addition, the twelvefold formula of conditioning links that explains dependent origination says craving is only part of the cause of suffering. Remember that this formula states that ignorance conditions formations, which condition consciousness, which conditions mentality-materiality, which conditions the sixfold base (the senses and the mind), which conditions contact, which conditions feeling, which conditions craving, which conditions clinging, which conditions being, which conditions birth, which conditions 'aging and death, sorrow, lamentation, pain, grief, and despair.' This, the Buddha says, 'is the origin of this whole mass of suffering' (M 927).

This formula purports to explain the origin of suffering, but it does not single out craving as the origin. Rather, it includes craving in a long list of conditions that begins with ignorance. In view of the prominence of the twelvefold formula, it is reasonable to understand it as a more comprehensive statement of the Second Noble Truth than that which appears in the first *sutta*. Moreover, the restatement of the formula in terms of cessations (beginning with the cessation of ignorance, passing through the cessation of craving, and ending with the cessation of suffering) suggests a more comprehensive expression of the Third Noble Truth (which in standard expressions makes giving up craving the key to the cessation of suffering). Recall that the Buddha declared that failure to understand the twelvefold formula in both variations was the reason people could not overcome suffering and the round of rebirth.

Nonetheless, despite its apparent importance, the twelvefold formula is perplexing in several respects. First, it seems to imply that ignorance is the first cause of suffering. But the Buddha does not think there are first causes, and he clearly says: 'A first beginning of ignorance . . . cannot be discerned . . . yet a specific condition of ignorance is discerned. Ignorance, too, has its nutriment' (N 254). In this respect, the twelvefold series is incomplete and misleading. Second, the formula appears to suggest a pair of linear sequences of elements, the cessation version the reverse order of the conditioning version (assumed in the interpretation in chapter 7, section 3). But the Buddha's considered view would seem to be that there are multiple relations of interdependence among the elements such that each element could directly condition several others (typically on the model of creating a strong propensity). For example, he says ignorance is conditioned by 'the five hindrances' (sensual desire, ill will, sloth and torpor, restlessness and remorse, and doubt). These hindrances (*nivarana*) are conditioned by 'the three ways of wrong conduct' (deeds, words, and thought), and these in turn are conditioned by lack of 'self-restraint,' lack of 'mindfulness and clear comprehension,' and 'improper attention' (N 255). In general, the Buddha suggests that such things as the formations (volitions), feelings, and cravings may all condition ignorance, and are in turn conditioned by ignorance. This is why the broad program outlined

131

in the Eightfold Path is required to achieve enlightenment. Third, related to this, the overall logic of the formula is far from obvious. For example, why do formations come so early on the first version, before such things as feelings and cravings? Finally, the formula stands in an odd relationship to the five aggregates: it explicitly mentions four of the aggregates, but leaves out the middle one (perceptions) and it includes several other elements that seem closely related to the aggregates. Moreover, mentality-materiality may be taken to refer to all of them.

In short, the principles behind the twelvefold formula are not clear. As a result, it has been understood in different ways. Most prominent is a traditional *Theravāda* interpretation that lends the formula greater intelligibility than may be immediately apparent. This interpretation declares that the formula concerns three successive lives of a person: the middle eight elements refer to our present life, while ignorance and formations refer to our previous life, and birth and aging, and so on refer to our next life. Thus, in our previous life, ignorance conditioned formations. Lacking enlightenment, good and bad actions were performed that would result in positive and negative features in the future. These forces of *kamma* propelled our consciousness to a new birth in our present life. This gives rise to our basic mental and physical make-up (mentality-materiality), and this affects the operation of our five senses and the mind (the sixfold base). With these faculties, we come into contact with the world, and this leads to feelings on the basis of which we come to crave and then cling to things. This results in our being a certain kind of person, and as a consequence of this we will be born again in the next life with its attendant suffering.

Nonetheless, this interpretation does not resolve all the aforementioned problems, and this deficiency might suggest other readings. Perhaps the twelvefold formula is a composite of earlier lists, or maybe it is merely a mnemonic device for remembering key elements of the Buddha's teaching, with no suggestion of a strict causal sequence. In various contexts, the Buddha regards each of the first eleven elements as important factors contributing to suffering.

In any case, taken together, the Second Noble Truth and the twelvefold formula clearly draw our attention to two important features of the Buddha's message: the origin of suffering particularly depends on craving (mentioned in both and featured in the Truth) and ignorance (the first member of the formula, and referred to in the burning simile as delusion). Though ignorance and craving are themselves conditioned, they are aspects of our lives the Buddha believed we are especially in a position to modify, by following the Eightfold Path, so as to overcome suffering. We will see that enlightenment requires a comprehensive transformation of the person that includes radically changing both our beliefs and our desires.

The primary way in which ignorance causes suffering is that we are ignorant of the Four Noble Truths. Ignorance is 'not knowing suffering, not knowing the origin of suffering, not knowing the cessation of suffering, not knowing the way leading to the cessation of suffering' (C I 535). However, the not-self doctrine is essential to understanding these truths. The false belief that we are substance-selves is a crucial reason why we crave things. Since each of us believes he or she is a distinct self with identity through time, we conceive of true happiness as a state of this self in which it permanently possesses a set of attributes it judges to be positive and permanently avoids other attributes it regards as negative. Since all these features are in a process of change, this permanent state of affairs can never be achieved. As a result, we constantly crave things. The incongruity between the permanent happiness we seek and the impermanence of the things in the world whose possession and avoidance we think will bring happiness results in a life of craving that is often frustrated and always at risk. The result is suffering. Moreover, even craving for *Nibbāna* is misguided insofar as it presupposes a substance-self that could possess *Nibbāna*. Since there is no such self, craving for *Nibbāna* can also be a source of suffering. We attain *Nibbāna* not by bringing our self in touch with it, but by realizing there is no self.

4 Is the Second Noble Truth true?

There are two ways stream-observers might question the Second Noble Truth. First, it might be said that the source of suffering is not our cravings but the fact that the world does not fulfill our cravings. The Buddha does not dispute this so far as it goes: he agrees that we suffer because the world does not provide what we crave. But his interest is in showing a way to overcome suffering, and his central idea is that the only way to truly accomplish this is by focusing on our cravings and not the fact that the world does not always respond to them. This is not what we typically do. We usually try to change the world to accommodate our desires rather than trying to change our desires to accommodate the world. The Buddha thinks this strategy may bring temporary and incomplete success, but it can never achieve real happiness. Since everything in the world is impermanent, no everlasting happiness can be found by trying to mold the world to satisfy our desires. Sooner or later, the inevitable processes of the world – especially aging, sickness, and death – will catch up with us or those we love, and our most important desires will be thwarted. The Buddha focuses on craving as the source of suffering because we have the capacity to achieve enlightenment and thereby bring an end to craving, and we do not have the capacity to render the world fully responsive to our desires. In addition, he thinks that even if the world did respond to our desires, it would not bring the kind of happiness we achieve when we attain *Nibbāna*. The happiness we really seek can only be found when we reach a condition of selflessness and are able to live without craving the things of this world.

Second, it might be objected that the depiction of people as consumed by craving is inaccurate, that in fact many people are fairly content with what

133

they have. The Buddha does not deny that there are differences among people with respect to craving. Some people are quite driven by their desires, always seeking new satisfactions, while others are fairly relaxed about theirs and are more inclined to accept what the world brings them. Nonetheless, he thinks there are basic facts about our nature and circumstances that, in the absence of enlightenment, render us all essentially creatures of craving. Since we seek permanent happiness in what is impermanent, our contentment is always precarious, and eventually we will crave changes in our lives. It is true that some people may achieve a relative degree of contentment insofar as the world has mostly cooperated with their desires and they have diverted attention away from the ways in which it has not. But such contentment is always partial and provisional. In time, the processes of change will erode it, and new, insatiable cravings will emerge. On the other hand, people who truly accepted what the world brings them, no matter what happens, would achieve complete and permanent happiness. However, the Buddha thinks this is possible only for those who have been fully liberated from their sense of self and its cravings, and so have attained *Nibbāna*.

SUGGESTED READING

Dependent origination and the twelvefold formula are explained in the *Mahānidāna Sutta* ('The Great Discourse on Origination'), L #15. See also the *Mahātaṇhāsankhaya Sutta* ('The Greater Discourse on the Destruction of Craving'), M #38 (recommended earlier) and the *Nidānasaṃyutta* ('Connected Discourses on Causation'), C I 533–620.

An important work on causality and dependent origination is Kalupahana (1975); on this topic, see also R. Gupta (1977), Inada (1985), Mitchell (1975), Streng (1975), and Watts (1982).

12

THE CESSATION OF
SUFFERING: *NIBBĀNA*-IN-LIFE

The Third Noble Truth depicts a state of health that is said to be free of suffering. In the first *sutta*, the Buddha says:

> Now this, *bhikkhus*, is the noble truth of the cessation of suffering: it is the remainderless fading away and cessation of that same craving, the giving up and relinquishing of it, freedom from it, nonreliance on it.
>
> (C II 1844)

In this and related formulations of the Third Noble Truth, the term '*Nibbāna*' does not appear. But there is no question that *Nibbāna* is what this truth concerns. This is evident in the Buddha's description of a person who, having seen the aggregates as impermanent, suffering and not-self, 'turns his mind away from those states and directs it towards the deathless element thus: "This is the peaceful, this is the sublime, that is, the stilling of all formations, the relinquishing of all attachments, the destruction of craving, dispassion, cessation, *Nibbāna*"' (M 540). To destroy craving is to attain *Nibbāna*, and this undermines suffering, which has its origin in craving. *Nibbāna* is the state of health that is the complete cure of the disease of suffering: 'The greatest of all gains is health. *Nibbāna* is the greatest bliss' (M 613). *Nibbāna* is clearly the focal point of the Buddha's teaching. He says he teaches the Four Noble Truths because they lead 'to disenchantment, to dispassion, to cessation, to peace, to direct knowledge, to enlightenment, to *Nibbāna*' (M 536). We are told that the Buddha 'has attained *Nibbāna* and he teaches the *Dhamma* for attaining *Nibbāna*' (M 330).

In view of the importance of *Nibbāna* in the Buddha's teaching, he says less about it than one might initially expect. Moreover, he stresses the difficulty the unenlightened face in trying to comprehend *Nibbāna*. Nonetheless, the challenge for stream-observers is to gain some preliminary understanding. In the absence of this, there could be no basis for undertaking the Eightfold Path that purports to lead to full enlightenment about *Nibbāna*. We will focus on *Nibbāna*-in-life in this chapter and *Nibbāna*-after-death in the next.

1 Senses of '*Nibbāna*'

The term '*Nibbāna*' literally means 'blowing out,' 'quenching,' or 'extinction.' In part, '*Nibbāna*' refers to the extinction of craving, as in the Third Noble Truth, or to the extinction of clinging or attachment (what craving conditions in the twelvefold formula). But it can also refer to something broader, to the end of the process-self, and with it the end of being a self in any sense. This and other depictions have led to the suspicion, frequent in Western assessments of Buddhism, that *Nibbāna* is non-existence or nothingness, and hence that the teaching of the Buddha is ultimately nihilistic. Yet much that the Buddha says concerning *Nibbāna* appears to counter this suspicion. We have just seen that he refers to it as the deathless element and a state of peace and bliss. Elsewhere, he calls *Nibbāna* the unborn, unaging, unailing, deathless, sorrowless, and undefiled 'supreme security from bondage' (M 259–60). These descriptions imply a state of reality beyond the cycle of rebirth, a state in which suffering is replaced by the highest happiness. Both aspects of the teaching of the Buddha are significant, those suggesting extinction and those suggesting the greatest bliss. An important question is whether they can be coherently reconciled.

The concept of *Nibbāna* has several different senses in the Buddha's teaching. In the *Itivuttaka*, he says there are 'two *Nibbāna*-elements' – that 'with residue left' and that 'with no residue left.' On the one hand, there is an *arahant* 'whose taints are destroyed' and who has been 'completely released through final knowledge.' But 'his five sense faculties remain unimpaired, by which he still experiences what is agreeable and disagreeable and feels pleasure and pain.' The Buddha says, 'It is the extinction of attachment, hate, and delusion in him that is called the *Nibbāna*-element with residue left [*sa-upādisesa-nibbānadhātu*].' On the other hand, he says, for an *arahant* 'here in this very life, all that is experienced, not being delighted in, will be extinguished.' This refers to 'the *Nibbāna*-element with no residue left [*anupādisesa-nibbānadhātu*]' (U/I 181). An *arahant* is a fully enlightened person. The distinction is between an *arahant* who is still alive physically and one who is not, between a person who has attained *Nibbāna*-in-life and one who has attained *Nibbāna*-after-death. Each of these persons – or we might say (from our unenlightened perspective) one person first in one state, then in the other – has in some sense attained *Nibbāna*. For example, in both 'attachment, hate, and delusion' are extinguished. But there are important differences between the two. For instance, the first 'experiences what is agreeable and disagreeable,' while the second does not.

An *arahant* after death is portrayed as having attained *Nibbāna*, understood as ultimate reality or *summum bonum* (highest good) that is unconditioned, unchanging, beyond space and time – and also empty of any self. In the next chapter, we will discuss *Nibbāna* in this sense and what it means to attain it after death. An *arahant* who is still alive has followed the Eightfold Path and achieved enlightenment. The moment of enlightenment is understood as a special state of mind in which *Nibbāna* as ultimate reality is experienced and comprehended. Subsequent to this moment, the *arahant* resumes his life transformed by this knowledge. Later, we will consider how meditation brings about the enlightenment moment (see chapter 16). Our purpose in this chapter is to explore the post-enlightenment life of a person, of an *arahant* who is still alive. This is the most immediate (though not the ultimate) concern of the Third Noble Truth – what it means to overcome suffering in this life – and the attraction of the life of an *arahant* is surely central to anyone drawn to the teaching of the Buddha. For stream-observers skeptical of the other-worldly aspects of Buddhism, of rebirth and *Nibbāna*-after-death, this life is the only respect in which Buddhism could appear attractive. Our primary model for understanding the life of an *arahant*, of course, is the life of the Buddha, of Siddhattha Gotama after his enlightenment.

The Buddha believed that it is extremely difficult to grasp *Nibbāna* and that it can be understood truly only by those who are fully enlightened. At the time of his enlightenment, he observed that his teaching and the truth of *Nibbāna* are 'hard to see' and can only 'be experienced by the wise' (M 260). In partic- ular, the Buddha thought *Nibbāna* could be comprehended only by those who undertake the intellectual, moral, and meditative disciplines of the Eightfold Path. For example, he said his teaching 'will never be perceived by those who live in lust and hate' (M 260), and he insisted that *Nibbāna* cannot be under- stood so long as a person thinks in terms of a self (see M 87). It is sometimes said that trying to explain *Nibbāna* to an unenlightened person is like trying to explain color to someone who has been blind from birth: in both cases any description is inadequate. It is also said that *Nibbāna*, insofar as it pertains to ultimate reality as unconditioned, unchanging, and beyond space and time, cannot be adequately described by the concepts in our language, since these were designed to depict the conditioned, changing, spatial-temporal world of ordinary experience. All this puts stream-observers in a precarious epistemo- logical position. On the other hand, the Buddha thought he could say enough, or show enough through his life, to give persons reason to begin the Eightfold Path and seek an understanding of *Nibbāna* for themselves. Our concern here is to see what reason he provides.

2 Life after enlightenment

A person who has achieved enlightenment ordinarily continues to live his (or her) life, as the Buddha himself did for forty-five years. Enlightenment is said to radically transform a person. In comparison with his unenlightened state, an *arahant* sees the world and lives his life in a new way. Most importantly, in some sense he overcomes suffering and achieves happiness: *Nibbāna* is the 'greatest bliss.' However, the life of an *arahant* is provisional and less than perfect. As a living person, he still experiences what is disagreeable and feels pain. For example, the Buddha is reported to have felt tired, to have had a sore back, to have found a particular location too crowded, and so on. The twelvefold formula states that suffering ends with the cessation of feelings of pleasure and pain as well as other aggregates such as material form and consciousness. But both the Buddha and the *arahants* maintained these aggregates during *Nibbāna*-in-life (though they may have been suspended during the meditative experiences of *Nibbāna* as ultimate reality). And, of course, the Buddha grew old, got sick, and died. Hence, overcoming suffering and achieving happiness *in a full sense* comes only after death. In this life, an *arahant* achieves this to a lesser extent, as a prelude to *Nibbāna*-after-death. Still, the happiness of an *arahant* is incommensurably better than that of an unenlightened person. Thus, the Buddha speaks of 'a delight apart from sensual pleasures' (M 610), and Sāriputta contrasts 'sensuous happiness' with a happiness 'not sensed' (G IV 280).

An *arahant* is in a state of transition between the cycle of rebirth and *Nibbāna*-after-death. As a living person, he still bears the fruits of his past actions in this or previous lives. Hence, his happiness is not perfect. However, as an enlightened person, his actions no longer produce such fruits. This does not mean his actions are not morally good. Indeed, they are best thought of as wholly good. But he has transcended the framework of *kamma* in which our actions bring about more or less relative happiness in future rebirths. His destiny is the immeasurable happiness found in *Nibbāna*-after-death, a state of being beyond the cycle of rebirth.

The *arahant* is described in a variety of ways, both in terms of what is absent and what is present. Among the depictions of absence, someone who has attained *Nibbāna* is said to have achieved dispassion and disenchantment. In addition, these words of Sāriputta are common: 'The destruction of lust, the destruction of hatred, the destruction of delusion: this, friend, is called *arahantship*' (C II 1295). Finally, great emphasis is placed on the absence of both craving and clinging or attachment. The Third Noble Truth depicts the cessation of suffering as freedom from craving. The Buddha also commonly says that with 'true knowledge' a person does not cling to sensual pleasures, views, rules and observances, or a doctrine of self. When this happens, the person 'is not agitated' and 'personally attains *Nibbāna*' (M 163).The *arahant* experiences what is agreeable and feels pleasure, but he does not crave these things nor is he attached to them. Likewise, he experiences what is disagreeable and feels pain, but he does not crave nor cling to the elimination of these things.

In terms of what is present, we have seen that an *arahant* is characterized as having peace and tranquility. He is also portrayed as possessing an 'immeasurable deliverance of mind' that includes states such as loving-kindness (*mettā*). 'He abides pervading the all-encompassing world with a mind imbued with loving-kindness, abundant, exalted, immeasurable, without hostility and without ill will' (M 1003). In a similar way, he is said to possess

138

compassion (*karuṇā*), appreciative joy (*muditā*), and equanimity (*upekkhā*). *Arahants* are also depicted as being fully focused on the present moment, undistracted by concerns about the past and the future: 'They do not sorrow over the past, nor do they hanker for the future. They maintain themselves with what is present' (C I 93).

In short, an *arahant* is free of lust, hatred and delusion; he does not crave or cling; he is dispassionate and disenchanted; he is peaceful and tranquil; he possesses loving-kindness, compassion, appreciative joy, and equanimity; and he focuses on the present moment. At the root of all of these characteristics is comprehension of the not-self doctrine. According to the Buddha, 'one who perceives non-self achieves the elimination of the conceit "I am" and attains *Nibbāna* in this very life' (N 229). The Buddha frequently points out that an *arahant* should conceive of nothing in terms of himself, including *Nibbāna*. For example:

> He directly knows *Nibbāna* as *Nibbāna*. Having directly known *Nibbāna* as *Nibbāna*, he should not conceive [himself as] *Nibbāna*, he should not conceive [himself] in *Nibbāna*, he should not conceive [himself apart] from *Nibbāna*, he should not conceive *Nibbāna* to be 'mine', he should not delight in *Nibbāna*. Why is that? So that he may fully understand it, I say.
>
> (M 87)

To be enlightened is to know that the belief that one is a substance-self is false, and to know this is to undermine the process-self that was sustained by this false belief. Due to the effects of past actions in accordance with *kamma*, an *arahant* who is still alive continues to be a process-self in some respects (only in *Nibbāna*-after-death does this self fully disappear). But he no longer perceives the world, nor lives in the world, solely from the perspective of that self. To modify Thomas Nagel's striking expression, he has achieved, or has come close to achieving, *the view from no one* (see Nagel 1986). To attain this view is to live selflessly in a quite literal sense. And living selflessly puts an end to lust and hate, to craving and clinging, and brings about peace, compassion, joy, and the like.

3 What selflessness involves

In many respects, the life of an *arahant* is an attractive ideal. Who would not want to live a life of peace, compassion, and joy? But there is a central aspect of this life that may arouse the suspicions of stream-observers. This troubling aspect is featured in the Third Noble Truth – that suffering is overcome by giving up craving – and it is also suggested by the references to dispassion and disenchantment. The life of an *arahant* seems to be a life without desires and feelings, and this, it might be thought, does not look like much of a life.

What about love?

139

The difficulty may be seen in the logic of the Second and Third Noble Truths. The origin of suffering is the fact that we crave to permanently possess or avoid things that are by nature impermanent. With respect to what we crave to possess, we suffer because we do not now possess it or fear that we will not in the future. With respect to what we crave to avoid, we suffer because we have not avoided it or fear that we will not in the future. If we stop craving in these ways, as the *arahant* does, we will not suffer in these respects. Assuming for the moment that we could bring about a general cessation of craving (we will discuss the prospects for this in Part 4), we might wonder whether this would really result in true happiness. Though much unhappiness is caused by unfulfilled desires, it may be said, is not much happiness also brought about through fulfilled desires? It seems that the *arahant* avoids the unhappiness of unfulfilled desires at the cost of the happiness of fulfilled desires – and this may not seem to be real happiness at all. Many people would probably prefer to take their chances and hope that in an admittedly impermanent world their fulfilled desires will generally outweigh their unfulfilled desires. A life without desires would seem to throw out the baby with the bath water: it would seem to be a life of passivity and indifference, not 'the greatest bliss.'

It is important to consider what the Buddha could say in response to this objection. Part of the response is a key argument for the Second Noble Truth, that taking our chances in this way will lead to a deeply unsatisfactory life in the long run. But the main response is that the full existential realization of selflessness brings about a fundamental transformation that opens up new sources of happiness – sources that are difficult, perhaps impossible, to fully comprehend for those who still believe they are selves. *Nibbāna* in this life is not merely the absence of the unhappiness of frustrated desires: it has a positive dimension the Buddha thought far exceeds the happiness of fulfilled desires. We need to try to understand why he thought this.

To begin, the belief that one is a self distinct from other selves is the source of much suffering. This belief is the origin of a fundamental and far-reaching orientation to the world in terms of a distinction between what is mine and serves my interests, and what is yours and serves your interests. The consequence of this orientation is a pattern of thought, desire, and emotion that is typically destructive and gives rise to such passions as greed, envy, lust, jealousy, vengefulness, ambition, intolerance, anger, hatred, pride, and the like. These bring unhappiness to the person driven by these passions and to others as well. According to the Buddha: 'When lust, hatred, and delusion have been abandoned, he neither plans for his own harm, nor for the harm of others, nor for the harm of both; and he does not experience in his mind suffering and grief. In this way . . . *Nibbāna* is directly visible' (N 57). The Buddha thought that the realization that we are not distinct selves would undermine the destructive emotions that separate us from one another *and* would release in us a latent but powerful capacity for compassion and loving-kindness. He does not argue from the premise of selflessness to the conclusion of compassion. Rather, he maintains that the discovery of selflessness will result in the disappearance of the negative passions and the emergence of our fundamentally compassionate nature. And this, he thought, would bring about a happiness that is far more than the mere absence of unfulfilled desires: a life expressing compassion and loving-kindness is a better life than one consumed by greed, ambition, hatred, and so on – better not only for others, but for the person possessing these characteristics.

key premise

An *arahant* does not have the desires and feelings associated with the destructive emotions just mentioned. However, given the broad meaning of these English terms, surely he has some desires and feelings in some sense (while living his life – both *Nibbāna*-after-death and momentary meditative experiences of *Nibbāna* as ultimate reality are another matter). The Buddha felt tired. Hence, there must have been a respect in which he had the desire for rest. Moreover, compassion and loving-kindness themselves would appear to involve feelings for other people and desires for their well-being. The Buddha spent forty-five years travelling and teaching in order to benefit people. So the *arahant* must have some desires and feelings in the sense of regarding some states of being as good and others as bad (in some sense), and of acting on the basis of these – for example, by lying down or offering help to someone in need. The *arahant* is not portrayed as living a life of complete inaction and utter indifference, and the Buddha himself clearly did not lead such a life. Whatever dispassion and the absence of craving mean, they do not mean this.

On the other hand, the *arahant* does not have desires and feelings in the way we ordinarily do, in a way that is often personally troubling, that involves craving, clinging, attachment, and the like. The desires he has do not result in suffering. According to the Buddha:

> Pleasant feeling arises in a well-taught noble disciple. Touched by that pleasant feeling, he does not lust after pleasure or continue to lust after pleasure. That pleasant feeling of his ceases. With the cessation of the pleasant feeling, painful feeling arises. Touched by that painful feeling, he does not sorrow, grieve, and lament, he does not weep beating his breast and become distraught.
>
> (M 334)

On another occasion, the Buddha said that whatever feeling an *arahant* has, 'whether pleasant or painful or neither-pleasant-nor-painful, he abides contemplating impermanence in those feelings,' and this leads him to 'not cling to anything in the world' (M 344). Though the *arahant* has pleasant and painful feelings, they do not lead him to crave the permanent possession or avoidance of things in the world that cause those feelings, and as a result he does not suffer.

141

The key to understanding this is that the realization of selflessness brings about a change of perspective that eliminates, or at least significantly reduces, the suffering of the *arahant*. First, lacking the belief that he is a substance-self, he regards the feelings and desires that we would ordinarily say are his as phenomena that are not in any real sense his own and to which he is not attached in any fundamental way. If feelings and desires are not properties of selves, but impersonal features of the universe, then there is no basis for maintaining any deep sense of identification with some of these in contrast with others. One way of seeing the effect of this may be to consider our reaction to seeing on television that someone in a distant part of the world has lost his or her home in a flood. We realize this is a bad thing and hope the person is able to recover. But, we typically think, because we are not personally involved, the intensity of our feelings, the degree to which we suffer, in the face of this news is substantially less than that of the person whose home has been destroyed. Now suppose that the person in the flood had feelings that were no more involved or intense than ours as distant observers. Something like this would actually be the case, the Buddha thought, if the person had come to the realization of selflessness. This realization would bring it about that the person would no longer be personally attached to his or her feelings and desires, which would consequently result in no more suffering than that felt by distant observers. An *arahant* flood victim would see that the lost home is in some sense bad vis-à-vis his or her relative happiness and would set about rebuilding. But the *arahant* would be no more agitated by this than anyone else with knowledge of the situation. The person would not be driven by the thought that *my happiness* is of primary importance and depends on permanently possessing a home. Nor would the person think, '*I* did not deserve this,' in part because he or she would recognize that the destruction of the home was a natural consequence of past actions (in accord with *kamma*), but mainly because he or she would realize that in a deep sense there is no 'I' to receive desert.

Second, without the belief that he is a substance-self with identity through time, the *arahant* is not preoccupied with the well-being of this self across time. In particular, he is not absorbed with regrets about frustrated desires in the past and anxieties about possible thwarted desires in the future. The realization of selflessness brings about a change in perspective in which there is no longer the intense focus of attention on one's past and future personal well-being. Liberated from these self-oriented concerns about past and future, the *arahant* is able to experience delight and enjoyment at whatever happens in the present moment. This is not merely the negative happiness that is the absence of unfulfilled desire; it is the positive happiness that becomes possible in the absence of preoccupation with desire. This is a crucial, if understated, aspect of the Buddha's teaching. Once we stop viewing the world from the perspective of incessant personal striving to bring about or maintain what we view as agreeable, and to avoid or get rid of what we regard as disagreeable, we will be freed to discover that there is something valuable, something good,

142

1	1	W	18	Dover Beach, Matthew Arnold
2	1	F	20	Nietzsche, Gay Science section 125 "God is Dead" On Truth and Lies in the Non-Moral Sense
3	1	M	23	Max Weber, Science as Vocation
4	1	W	25	James, The Will to Believe
5	1	F	27	Gowan preface, 3-27 Life of Buddha
6	1	M	30	Gowan 28-49 Teachings and Practice
7	2	1	W	Read first five of eight suttas on Blackboard: Setting the Wheel in Motion, All the Fermentations, the Not-self Characteristic, The Noble Search, Fear and Dread, and The Longer Discourse to Saccaka
	2	2	R	Movie, *The Flight from Death: the quest for immortality* 6:00. HS 216 Pizza
8	2	3	F	Gowan 50-69* Theoretical Dimensions
9	2	6	M	"Epicurus," An encyclopedia of philosophy Letter to Menoeceus, Blackboard
10	2	8	W	Epicurus, Principal Doctrines Blackboard Aurelius, Meditation 4 Blackboard
11	2	10	F	Gowan 69*-89* Not-Self
12	2	13	M	Gowan 91-116 Not-Self
13	2	15	W	Rescher, Process Phil. (on HD, 9 pages)
14	2	17	F	Hume, Of Personal Identity Blackboard Giles, No-Self Theory, Blackboard
15	2	20	M	Giles, No-Self Theory
16	2	22	W	Goodman, "Vaibhasika Metaphoricalism" Blackboard
17	2	24	F	
18	2	27	M	Gowan 119-139* Dukkha
19	3	1	W	Gowan 139*-157 Nibbana
20	3	3	F	
21	3	6	M	Gowan 161-179 Eightfold path
22	3	8	W	Gowan 180-200 Meditation
23	3	10	F	Gowan Conclusion (review book)

Empricism, Fallibilism, Pragmatism, Skepticism, Nietzsche, etc.

Audi, R. (1995). The Cambridge dictionary of philosophy. Cambridge ; New York,
Cambridge University Press. B41 .C35 1995

Stanford Online Encyclopedia of Philosophy

Routledge Encyclopedia of Philosophy B51 .R68 1998 (non-circulating)

www.accesstoinsight.org

google<befriending suttas>

↶ another key assumption
√

Zen
tiger
story

in each moment. One indication of this is the earlier reference to appreciative joy, part of the immeasurable deliverance of mind. This has traditionally been interpreted as taking joy in the happiness of others (see Buddhaghosa 1999: 308–9). But I believe it may be understood to exemplify a broader and somewhat different point: every moment is always an occasion to rejoice in what is good in the world. As before, that this is so is not to be discovered by reasoning; it is to be revealed by the experience of selflessness (and is ordinarily obscured by our self-centered perspective on the world). The Buddha's insight is suggested in this Japanese haiku by Ryôkan:

> Still on my window-sill the moon is left:
> The thief has overlooked it in his theft.
>
> (Stewart 1993: 71)

We all recognize how preoccupation with the past and future sometimes robs us of the pleasure of the present moment. The Buddha thought that the recognition of selflessness would dissolve all such preoccupations and that from this perspective we would see there is something of great value to be found in every moment – even when our home is burglarized or washed downstream. This is in part because from the standpoint of selflessness there is always something good to be found somewhere in terms of our ordinary conception of happiness. But more fundamentally it is because, from the apprehension of *Nibbāna* as ultimate reality revealed by selflessness, everything has a form of goodness no matter how bad it looks in terms of our ordinary conception.

In short, the Buddha taught that the full realization of selflessness – in particular, that we are not distinct substances with identity – would enable us to become compassionate towards other persons, to no longer be agitated by deep attachment to our feelings and desires, and to find cause for joy at every moment in our lives. And he taught that these together would bring us peace and tranquility. Compassion, freedom from agitation, joy, peace – this is not merely the lack of unhappiness that comes from the absence of unfulfilled personal desires. It is the supreme, positive happiness that abandoning the preoccupation with these desires makes possible, and the Buddha maintained that it exceeds immeasurably any happiness that comes from the fulfillment of desires. It is for this reason that he believed the attainment of *Nibbāna* in this life was the 'greatest bliss.'

4 Would the life of an *arahant* be a good life?

According to the Buddha, our nature is such that at a deep level it would be good for each of us to live the life of an *arahant*. Assuming it is possible, would this really be a good life? Would it overcome suffering? Would an *arahant* be a good person? Would the life of an *arahant* really be better than the life we have now? There are numerous issues stream-observers may wish

143

to raise here. Let us briefly consider what the Buddha might say in response to some of them.

It may be claimed that there are more accessible and metaphysically less problematic avenues to compassion and loving-kindness than the realization of selflessness. For example, these sentiments might be based on the belief that each person is a substance-self that has great and equal worth, and so deserves the same concern and respect. In short, altruism does not require the extraordinary life of an *arahant*. In response, the Buddha thought that, as long as we regard ourselves as distinct substance-selves, we will inevitably view the world from a self-centered perspective, and our capacity for altruistic feelings will be quite limited and imperfect. Only the realization of selflessness will *fully* develop this capacity.

Related to this, it may also be suggested that the Buddha's teaching provides no basis for opposing injustice and fighting oppression. Justice involves the impartial treatment of distinct individuals, and typically this has been brought about on account of people's anger and outrage at injustice in the world. The Buddha's denial that we are distinct substance-selves and his emphasis on dispassion and overcoming anger would undermine the struggle for justice. In reply, it should be said that the Buddha's outlook does imply an alternative approach to these issues, one based on recognizing the interdependence of all persons rather than their distinctness, and one motivated by loving-kindness and compassion rather than anger and outrage. However, it must be admitted that the Buddha did little to develop this approach. His emphasis was more on personal transformation than social reform. In recent years, a movement of 'Socially Engaged Buddhists' has tried to articulate a vision for social justice on the basis of his teaching.

To turn to a rather different topic, it might be thought that, on account of selflessness, intimate personal relations among *arahants* either would not exist or would have greatly diminished value: if there are no selves, what are we to make of the special concern for particular persons that is characteristic of love and friendship? On the Buddha's behalf, it may be said that the destructive passions the realization of selflessness enables us to overcome (envy, lust, jealousy, anger, and so on) are especially harmful in personal relationships, and that the replacement of these passions by compassion and loving-kindness would greatly enhance the value of these relationships. And it might be supposed that an *arahant*'s compassionate disposition could be focused on particular persons in relations of love and friendship as much as on humanity in general. However, it must be acknowledged that the Buddha was not much concerned with intimate personal relations and, in fact, seemed to regard them as a significant obstacle to enlightenment. We will see later (chapter 15, section 2) that he did outline some moral responsibilities for spouses, parents, children, friends, and the like. But this discussion does not address the question of whether, or in what respects, the realization of selflessness would fundamentally alter these relationships.

144

We might also wonder whether non-attachment to one's own feelings and desires would undermine a person's sense of identity, the self-understanding of who in particular he or she is, in a way that would be damaging to personal well-being. Here it may be observed that from the outside many Buddhists appear to have a rather strong sense of identity. For example, the Dalai Lama seems to have a coherent and integrated understanding of who he is, where he comes from, what he believes in, what his values are, what he is trying to accomplish, and so on. He does not look to have an 'identity problem.' The same may be said of the Buddha himself. However, the Buddha thought there was a danger in being preoccupied with one's own identity. An *arahant* would not even have thoughts such as 'I have attained *Nibbāna*.' On the face of it, the importance often assigned to having a strong sense of identity would not survive the realization of selflessness in a form we are likely to recognize.

A related concern is whether an *arahant* would have a proper sense of self-esteem and self-respect. It might be objected that a person who realizes his or her selflessness would no longer believe he or she is important, has legitimate interests and needs, and deserves to be treated with respect and appropriate regard. In support of the Buddha, it may be said that there is no suggestion here of totally losing oneself in, or sacrificing oneself for, others (as ordinarily understood, these notions presuppose the existence of distinct selves). The metaphysics of interdependence and the ethic of loving-kindness do not have these implications. Though the Buddha rejects the interpretation of persons as selves, his entire teaching is premised on the belief that there is a significant sense in which, as we might put it, each individual person is equally important and valuable. He taught, he said, 'out of compassion for beings' (M 261). Though presumably the *arahant* would regard the language of self-esteem and self-respect as misleading in some regards, there would be no thought of being worthless, either absolutely or in comparison with others. On the other hand, an *arahant* who was insulted or treated in a degrading manner may be expected to focus not on righting a personal affront, but on encouraging the offending person to be more considerate to people. The Buddha's outlook does challenge some conceptions of why and how we should stand up for ourselves.

On a somewhat different issue, it might be suspected that selflessness would mean not simply that we are no longer attached to our own feelings, but that we are affected by the feelings of everyone. Since compassion involves being concerned about the plight of all persons, would this not increase rather than decrease the *arahant*'s suffering? Now, if we take being concerned about another person's plight to mean feeling what the other person feels, with a similar sense of intense personal ownership, this might be a serious objection. A person who felt compassion towards all persons in this way might seem to be overwhelmed by the suffering of others. But the Buddha plainly has some-thing else in mind – perhaps something closer to the dispassionate concern of a social worker whose personal life is not ordinarily broken up by worries

(handwritten margin note: Zen story of wrongly accused monk.)

about his caseload than the impassioned concern of a person who lies awake worrying about her best friend's marital problems. The *arahant* is portrayed as being compassionate, but also as being peaceful and not agitated. Though we sometimes take the absence of agitation as a sign of lack of concern, the Buddha's contention is that the realization of selflessness makes it possible to be both fully concerned and at peace.

Related to this, we might wonder whether selflessness would preclude acting in the world with an appropriate concern for the past and future. The *arahauts'* realization that they are not substance-selves with identity is supposed to make it possible to focus on and find value in the present moment: 'They maintain themselves with what is present.' But does not any worthwhile (or even intelligible) human life require some attention to past and future – for example, in order to act to fulfill promises to others and commitments to ourselves? The Buddha's own post-enlightenment life suggests that he was capable of forming intentions and carrying them out over time. Hence, *Nibbāna*-in-life apparently does not preclude action in this sense. Since in this life an *arahant* persists in some respects as a process-self (full selflessness is attained only with *Nibbāna*-after death), the continuity of processes through time must be sufficient to account for a level of concern with his or her own past and future. The realization that there is no identity diminishes this concern, but at this transitional stage it does not eliminate it. Still, there are perplexing questions on the horizon here. Since wholesome and unwholesome intentional actions are said to perpetuate the cycle of rebirth, the Buddha did not perform intentional actions in this sense (see M 650). This is because his actions were in no way expressions of craving, clinging, lust, hatred, delusion, and so on. We might say that the *arahant* performs something like intentional actions (for example, actions oriented towards goals on the basis of reasons). However, since these are not merely wholesome but incommensurably good, no future effects via *kamma* are created.

It might also be objected that there is no reason to think there is something good in every moment. Are not some moments simply bad? The Buddha acknowledged that this is how it appears to those caught up in the cycle of rebirth. This is part of the point of the First Noble Truth. But those who have realized selflessness are able to see that there is always goodness to be found. There is no argument for this in the Buddha. All that is claimed is that if we attain this perspective we will see that this is true. The *arahant* does not accept and endure things no matter how bad they are. Rather, he has the conviction grounded in knowledge that there is good in things no matter how bad they seem (from a self-centered standpoint). We glimpsed the possibility of this in the discussion of appreciative joy. Perhaps the belief that each person is capable of attaining *Nibbāna* is also relevant. Probably the experience of *Nibbāna* as what is beyond conditioning is most important of all.

Finally, it might be thought that there is much happiness to be gained from fulfilled desires, and that the *arahant*, unconcerned with desires, loses out on this. Think of how great it can feel to get something we really want. Even if there is much that appears attractive in the life of the *arahant*, it might be said, there is also a good deal of what ordinarily is considered happiness that is missing. One possibility is that, compared with an ordinary life, the life of an *arahant* has real losses, but is much better overall. However, the Buddha did not see it this way. To attain *Nibbāna* is to reach an unequivocally better state, not one in which the gains outweigh the losses. An analogy might help here. As adults we feel no loss in the fact that we can no longer enjoy tic-tac-toe. We have found far more engaging pursuits that render this inability irrelevant. But a young child who loves tic-tac-toe may find our perspective hard to appreciate. From the standpoint of the unenlightened, it may appear that there are losses in the life of an *arahant*. Indeed, it may appear that in some respects this life is hardly a human life at all. According to the Buddha, this is because the unenlightened, believing they are selves, have inherently flawed perceptions. For those who have realized selflessness, there is a life that is far better than this merely 'human' life to which we are so accustomed and attached. This is probably not an easy point for stream-observers to appreciate – as the Buddha himself at least partly acknowledges.

SUGGESTED READING

On the nature of the life of the *arahant*, see the *Dhātuvibhanga Sutta* ('The Exposition of the Elements'), M #140.

The *arahant*'s life is discussed in Bastow (1969), Gruzalski (1996), Gudmunsen (1972), Ling (1965), Mahinda (1996) and Rupp (1971). On Socially Engaged Buddhism, see Chappell (1999), Eppsteiner (1988), and Queen (2000).

13

THE CESSATION OF SUFFERING: *NIBBĀNA*-AFTER-DEATH

We have seen that the Buddha spoke rather briefly and elusively about *Nibbāna*-in-life. This is true to an even greater extent with respect to *Nibbāna*-after-death. On this topic, there are two issues we need to consider: *Nibbāna* as ultimate reality, and the *arahant's* attainment of this reality after death. In addition, there are several philosophical perplexities concerning the attainment of *Nibbāna* we should examine in view of the meaning of *Nibbāna* and the not-self teaching.

1 *Nibbāna* as ultimate reality

Nibbāna as ultimate reality is in many respects the opposite of reality as we commonly know it. This is especially true with respect to suffering. Just as our unenlightened lives are portrayed as fundamentally unsatisfactory, so *Nibbāna* is the polar opposite of this – a state of perfection that may be thought of as the highest good and the highest happiness. Similarly, just as the world of ordinary experience and our own lives are depicted as being impermanent and conditioned, so *Nibbāna* is ultimate reality beyond change and conditioning: '*Nibbāna* is cessation of becoming' (N 240). However, it is *not* the case that just as there is no self in this world so there is a self in *Nibbāna*. For the Buddha, there are no substances-selves in any sense, and process-selves exist only insofar as we falsely believe we are substance-selves. A person's process-self has no independent reality, and once the person is enlightened and escapes the cycle of rebirth the process-self has no dependent reality either. Since *Nibbāna* is the ultimate reality, it does not in any way contain selves or a self. As we have seen, 'it cannot happen that a person possessing right view could treat anything as self' (M 928), and a person who has attained *Nibbāna* cannot say anything self-referential such as '*I* have attained *Nibbāna*' (M 846). About himself, the Buddha said, 'I-making, mine-making . . . have been eradicated in me' (M 908).

The most extensive and best-known descriptions of *Nibbāna* as ultimate reality are found in the *Udāna*. In four brief sections, the Buddha is said to have instructed and inspired 'the *bhikkhus* with a *Dhamma* talk connected with *Nibbāna*.' In the first section, he says:

148

There is, *bhikkhus*, that base [or sphere] where there is no earth, no water, no fire, no air; no base consisting of the infinity of space, no base consisting of the infinity of consciousness, no base consisting of nothingness, no base consisting of neither-perception-nor-non-perception; neither this world nor another world nor both; neither sun nor moon. Here, *bhikkhus*, I say there is no coming, no going, no staying, no deceasing, no uprising. Not fixed, not movable, it has no support. Just this is the end of suffering.

(U/I 102)

This clearly implies that *Nibbāna* is a reality that stands in sharp contrast to the reality of ordinary experience. As is often the case in accounts of *Nibbāna*, the entire description is in terms of what is *not* the case. *Nibbāna* is not a physical realm at all, and it is beyond all that is conditioned and impermanent. Hence, it is timeless not in the sense of lasting forever, but in the sense of being outside of time. The four bases – infinite space, infinite consciousness, nothingness, and neither-perception-nor-non-perception – refer to the four spheres of formlessness that stand at the top of the Buddha's cosmology. Hence, *Nibbāna* is a reality entirely beyond the whole cycle of rebirth. (In one form of meditation, these four spheres correspond to the four highest levels of attainment short of *Nibbāna*.) However, though *Nibbāna* itself is not conditioned, we conditioned beings can in some sense know and attain it.

The second section is a brief verse that contains familiar ideas. Craving is said to be 'penetrated by one who knows,' but 'the truth is not easy to see' (U/I 103). The third section is the most widely quoted and seems to suggest an argument:

There is, *bhikkhus*, a not-born, a not-brought-to-being, a not-made, a not-conditioned. If, *bhikkhus*, there were no not-born, not-brought-to-being, not-made, not-conditioned, no escape would be discerned from what is born, brought-to-being, made, conditioned. But since there is a not-born, a not-brought-to-being, a not-made, a not-conditioned, therefore an escape is discerned from what is born, brought-to-being, made, conditioned.

(U/I 103; see also 180)

The phrases 'not-born,' 'not-brought-to-being,' 'not-made,' and 'not-conditioned' are common descriptions of *Nibbāna*. Let us summarize them with the term 'Unconditioned.' Their opposites – what is born, brought-to-being, made, and conditioned – are typical descriptions of everyday reality. Let us summarize these with the term 'Conditioned.' The text consists of the following statements.

(1) There is the Unconditioned.
(2) If there were no Unconditioned, no escape would be discerned from the Conditioned.
(3) But since there is an Unconditioned, an escape is discerned from the Conditioned.

This looks like an argument for the conclusion that an escape is discerned from the Conditioned. However, if it is interpreted in this way, the argument is plainly a fallacy (C cannot be inferred from U and 'If not-U, then not-C'). But perhaps it should be interpreted differently. One alternative would be to take (2) and (3) together as stating that there is an Unconditioned if, and only if, an escape from the Conditioned has been discerned. Since it is assumed that the Buddha has discerned such an escape, this would prove that there is an Unconditioned, as stated in (1). A variation on this would interpret the argument as proving that there is an escape, given (1) and the equivalence shown in (2) and (3). Either way, nothing would have been said to support the key premises. Another alternative would be to interpret (2) as stating that we could escape from the Conditioned only if there were something to escape to, namely the Unconditioned, and (3) as emphasizing that the existence of the Unconditioned has made it possible for the Buddha to discern an escape. The passage may be a reminder that a circumstance necessary for escape is real, perhaps in response to those who doubt escape is possible.

The fourth and final section says:

> For the supported [attached or clinging] there is instability, for the unsupported there is no instability; when there is no instability there is serenity; when there is serenity there is no inclination; when there is no inclination there is no coming-and-going; when there is no coming-and-going there is no decease-and-uprising; when there is no decease-and-uprising there is neither 'here' nor 'beyond' nor 'in between the two.' Just this is the end of suffering.
>
> (U/I 104)

This is a familiar depiction of *Nibbāna* as tranquil, beyond instability, inclination, and change. The last expression – 'neither "here" nor "beyond" nor "in between the two"' – presumably means neither in this life, nor in another rebirth, nor in between the two: *Nibbāna* is not a stage in the cycle of rebirth, but is completely beyond this cycle.

It is evident from these passages in *The Udāna* that *Nibbāna* is something real. Therefore, the contention that *Nibbāna* is simply nothingness, and hence that in this respect Buddhism is ultimately nihilistic, is mistaken. The terminology of absence – *Nibbāna* as not earth, not born, and so on – is intended to show that *Nibbāna* is completely beyond the conditioned world, not that it is nothing at all. On the other hand, insofar as *Nibbāna* is portrayed as ultimate reality that is beyond change and conditioning, and that, when attained, enables us to overcome suffering, it might invite comparison with the God of the theistic traditions of Judaism, Christianity, and Islam. There are points of similarity. As we saw in chapter 5, *Nibbāna* is transcendent reality in a broad sense of the term: it is beyond the ordinary world of sense-experience and may be approached only via meditation. But the differences are quite significant. The most important are that, unlike God, *Nibbāna* is not the ultimate cause of the universe, and it is not a personal being who is omnipotent, omniscient, and all-loving. Hence, it is not a reality on which human beings depend or with whom they could form a personal relationship. Since the orthodox descriptions of God and *Nibbāna* are incompatible, it does not seem that they could refer to the same thing. Of course, it might be said that these descriptions are culturally diverse attempts to understand the same transcendent reality, that they are two limited human responses to it. Though this may be true, prima facie they cannot be said to be two equally successful attempts. At any rate, from our human perspective, at least one of them must be partly or wholly mistaken. Various lessons may be drawn from this. But a dialogue – for example, between Buddhists (rooted in the *Pāli* canon) and Christians – would have to take this metaphysical divide as an initial point of difference, whatever other similarities there might be.

The Buddha thought we could know *Nibbāna* as ultimate reality only through meditation. There is no indication that there is a rational argument for *Nibbāna* in any way similar to classical arguments for God's existence such as the cosmological argument. The epistemological emphasis is on a long training that crucially involves meditation and culminates in an enlightenment experience in which *Nibbāna* is glimpsed. The closest theistic analogue to this would be arguments for God from religious experience – for example, see Alston (1991), Davis (1989), Swinburne (1979: chapter 13), and Yandell (1993).

A skeptical stream-observer might observe that the reality of *Nibbāna* is as implausible as the idea of rebirth. However, there is an epistemic difference between them. If rebirth were true, it would seem that much evidence ought to be available that apparently is not. This cannot be said of *Nibbāna*: it could only be understood by extraordinary means. By contrast, it is conceivable that rebirth could be comprehended by relatively ordinary means. For example, we might all remember past lives. This does not mean there is more evidence for *Nibbāna*, only that it is not open to an objection that is relevant to rebirth. The skeptic might reply that this is because *Nibbāna* is so far outside normal experience that nothing could count for or against it. Perhaps this is true, but the Buddha would respond that normal experience is not the only experience available to us. Moreover, the lives of *arahants* might provide indirect evidence of *Nibbāna*: perhaps these lives are so extraordinary that it is unlikely they are based on an illusory experience.

2 The *arahant* after death

What does it mean for an *arahant* to attain *Nibbāna*-after-death? It is evident that the *arahant* permanently escapes the cycle of rebirth. But to what, so to speak, does he or she escape? This is not an easy question to answer. It is clear that the *arahant* does not fully and in every respect simply cease to exist: the physical death of an *arahant* is not complete annihilation, and in fact one of the standard depictions of *Nibbāna* is that it is 'deathless.' On the other hand, the Buddha was extremely reluctant to provide a positive account of the *arahant* after physical death, and what he does say is sometimes mistakenly interpreted as implying annihilation.

An essential class of texts in this regard are those in which the Buddha refuses to affirm a series of metaphysical propositions. (We have discussed these in chapter 3, section 2, chapter 6, section 2, and chapter 9, section 4.) These propositions include the following (for the passages in this paragraph, see M 591–3).

(1) After death a *Tathāgata* exists: only this is true, anything else is wrong.
(2) After death a *Tathāgata* does not exist: only this is true, anything else is wrong.
(3) After death a *Tathāgata* both exists and does not exist: only this is true, anything else is wrong.
(4) After death a *Tathāgata* neither exists nor does not exist: only this is true, anything else is wrong.

'*Tathāgata*' is an epithet for the Buddha, but it may be taken to refer to the existence of any *arahant*. The Buddha says each of these propositions is a 'thicket of views' that is 'beset by suffering' and 'does not lead . . . to peace, to direct knowledge, to enlightenment, to *Nibbāna*.' He concludes that, 'seeing this danger, I do not take up any of these speculative views.' Since these four statements exhaust the logical possibilities, the Buddha appears to be refusing to take a stand on whether or not an *arahant* exists after death. When his interlocutor Vacchagotta presses him on this refusal, the Buddha responds by referring to the changing state of the aggregates and saying that with the 'relinquishing of all conceivings, all excogitations, all I-making, mine-making, and the underlying tendency to conceit, the *Tathāgata* is liberated through not clinging.' Vacchagotta then asks, 'When a *bhikkhu*'s mind is liberated thus, Master Gotama, where does he reappear (after death)?' The Buddha again refuses to affirm any statement, positive or negative, that employs the term 'reappears' in this connection. Vacchagotta expresses bewilderment about this, and the Buddha says his teaching is 'hard to understand . . . unattainable by mere reasoning, subtle, to be experienced by the wise.' He then offers a simile: if we asked about an extinguished fire 'To which direction did it go: to the east, the west, the north, or the south?,' the proper answer would be 'That does not apply.' The Buddha concludes:

152

So, too, Vacchagotta, the *Tathāgata* has abandoned that material form by which one describing the *Tathāgata* might describe him . . . .The *Tathāgata* is liberated from reckoning in terms of material form, Vaccha, he is profound, immeasurable, hard to fathom like the ocean. The term 'reappears' does not apply [in any negative or positive form].

Three themes may be discerned in these remarks. First, to ask whether the *Tathāgata* exists after death, or where he reappears after death, does not lead to *Nibbāna* and in fact contributes to suffering (a point emphasized in the simile of the poison arrow, where the Buddha also declined to comment on the *Tathāgata's* existence after death; see M 533–6). Concern with these questions betrays preoccupation with one's self. Second, the Buddha's teaching on this subject is difficult to understand, especially from a rational perspective. Finally, and most importantly, one reason it is hard to understand is because terms such as 'exists' and 'reappears' cannot be applied properly in this context. Just as it would not make sense to say an extinguished fire went in one direction or another, so it does not make sense to say the *Tathāgata* exists or does not exist, and so on. It does not make sense because 'the *Tathāgata* has abandoned that material form by which one describing the *Tathāgata* might describe him' and similarly for the other aggregates. The implication is that the only terms we have to refer to a person are the aggregate terms. Since a *Tathāgata* after death has no aggregates, there are no terms by which we can say whether or not he exists, and so on. More generally, when we speak of the existence and reappearance of things we presuppose the conditioned world of becoming of our ordinary experience. For this reason, these expressions cannot be meaningfully applied to the attainment of *Nibbāna* as ultimate reality beyond conditioning and change. Hence, the *Tathāgata* after death is 'immeasurable, hard to fathom like the ocean.'

In another text, the Buddha says nothing can be found of which it can be said: ' "The consciousness of one thus gone [a liberated *bhikkhu*] is supported by this." Why is that? One thus gone, I say, is untraceable here and now' (M 233–4). A related aspect of his refusal is rooted in the not-self teaching: to say that the *Tathāgata* exists after death might be misinterpreted as eternalism (the view that the self exists eternally after death), while to say that the *Tathāgata* does not exist after death might be misinterpreted as annihilationism (the view that the self ceases to exist after death). Both eternalism and annihilationism falsely presuppose that there is a self. The Buddha often presented his own view – that there is no self, but an enlightened person attains *Nibbāna* after death – as an alternative to these two positions (see M 839).

In short, the Buddha's reluctance to speak positively about the state of the *arahant* after death was rooted in the philosophical conviction that our concepts are designed to describe the impermanent and conditioned world, and hence are inappropriate for depicting *Nibbāna*-after-death. Of course, we cannot speak at all without employing some concepts. On the rare occasions when the Buddha spoke of *Nibbāna*, he tried to indicate the limitation of language by using concepts in unusual ways, as in the descriptions of *Nibbāna* in terms of what it is not, and the similes such as that of the extinguished fire and the ocean. It is a mistake to conclude from this that the attainment of *Nibbāna* is a state of nothingness (in particular, the simile of the extinguished fire should not be interpreted in this way). However, there is little that can be said positively to describe this state. For one who has attained enlightenment, such descriptions are unnecessary, while for one who has not, they are not very helpful.

3 Some philosophical perplexities

In an important respect, stream-observers are in a better position to evaluate the life of an *arahant* who is still alive than they are to assess the state of an *arahant* who has died. We could observe a living *arahant* and judge whether he has a truly good life. However, we cannot directly observe the state of an *arahant* after death. From the Buddha's perspective, an unenlightened person cannot fully comprehend the worth of an *arahant*'s life before or after death. But he thought stream-observers could comprehend enough to conclude that it would be worthwhile to undertake the Eightfold Path. We now need to consider whether or not the state of an *arahant* beyond this life is sufficiently coherent to make this preliminary assessment. There are several philosophical perplexities on the horizon.

The most important problem concerns what it means to say a person has attained *Nibbāna*-after-death. Since *Nibbāna* as ultimate reality is beyond change and conditioning, the fact that a person attains *Nibbāna* cannot result in a change to *Nibbāna* itself: it does not change. Hence, a person's attainment of *Nibbāna*-after-death must involve a transformation within the person. But the Buddha regularly speaks as if a person in this life is nothing more than the aggregates, and he says a person who attains *Nibbāna*-after-death abandons all the aggregates (in my terminology, the person is not a substance-self, and the process-self is completely dissolved with the attainment of *Nibbāna*-after-death). The consequence is that there does not seem to be anything left of a person who attains *Nibbāna*-after-death. However, there must be something left or attainment of *Nibbāna*-after-death would be annihilation – and this the Buddha denies.

There are four main responses to this problem. First, it may be contended that, despite what the Buddha says, *Nibbāna*-after-death really is annihilation of the person. Even if what he claims about *Nibbāna* as ultimate reality is correct, his overall position entails that attainment of *Nibbāna*-after-death could be nothing else but the complete cessation of the person. Second, it may be argued that, in spite of the Buddha's not-self doctrine, there surely is a self *in some sense* that permanently exists through this life and attains *Nibbāna*-after-death. If this attainment is not annihilation, then there must be a self that attains *Nibbāna*. Both of these interpretations attribute an unintended inconsistency to the Buddha's teaching. The remaining interpretations take a different approach. The third says the rational irresolvability of this problem is part of the Buddha's teaching. Though it is true from a rational standpoint that this is a problem, the Buddha acknowledges that his teaching concerning *Nibbāna* is 'unattainable by mere reasoning.' For one who is enlightened all will be clear, but for others nothing more can be said than this. The difficulty with this interpretation is that it seems to deprive stream-observers of a solid rationale for undertaking the Eightfold Path. It requires them to have considerable faith in the Buddha as a prelude to achieving enlightenment for themselves.

The fourth interpretation maintains that there is an aspect of the person that, like *Nibbāna* as ultimate reality, is beyond space and time, change and conditioning, and so on. Though any label misleads, it will be convenient to call this aspect of the person its *liberated dimension*. This dimension cannot be identified with the aggregates and it cannot be described as any kind of self: both the process-self and the substance-self presuppose categories that the liberated dimension is beyond. On this interpretation, it is the liberated dimension that persists in *Nibbāna*-after-death. If this were the case, the Buddha could consistently maintain both the not-self doctrine and the view that attainment of *Nibbāna* is not complete annihilation. But if both *Nibbāna* and the liberated dimension are beyond change and conditioning, what would it mean for a person to attain *Nibbāna*? Attainment involves change, and both *Nibbāna* and the liberated dimension do not change. What would have to be said is that *Nibbāna* and the liberated dimension have always been united in the appropriate way (however union might be understood). This does not change. To attain *Nibbāna* means that the person dissolves all sense of selfhood as an illusion and thereby discovers the previously hidden fact that the liberated dimension and *Nibbāna* have always been united. Here an analogy may help. Suppose your living room window overlooks a beautiful mountain valley, but nothing can be seen because the window is too dirty. Cleaning the window enables you to see the valley. But this does not create the fact that your living room overlooks the valley. It merely reveals what was already the case. Similarly, on this interpretation, enlightenment creates no new reality, but by cleansing the person of the illusion of selfhood it reveals the fact that the liberated dimension has always been united with *Nibbāna* – and this ends suffering and brings the greatest bliss.

In support of this interpretation is the fact that a fundamental premise of the Buddha's teaching is that the person, though not a self, is capable of attaining the highest happiness of *Nibbāna*-after-death. This suggests that the Buddha was committed to this view or something close to it. On the other hand, he did not directly formulate the problem about the meaning of the attainment of *Nibbāna*, and he did not explicitly articulate this understanding of the person as a resolution of that problem (nor for any other reason). His primary instinct was to say little about *Nibbāna* and to focus on the means to its attainment. This interpretation could be defended only on the ground that it makes the best overall sense of the Buddha's teaching in comparison with the other three.

Two related perplexities should also be mentioned. They both are rooted in the fact that an *arahant* who attains *Nibbāna*-after-death has abandoned all the aggregates. First, one of the aggregates is consciousness (*viññāṇa*). Hence, it seems that an *arahant* who attains *Nibbāna*-after-death is not conscious. But what could it mean to attain *Nibbāna* without being conscious? Would this be any different than annihilation? It might be said that consciousness, as one of the aggregates, is inescapably tied up with the illusion of selfhood. For this reason, one who attains *Nibbāna* cannot be conscious in this sense. However, there might be another form of consciousness that involves no notion of selfhood and is present in one who attains *Nibbāna*. This consciousness-with-out-selfhood might be part of the liberated dimension of the person discussed on page 155.[1] Of course, we might wonder whether consciousness-without-selfhood is really possible. Perhaps animals have such consciousness. But it seems unlikely that our liberated dimension is akin to animal consciousness: animals are below humans in the Buddha's cosmology. In the end, the Buddha might respond in this way: the distinction between what is and is not conscious applies to the conditioned world of our experience, and since *Nibbāna* is beyond this world, in this respect nothing meaningful can be said about the *arahant* after death.

Second, another of the aggregates is feelings or sensations (*vedanā*). Attaining *Nibbāna* is said to be the highest happiness, but how is happiness possible in the absence of feelings? The Buddha has something to say in response to this question. The happiness of *Nibbāna*-after-death is not a matter of pleasant feelings, and it is immeasurably higher than any form of happiness available to the unenlightened in the cycle of rebirth. For example, we hear of a happiness that comes with 'the ending of perception and feeling' (G IV 281) and a 'delight apart from sensual pleasures' (M 610). Most people would probably acknowledge that happiness is not merely pleasant feelings (and the absence of painful ones). Much that is ordinarily associated with happiness, such as a fulfilling family life or a satisfying job, cannot plausibly be understood simply in terms of pleasant feelings. But it is another matter whether we can envision a form of happiness in the absence of *any* of the aggregates. The issue here is closely related to the last: it is hard to imagine a state we would consider the highest happiness without some form of consciousness. As before, the Buddha was less inclined to explain this than to encourage us to experience it for ourselves by following the Eightfold Path.

SUGGESTED READING

For descriptions of *Nibbāna*, see U/I 102–4. The fate of an *arahant* after death is discussed in the *Aggivacchagotta Sutta* ('To Vacchagotta on Fire'), M #72.

Nibbāna is discussed in Collins (1998), Cruise (1983), Doore (1979), Harvey (1995a), Johansson (1969), and Welbon (1968).

NOTE

1   There may be some hint of this at L 179 and M 428. In this connection, see Harvey 1995a: chapter 12.

Part 4

THE WAY TO THE
CESSATION OF SUFFERING

14

THE EIGHTFOLD PATH:
WISDOM

The first three Noble Truths depict the nature of suffering, its origin, and its cessation. These comprise the theoretical dimension of the Buddha's teaching. But they are all preliminary to what is most important: the practical teaching that explains the path by which suffering is overcome and *Nibbāna* attained. This is summarized in the Fourth Noble Truth:

> Now this, *bhikkhus*, is the noble truth of the way leading to the cessation of suffering. It is this Noble Eightfold Path; that is, right view, right intention, right speech, right action, right livelihood, right effort, right mindfulness, right concentration.
>
> (C II 1844)

The Buddha says the 'good practice' of this path 'leads to complete disenchantment, to dispassion, to cessation, to peace, to direct knowledge, to enlightenment, to *Nibbāna*' (M 697). Though the Eightfold Path pertains primarily to practice, it is based on the diagnosis of the first three truths. Moreover, we cannot fully understand these truths without comprehending the Path. In particular, we will better understand the life of the *arahant* if we inquire into the training that leads to this life. The Buddha divided the eight steps of the path into three groups as follows.[1]

Wisdom (*paññā*)	Right View (*sammā diṭṭhi*)
	Right Intention (*sammā sankappa*)
Virtue (*sīla*)	Right Speech (*sammā vācā*)
	Right Action (*sammā kammanta*)
	Right Livelihood (*sammā ājīva*)
Concentration (*samādhi*)	Right Effort (*sammā vāyāma*)
	Right Mindfulness (*sammā sati*)
	Right Concentration (*sammā samādhi*)

The term '*sammā*' means right in the sense of correct. Each of the eight aspects of the path describes a part of the proper training that is required to achieve enlightenment. On occasion, the Buddha drew a distinction between the eightfold path of 'the disciple in higher training' and the tenfold path of the *arahant*. The tenfold path adds right knowledge (*sammā ñāṇa*) and right deliverance (*sammā vimutti*) to the original eight steps (see M 939). But these additional steps do not seem to add anything of great substance, and the Buddha almost always spoke of the eight on page 161. Hence, we may focus on these eight, divided into their customary groups of wisdom, virtue, and concentration.

We will consider virtue and concentration in chapters 15 and 16. In this chapter, we will discuss wisdom along with several preliminary issues important for properly understanding the Path: the idea that it is a middle way on which gradual progress is possible, and its significance for women and lay followers of the Buddha.

1 Stages on the middle way

In the first *sutta*, the Buddha described the Eightfold Path as a 'middle way' between the extremes of pursuing 'sensual happiness' and pursuing 'self-mortification' (C II 1844). In that discourse, the Buddha was addressing the ascetic *samaṇas* he had abandoned before seeking enlightenment on his own, and he wanted to assure them that he had not reverted to a life of luxury. Hence, he presented his practice as falling between the extreme asceticism of the *samaṇas* and the worldly pursuits of most people. Beyond this, the idea of the middle way functions as something of a motif in the Buddha's teaching. For example, he said that a *bhikkhu* engaged in fruitful striving 'does not give up the pleasure that accords with *Dhamma*, yet he is not infatuated with that pleasure' (M 833–4), and he declared that 'one should neither extol nor disparage, but should teach only the *Dhamma*' (M 1080). On the metaphysical plane, the Buddha said: ' "All exists": Kaccāna, this is one extreme. "All does not exist": this is the second extreme. Without veering towards either of these extremes, the *Tathāgata* teaches the *Dhamma* by the middle' (C I 544). The two extremes refer to eternalism and annihilationism. The middle way is the twelvefold formula of dependent origination.

The idea that the Eightfold Path is a middle way between the pursuit of sensual pleasures and asceticism invites comparison with Aristotle's doctrine that virtue is 'a mean between two vices, one of excess and one of deficiency' (Aristotle 1999: 1107a3). This comparison seems particularly apt with respect to temperance, the Aristotelian virtue that is an intermediate state concerning the bodily pleasures of eating, drinking, and sex. Nonetheless, though there is a formal similarity here (for both, the correct avenue to happiness negotiates between extremes), there are also significant differences. The most revealing is shown in this remark by Aristotle: 'People who are deficient in pleasures and enjoy them less than is right are not found very much. For that sort of insensibility is not human.' He adds: 'If someone finds nothing pleasant . . .

he is far from being human. The reason he has no name is that he is not found much' (1119a7–11). For the Buddha, such persons were found easily and they had a name. Indeed, the Buddha had once been a *samaṇa* himself. Moreover, the extent of the *samaṇas'* asceticism was so extreme that a middle way between that and the typical pursuit of pleasure would probably look rather ascetic by the ordinary standards of the world. Certainly the life of the *bhikkhu* and *bhikkhunī* is quite ascetic by this measure (for example, see M 449). Aristotle himself had a fairly austere understanding of temperance – the temperate person 'finds no intense pleasure in any (bodily pleasures)' (1119a14) – but overall the moderation conveyed by the doctrine of the mean does not come close to capturing the radical transformation the Buddha thought was required to attain *Nibbāna*. For the Buddha, our unenlightened nature is deeply flawed, and only extraordinary measures can overcome this. Aristotle's conception of human nature is quite different: the virtues develop our nature, but they do not radically transform it. For this reason, perhaps, the virtues emphasized by the Buddha are not generally explained on the model of a mean between excess and deficiency (we will return to Aristotle in chapter 15, section 3).

The ultimate goal of the Eightfold Path is to become an *arahant*. However, the Buddha envisioned three preliminary stages of progress towards this goal: that of the stream-enterer (*sotāpanna*), the once-returner (*sakadāgāmin*), and the non-returner (*anāgāmin*). In each case, there is a distinction between beginning the stage and bearing its fruit. Hence, the Buddha spoke of 'four pairs of persons' on the road to enlightenment (M 119). The stream-enterer has some understanding of the Four Noble Truths and some grasp of *Nibbāna*, on the basis of wisdom or at least faith (see M 236). In addition, he has eliminated three of the ten fetters to enlightenment: he recognizes that there is no substance-self among the aggregates (personality view), he does not doubt the Buddha's teaching, and he realizes that merely following rules and observances is not sufficient for enlightenment. The Buddha said the stream-enterer will be reborn at most seven times, always at a human level or higher, and will then attain *Nibbāna*. The once-returner makes progress in eradicating the two fetters of sensual desire and ill will (and hence in attenuating lust, hatred, and delusion). According to the Buddha, he will be reborn only once, in the sense-sphere realm as a human or a god, and will then attain *Nibbāna*. The non-returner completely eliminates the fetters of sensual desire and ill-will. The Buddha thought he will reappear in one of the Pure Abodes (the highest planes of the form realm) and will then attain *Nibbāna*. Finally, the *arahant* destroys the remaining five fetters: craving for rebirth in the fine-material realm, craving for rebirth in the immaterial realm, conceit, restlessness, and ignorance. As we have seen, the Buddha said the *arahant* provisionally attains *Nibbāna* in this life and upon the death of the body will attain *Nibbāna*-after-death. He believed everyone could attain *Nibbāna* eventually, but he held that in this life, for the most part, only *bhikkhus* and

bhikkhunīs could become *arahants*. Laypersons could attain the three preliminary stages, but it was very exceptional that they attained *arahantship*.

What is most important in this hierarchy of levels of enlightenment is that
the Buddha believed we can make gradual progress towards enlightenment
both within this lifetime and through several lifetimes. According to the
Buddha:

> Just as the great ocean slopes away gradually, falls gradually, inclines
> gradually, not in an abrupt way like a precipice; even so, Pahārāda,
> is this *Dhamma* and Discipline: there is a gradual training, gradual
> practice, gradual progress; there is no penetration to final knowledge
> in an abrupt way.

> (N 203)

Enlightenment is not an all-or-nothing affair. It is something we can work
towards in stages by following the Eightfold Path, and the more we progress,
the better off we are. By analogy, it is less like learning how to stay afloat
in the water, which is pretty much an all-or-nothing skill, than it is like gradually becoming fluent in a foreign language, where every bit of learning helps
– except that eventually there is a decisive attainment of enlightenment.
Though there are reports of persons gaining enlightenment in an instant,
presumably on account of preparation in previous lives, the overall tenor of
the Buddha's teaching implies that for most persons enlightenment will
require a long and difficult journey. However, progress should not be understood merely in terms of moving from one step of the path to another (there
is no simple correlation between the eight steps and the four levels of enlightenment). Rather, the eight steps should be undertaken more or less as a whole,
and each step should be seen as dependent on, and reinforcing, the others.
For example, full wisdom cannot be attained without virtue, but without some
wisdom no virtue could be achieved.

Together, the eight aspects of the path are intended to bring about a fundamental and multifaceted transformation of the person involving intellectual,
emotional, and moral dimensions. It is broadly speaking a rigorous, spiritual
enterprise, the purpose of which is to dismantle the conditions that lead
to rebirth and suffering, specifically to move us from craving and clinging to
non-attachment, from hatred to compassion, and from delusion to wisdom.
From a Western perspective, the most distinctive feature of the Eightfold Path
is concentration. The idea that our ultimate well-being or salvation requires
a basic metamorphosis of our beliefs, feelings, and values is not unfamiliar
in Western traditions (it is a basic theme of Hellenistic philosophy). But that
this can be brought about fully only through the mental disciplines the Buddha
calls right effort, mindfulness, and concentration – what is usually referred
to as meditation in the West – is not so familiar. In some respects, these mental
disciplines may appear similar to introspective observation or prayer, but they

should not be reduced to these activities. We need to try to understand them on their own terms.

2 The universality of the Path: women

The Eightfold Path is ordinarily presented as important for, and available to, all human beings. For this reason, the universality of the Buddha's teaching is often stressed. Nonetheless, the Buddha customarily divided his disciples into four categories defined by gender and position in or out of the *Sangha*. Hence, there were *bhikkhus* and *bhikkhunīs* as well as male and female lay followers (*upāsakas* and *upāsikās*). It is clear that the Buddha taught persons in all four groups. He said he would not pass to *Nibbāna*-after-death until he had persons in each of these groups who were 'correctly trained and walking in the path the *Dhamma*' (L 246–7). Moreover, he sometimes placed the four groups on a par with one another – a *bhikkhu*, a *bhikkhunī*, a male lay follower, and a female lay follower, 'these are the four who, being accomplished in wisdom, disciplined, confident, deeply learned, *Dhamma*-bearers, living in accordance with *Dhamma*, illuminate the Order' (G II 8). On the other hand, the Buddha primarily taught the *bhikkhus*, and questions may be raised as to the relevance of the path for women and lay followers. Though the pertinent issues are partly related, it will be best to consider women in this section and lay followers in the next.

The role of women in Buddhism is a large topic. Our concern here is with the representation of women in the Buddha's teaching as expressed in the *Sutta Piṭaka*. Overall, this portrayal contains ambiguities and has given rise to different interpretations. Some passages explicitly state that women as well as men can approach *Nibbāna* – for example, 'I call the *Dhamma* the charioteer, with right view running out in front. One who has such a vehicle – whether a woman or a man – has, by means of this vehicle, drawn close to *Nibbāna*' (C I 122). Moreover, the Buddha made it clear that both *bhikkhus* and *bhikkhunīs* could become *arahants*. He stated that there were over five hundred of each 'who by realizing for themselves with direct knowledge here and now enter upon and abide in the deliverance of mind' (M 596). The *bhikkhunī* Somā says: 'What does womanhood matter at all when the mind is concentrated well, when knowledge flows on steadily as one sees correctly into *Dhamma*. One to whom it might occur, "I'm a woman" or "I'm a man" or "I'm anything at all" – is fit for Māra to address' (C I 222–3). Since Māra's primary role is to present obstacles to enlightenment, the implication is that gender is irrelevant to attaining *Nibbāna*. There are also texts in which the Buddha appears to criticize prevailing prejudices against women. For example, he notes that for a woman success 'in this world' requires being able in her work, managing domestics, behaving agreeably to her husband, and protecting his earnings. Nevertheless, the Buddha adds, a woman 'is successful in regard to the other world' if she is 'accomplished in faith, virtue,

generosity, and wisdom,' where each of these is understood by direct reference to the Buddha's teaching (N 219).

However, though the Buddha expresses a commitment to gender equality
regarding the attainment of *Nibbāna*, there are other passages in which he
affirms patriarchal attitudes. For example, he declares that 'womenfolk do not
sit in a court of justice, do not embark on business' because they are uncontrolled, envious, greedy, and weak in wisdom (G II 93). Rita M. Gross, writing
as both a feminist and a Buddhist, says: 'No major Buddhist teaching provides
any basis for gender privilege or gender hierarchy.' But she also claims that
'Buddhist institutions, both lay and monastic, are riddled with male domi-
nance.' Additionally, she argues that 'to be true to its own vision, Buddhism
needs to transcend its androcentrism and patriarchy' (Gross 1993: 153). To
determine whether the *Sutta Piṭaka* could support such a feminist reconstruction of Buddhism would require examination of the Buddha's founding
of the order of *bhikkhunīs*, the whole of his various comments about women,
and the question of whether or not, in light of our knowledge of the needs
and capacities of men and women, his central teachings are fundamentally
gender-neutral. Here we can touch only briefly on each of these points.

The idea of a *Sangha* for women came from the Buddha's stepmother
Mahāpajāpatī and was supported by his attendant Ānanda. Three times each
of them asked the Buddha to sanction a monastic order of women and on
each occasion he refused. Ānanda then asked the Buddha: 'If women go forth
from the home to the homeless life into the discipline of *Dhamma* . . . can
they realize the fruit of Stream-entry, of Once-returning, of Non-returning
and of *Arahantship*?' (G IV 183.) The Buddha replied that they could, and he
then agreed to establish the order as long as Mahāpajāpatī consented to follow
eight special rules. These rules were plainly prejudiced against women. For
example, they stated that a *bhikkhunī* must be admitted by both orders (while
bhikkhus needed to be admitted only by the male order) and that 'admonition
by *bhikkhunīs* of *bhikkhus* is forbidden, but admonition of *bhikkhunīs* by
bhikkhus is not forbidden' (G IV 184). Nonetheless, Mahāpajāpatī agreed and
the order was founded.

This account brings out the ambivalence in the Buddha's attitude towards
women. He agreed that women could become *arahants* and attain *Nibbāna*, yet
the eight rules placed the *bhikkhunīs* in an institutional position subordinate to
the *bhikkhus*. On behalf of the Buddha, it may be said that he had reasonable
grounds for fearing the entry of women into a celibate order of men. But
this concern would only justify a measure of separation, not subordination. It
may also be true that, despite the rules, establishing the order at all went against
prevailing norms of the Brahmanical tradition and marked an improvement
in the status of women. The Buddha's teaching did radically challenge his
contemporaries in many respects, but he was not primarily a social reformer.

The most important manifestation of the order of *bhikkhunīs* is the
Therīgāthā, a text in which over a hundred *bhikkhunīs* from a variety of

circumstances testified to their aspirations for, and attainments of, Buddhist enlightenment. For example, Sundarī declared to the Buddha: 'Buddha, teacher, I am your daughter, your true child, born of your mouth. My mind is free of clinging. My task is done.' The Buddha gave words of welcome and agreed, 'Your mind is free of clinging, your task is done' (Murcott translation: 189). That there were *bhikkhunīs* who expressed themselves in the *Therīgāthā*, and that their words have survived as part of the *Sutta Piṭaka*, is the greatest evidence of the positive role of women in early Buddhism and is an important resource for a feminist reassessment of Buddhism.

In many respects, the Buddha did not question the social understandings of gender in his culture, and his comments concerning women are mixed. There are passages in which he speaks highly of women. For example, he praises three female lay followers: Khujjuttarā for her 'wide knowledge,' Sāmāvatī for her 'kindliness,' and Uttarā for her 'meditative power' (G I 24). On the other hand, there are also texts that express a negative assessment of women. In some cases, these are balanced by parallel assessments of men. For instance, women are often portrayed as seeking to sexually entice the *bhikkhus*; but men are also presented as posing the same threat to the *bhikkhunīs*. However, in other cases, his comments evince a clear prejudice against women. Thus, after establishing the order of *bhikkhunīs*, the Buddha told Ānanda that now his teaching would last 500 rather than 1,000 years (see G IV 184–5). Again, he declared that a woman could not be 'an Accomplished One, a Fully Enlightened One' – that is, someone who introduces the *Dhamma* to the world (M 929; cf. G I 26).

The most important question regarding women is whether or not the Buddha's fundamental teaching betrays patriarchal attitudes. Are gender biases contained in the Four Noble Truths or the basic philosophical doctrines of *kamma*, rebirth, not-self, the five aggregates, dependent origination, and so on? One indication of bias might be an argument, traditional among some Buddhists, that women are in a less fortunate situation than men because of the moral character of their past lives, in accord with *kamma* and rebirth (see Gross 1993: 142–6). The Buddha sometimes did depict the lives of women as more difficult than those of men (for example, see C II 1287). But there is no evidence that he explained this situation in terms of *kamma* and rebirth. In any case, such an argument could not properly be used to justify the oppression of women. However, the currency of this argument does show that the doctrines of *kamma* and rebirth are subject to abusive misuse: any misfortune could be attributed to bad character in a previous life, and this might be cited as an excuse to aggravate or fail to alleviate the misfortune – contrary to the Buddha's emphasis on compassion. But the Buddha did not abuse the doctrines in this way, nor did he encourage his followers to do so (see page 111).

A more significant criticism is the claim that the Buddha's not-self teaching addresses needs more characteristic of men than women. According to this argument, men commonly have too great a sense of self or ego, and the

167

not-self doctrine may be a useful corrective to this. But women often have the opposite problem (at least under patriarchal conditions): they tend to have too small a sense of self or ego. Hence, for women the not-self doctrine points in the opposite direction from what is needed. One difficulty in evaluating this argument is that it presupposes that men and women both have a self and need a proper sense of self-worth. Since the Buddha denied that we have a self in any ultimate sense, a Buddhist response in the precise terms of the argument cannot be given. For the Buddha, the root of suffering is not having too much or too little self-worth, but thinking about life in terms of a self at all. The Buddha thought that the realization of selflessness puts any human being – male or female – in an immeasurably better state, but this cannot be described correctly by saying that he or she has a proper sense of self-worth. However, we can ask whether female *arahants* have, in non-Buddhist terms, a strong sense of self-respect, self-esteem, and the like. In view of the earlier discussion of the *arahant* (chapter 12, section 4), the answer may well be 'Yes.' A female *arahant* is surely not someone who feels worthless or is unable to act effectively in the world.

There is one line of feminist analysis that bears some resemblance to the Buddhist perspective. In opposition to the emphasis on autonomy in much modern Western philosophy (especially Kant), some feminists have stressed, often as a typical feature of women's moral experience, the importance of interdependence and relationships among persons (for example, see Gilligan 1987). This 'care perspective' is similar to, but not identical with, the Buddha's idea that all persons are interconnected and should show compassion to one another. On this point, there may be a basis for some productive dialogue between feminism and Buddhism.

Whatever may be concluded about the representation of women in the Buddha's teaching, it must be acknowledged that Buddhism has many women followers, and some feminist followers, in Asian as well as Western countries. This is not to say that feminist critiques of Buddhism have not raised serious issues, but that many women have found value in the teaching of the Buddha despite these critiques.

3 The universality of the Path: lay followers

The Buddha drew a sharp distinction between followers who belonged to the *Sangha* – *bhikkhus* and *bhikkhunīs* – and lay followers who did not. The two groups lived in a reciprocal relationship: members of the *Sangha* offered spiritual instruction to the laity, and laypersons provided material support to the *Sangha*. But the Buddha made it clear that *bhikkhus* and *bhikkhunīs* were higher than lay men and women in two key respects: they were better able to achieve full enlightenment, and their way of life was more compatible with being enlightened. According to the Buddha, 'Household life is crowded and dusty . . . it is not easy, while living in a home, to lead the holy-life' (M 448).

In contrast to members of the *Sangha*, lay followers have 'a great deal of activity, great functions, great engagements, and great undertakings.' As a result, the Buddha said, laypersons do 'not constantly and invariably speak the truth, practice asceticism, observe celibacy, engage in study, or engage in generosity' (M 815). It is not surprising that the Buddha directed his teaching primarily to the *bhikkhus*, and to a lesser extent the *bhikkhunīs*, rather than to laypersons. 'There are two kinds of happiness,' he said, 'the happiness of the home life and the happiness of monkhood.' However, 'the happiness of monkhood is the higher of the two' (N 44).

Still, the Buddha did support and teach laypersons. No aspect of the Eightfold Path was barred to them: lay followers were encouraged to listen to, retain, and carefully reflect on the meaning of the *Dhamma* (see N 208); they were advised to follow the Buddha's basic moral precepts (see C II 1825); and it was said that they sometimes engaged in 'the four foundations of mindfulness,' an important form of meditation (M 444). In fact, one step of the Eightfold Path, right livelihood, appears especially designed for the laity. Moreover, the Buddha said that laypersons could and did attain the levels of stream-enterer, once-returner, and non-returner (see M 570). In a few cases, lay followers even became *arahants* (see G III 314).

It is sometimes said that in contemporary Buddhist cultures laypersons aim only for a better rebirth while the pursuit of *Nibbāna* is reserved for the *bhikkhus* and *bhikkhunīs*. The Buddha encouraged this dichotomy, though he allowed that, strictly speaking, any degree of progress up to the attainment of *Nibbāna* is available in principle to lay followers. On the whole, however, he made it clear that life outside the *Sangha* is not really conducive to achieving and living in accordance with full enlightenment. We need to understand why he thought this and what, realistically, his teaching offers to those who are not prepared to become a *bhikkhu* or *bhikkhunī* in this lifetime (this concerns what I called the 'integration question' in chapter 2, section 5).

The tradition of the *samaṇas* as well as his own personal experience made the advantages of the *Sangha* appear natural to the Buddha. But our concern is with the reasons he had for endorsing these advantages. The issues here go to the heart of the Buddha's teaching. He believed suffering was an inherent feature of the cycle of rebirth. Though suffering could be reduced to some extent by achieving a better rebirth, it could be overcome fully only by escaping the cycle of rebirth altogether – by attaining *Nibbāna*. In this lifetime, monastic life appears to be the closest we can come to *Nibbāna*. By not producing and raising children, those in the *Sangha* withdraw in an important respect from the cycle of rebirth. This suggests that life outside the *Sangha* is almost inevitably second-best. The activities of everyday life are replete with reinforcements to our sense of selfhood and consequent temptations to attachment. Hence, significant progress to enlightenment appears unlikely within such a life. Moreover, a fully enlightened person has achieved a state of selfless non-attachment, and it would seem difficult to integrate this state into the activities of ordinary life. In short, the Buddha's basic teaching gave him substantial reasons to believe monastic life was superior to lay life.

Nonetheless, though many persons are suited to be *bhikkhus* or *bhikkhunīs*, it seems most are not. Are there grounds for challenging the Buddha's belief that life in the *Sangha* is a much surer route to enlightenment than life outside it? It is evident that the Eightfold Path is not easily reconciled with the ordinary lives of most people. But perhaps the path could transform these lives into more fruitful pursuits of enlightenment than the Buddha thought likely.

A central issue is celibacy. The fetter of sensual desire must be completely eliminated to reach the levels of non-returner and *arahant*. The most important sensual desire is sexual desire, and the Buddha believed celibacy was required for these levels of enlightenment (see M 596–7). In general, his attitude towards sexual relationships was unqualifiedly negative. In a revealing passage, Ānanda compares the temptations of food and sex. With respect to food, he suggests, it is possible to achieve non-attachment without giving up eating. But with respect to sex, non-attachment cannot be attained without giving up sexual relations: 'In regard to the sexual act the Blessed One has advised the destruction of the bridge' (N 111). The Buddha also described sexual intercourse as a 'vulgar practice' (M 449). 'Inflamed by sensual passions and in bondage to lustful desire,' he said, 'one is free neither of the perils of this world nor of the perils of the next world' (N 155). In short, sex is singled out as an unsurpassable obstacle to the highest stages of enlightenment. More than anything else, this is why the Buddha believed monastic life was superior to lay life. Life in the *Sangha* is based on a commitment to celibacy, and lay life typically is not.

The Buddha thought his own enlightenment required abandoning all sexual activity, and others may rightly think this as well. But why suppose that this is universally the case, that no one can become enlightened without celibacy? And why suppose the obstacle sexual desire presents to enlightenment is so much greater than the dangers of the desires for wealth, power, status, and so on? A more fundamental theme in the Buddha is that the main problem is craving and clinging themselves, not any particular object of these. A more balanced evaluation might suggest that there are many potential objects of craving and clinging, but that no one of them is a critical obstacle for all persons. Moreover, a less pejorative attitude towards sexual activity would make it possible to see its positive dimensions – for example, as part of a loving relationship between persons. If these reevaluations were sound, they might clear the way for a more optimistic estimation of the potential for achieving and living an enlightened life within the context of everyday activities that include sexual relations as well as other pursuits the Buddha regarded as less problematic.

Such a reassessment would need to challenge the Buddha by stressing the advantages of lay life and perhaps also by noting some disadvantages of monastic life. For example, it may be pointed out that the life of work and family offers not simply obstacles to, but unique possibilities for, the development and expression of important Buddhist values. Earning a living may generate greed, one of the three unwholesome roots that preclude enlightenment. But it may also provide an opportunity for generosity or liberality (*dāna*). Raising children is sometimes little more than an extended way of being self-interested, but it can be an occasion for manifesting and teaching selfless compassion and loving-kindness. Moreover, we will see in chapter 16 that insight meditation may be practiced in every aspect of our lives. On the other side, it might be argued that monastic life has its own distinctive dangers. The Buddha said two of the four main forms of clinging are clinging to views and clinging to rules and observances. The roles of *bhikkhus* and *bhikkhunīs* may give rise to these. Likewise, there could be attachment to the prestige, power, or wealth of the monastery, or to one's position in it, or to the higher road to enlightenment itself.

A reassessment along these lines might show that lay life is not necessarily inferior to monastic life. This would not mean the *Sangha* is without its special importance. It offers obvious advantages for pursuing the Eightfold Path, and for some persons it may be essential. Moreover, the *Sangha* may have much to contribute to the Buddhist community as a whole – for example, in teaching and providing opportunities for retreats. It should also not be denied that everyday life presents substantial challenges and obstacles to achieving enlightenment. Most persons are quite consumed by the demands of earning a living, raising a family, and pursuing other important activities. These endeavors typically require a great deal of time, energy, and attention. As the Buddha said, our lives are often 'crowded and dusty.' In these circumstances, following the Eightfold Path is not likely to be easy. It should also be emphasized that, from the Buddha's perspective, some people's lives are filled with activities that are counterproductive. For example, his teaching implies a critique of the relentless pursuit of wealth, status, entertainment, and sex that preoccupies some persons in the world today. However it may be achieved, the Buddha thought a radical transformation of the lives that most people live is necessary to bring about the state of selfless freedom from craving and attachment that would overcome suffering.

Though the Buddha believed enlightenment was much better pursued in the *Sangha* than outside it, he also believed the Eightfold Path was a middle way between asceticism and indulgence in sensual pleasures. Perhaps the middle way is wider and contains more alternative approaches than he envisioned. In this respect, later Buddhist traditions sometimes offer grounds for encouragement. A striking, albeit unusual, example indicates the lengths some Buddhists have been prepared to go in modifying the teaching of the Buddha: the *Vajrayāna* tradition maintains that in very special circumstances the Tantric practice of sexual yoga may be used as a means of attaining enlightenment. More representative of later traditions, and more broadly significant, is the series of *Ten Oxherding Pictures* in Ch'an (Zen) Buddhism. The pictures portray a man searching for a lost ox as a symbolic enactment of the search for enlightenment. What is significant here is the last picture: after capturing the ox – achieving enlightenment – the caption depicts the man as 'Entering the City with Bliss-bestowing Hands.' The commentary reads: 'Carrying a gourd he goes out into the market, leaning against a staff he comes home. He is found in company with wine-bibbers and butchers, he and they are all converted into Buddhas' (Suzuki 1999: Plate XI and 134). This implies a model of integrating enlightenment with everyday life that goes beyond what the Buddha himself thought possible (see also Watson 1997).

4 Right view and intention

Let us now begin an examination of the Eightfold Path. The first two steps – right views and right intention – are placed in the category of wisdom. It will come as no surprise that right view is standardly described as knowledge of the Four Noble Truths. Right intention is depicted as 'intention of renunciation, intention of non-ill will, and intention of non-cruelty' (M 1100). Both of these may be understood at two levels: as preliminary states that are required to begin the Eightfold Path, and as higher states that are gradually attained as one progresses towards enlightenment.

With respect to right view, a person must begin with some knowledge of the Four Noble Truths. This is clearly fundamental to achieving enlightenment. At first, this knowledge may be based on intellectual understanding, or it may come more from faith or confidence in the Buddha, though not blind faith. In any case, the ultimate knowledge of the Four Noble Truths that enlightenment brings goes beyond both intellectual understanding and faith. This is the direct knowledge that is acquired only through concentration. Here is another respect in which the eight steps of the path are interdependent. For example, the Buddha said that 'these three states run and circle around right view, that is, right view, right effort, and right mindfulness' (M 935). To achieve direct knowledge, some measure of intellectual comprehension and confidence in the Buddha are typically necessary. But they are not sufficient, and they cannot replace the ultimate wisdom that is attained by means of the concentration disciplines.

Full knowledge of the Four Noble Truths requires more than comprehension of the basic statement of these truths. It also includes understanding of the not-self doctrine, impermanence, dependent origination, the five aggregates, *kamma* and rebirth, and so on. For this reason, in some descriptions of right view other aspects of the Buddha's teaching are emphasized. Sometimes a lower form of right view, focusing mainly on *kamma* and rebirth, is distinguished from the 'supramundane' form that is central to attaining *Nibbāna* (see M 934–5). On occasion, right view refers to other aspects of the Eightfold Path – for example, to the ethical dimensions. This is only to be expected, since the aspects are interconnected and the Eightfold Path is itself the last of the Four Noble Truths. In some contexts, the Buddha discussed various ways in which right view may be acquired. Thus he said that five factors by which right view is promoted are 'virtue, learning, discussion, serenity, and insight' and that 'two conditions for the arising of right view' are 'the voice of another [teaching the *Dhamma*] and wise attention' (M 390).

Right view is essentially the possession of knowledge. It should be expected that this is the first step of the Eightfold Path since, in the twelvefold formula of dependent origination, ignorance is the first condition that ultimately leads to suffering. The Buddha's entire teaching emphasizes the importance of knowledge in attaining *Nibbāna*. However, the knowledge in question is not knowledge per se, nor knowledge of just anything, nor the mere knowledge that some propositions are true. The Buddha did not encourage the acquisition of knowledge unrelated to attaining *Nibbāna* (remember the simile of the poison arrow). And he held that *Nibbāna* may be attained only on the basis of a deep, existential comprehension of the Four Noble Truths and all that they involve.

Right intention involves a threefold commitment to renounce sensual desire, to reject ill will, and to repudiate cruelty. Expressed in positive terms, right intention is commitment to non-attachment with respect to sensual desires, devotion to loving-kindness, and dedication to compassion. The Buddha's main point is that sensuous desire, ill will, and cruelty are obstacles to enlightenment. Insofar as we are consumed by these, we will find it difficult to acquire the knowledge that leads to *Nibbāna*. Conversely, insofar as we commit ourselves to non-attachment, loving-kindness, and compassion, the path to *Nibbāna* will be facilitated. These three pairs of states are, broadly speaking, moral characteristics. Attachment and non-attachment to desires, ill will and loving-kindness, and cruelty and compassion are coordinate vices and virtues. A basic conviction of the Buddha is that the extent to which we are virtuous rather than vicious is an important factor in gaining wisdom. This is another respect in which the knowledge we need for enlightenment is not merely intellectual knowledge. Practical knowledge, knowledge of how to live well, is also required. It is obvious that a person who is morally deficient could know many things. The Buddha did not deny this. What he denied is that such a person could know the Four Noble Truths. Hence, what is required at the beginning of the path to enlightenment is a commitment to acquire the virtues of non-attachment, loving-kindness, and compassion. As a person progresses along the path, this commitment is expected to grow deeper (by becoming better understood, more firm, more natural, and so on) and eventually to result in the full acquisition of these virtues (see page 181).

The three virtues are important because they enable us to overcome various forms of preoccupation with the substance-self each of us mistakenly supposes he or she is. Attachment to sensual desires focuses attention on bringing pleasure to one's own self and thus reinforces the belief that this self is important. Ill will and cruelty emphasizes one's separation from and superiority over others, and this too contributes to one's sense of self-importance. For the Buddha, the realization that we are not substance-selves requires more than intellectual understanding: it also requires living our lives in such a way that our daily pursuits do not constantly foster the illusion of this self. Achieving non-attachment to sensual desires, loving-kindness, and compassion enable us to do this. At first, these virtues may be difficult to acquire. But they will come naturally once the realization that one is not a substance-self is gained.

It may be objected that there is something paradoxical in right intention and the Eightfold Path generally. The aim is to free ourselves from all craving, clinging, attachment, and the like. But the means to achieving this aim require considerable exertion, and this exertion would seem to require the very things we are trying to eliminate. For example, it appears that we would have to be quite attached to pursuing *Nibbāna* in order to attain the state of non-attachment that is *Nibbāna*. Does not this procedure give us one more attachment, and if so, would we not need yet a further attachment to get rid of this one (and so on)?

This is sometimes called the paradox of desire. However, insofar as there is a problem here, it is more an issue of psychology than logic. If the Buddha had said that the ideal is attachment to non-attachment, this would be conceptually problematic in a manner similar to the inconsistency involved in a skeptic's claim to know that we know nothing. But this is not the ideal. To attain *Nibbāna* is to not be attached to anything, including non-attachment. We might wonder whether pure non-attachment is humanly possible, but this is another matter that concerns the feasibility of the goal. The issue here concerns the plausibility of attaining the goal of non-attachment by means of attachment. In general, there is no incoherence in having a goal that can only be achieved by means that the attainment of the goal renders impossible. For example, the goal to reach a place where it is not possible to walk any higher can only be achieved by walking higher. There is no paradox here. The Eightfold Path to *Nibbāna* is somewhat like this. According to Ānanda, who explicitly responded to this question, a *bhikkhu* 'earlier had the desire for the attainment of *arahantship*, and when he attained *arahantship*, the corresponding desire subsided' (C II 1733). Since we begin within the cycle of rebirth, the only way to undertake the path is with a measure of attachment to attaining *Nibbāna*. But as we successfully pursue the path, selflessness is progressively realized and attachment gradually drops away. Once *Nibbāna* is fully attained, attachment disappears altogether, and there are no longer any grounds for being attached to attaining it (recall the simile of the raft). By analogy, imagine walking to the top of a rounded hill: we continue going up by decreasing degrees until finally we stop going up altogether. Whether the realization of selflessness actually brings about non-attachment is a further question, but there is nothing problematic in supposing that attachment to this realization could culminate in complete non-attachment.

SUGGESTED READING

For a dialogue between a *bhikkhunī* and a lay follower that places the Eight-fold Path in the context of the Buddha's overall teaching, see the *Cūḷavedalla Sutta* ('The Shorter Series of Questions and Answers'), M #44. On the Eightfold Path, see also the *Mahācattārīsaka Sutta* ('The Great Forty'), M #117 and the *Araṇavibhanga Sutta* ('The Exposition of Non-conflict'), M #139. Voices of female followers of the Buddha are expressed in the *Bhikkhunīsaṃyutta* ('Connected Discourses with *Bhikkhunīs*'), C I 221–30 and the *Therīgāthā* (see page 207 of the Bibliography for two editions).

The Eightfold Path is examined in Bastow (1988) and Habito (1988). For discussions of Buddhism and women, see Dalmiya (2001), Gross (1993 and 1999), Paul (1979), Powers and Curtin (1994), and V. Rajapakse (1992). On lay life, see Aronson (1979), Bond (1996), Hershock (2000), and Reynolds (1979). The paradox of desire is discussed in Alt (1980), Gruzalski (1996), Herman (1979 and 1980), and Visvader (1978 and 1980).

NOTE

1   The eight steps are standardly presented in the order given here. However, confus-edly, the threefold division is presented in the order virtue, concentration, and wisdom (see M 398). It is probably a mistake to assign much significance to either ordering.

15

THE EIGHTFOLD PATH:
VIRTUE

In the threefold division of the Eightfold Path, the middle section is entitled 'virtue' and is said to include right speech, right action, and right livelihood. In fact, however, all three sections include moral dimensions. We have just seen this with respect to right intention (classified under 'wisdom') and we will see it again in regard to right effort (classified under 'concentration'). The interdependence of the three sections is illustrated by the Buddha's comment that 'wisdom is purified by morality, and morality is purified by wisdom' (L 131). Generally speaking, in the Buddha's teaching morality functions at two levels. On the one hand, in order to achieve enlightenment, a significant moral transformation is required. 'Virtuous ways of conduct,' the Buddha said, 'lead step by step to the highest' (N 238). For this reason, morality plays a large role in the Eightfold Path. On the other hand, someone who is enlightened, who has attained *Nibbāna*-in-life, will be a morally good person to the greatest degree. Hence, morality is both a means to enlightenment (in preliminary form) and a product of it (in its highest manifestation). Since the primary aim of the Buddha's message is the achievement of enlightenment, and since the fully enlightened person is both virtuous and happy, his teaching centrally includes a moral teaching.

1 Right speech, action, and livelihood

In a standard depiction, right speech is described as 'abstaining from false speech, abstaining from malicious speech, abstaining from harsh speech, and abstaining from idle chatter.' Right action is said to be 'abstaining from killing living beings, abstaining from taking what is not given, and abstaining from misconduct in sensual pleasures' (M 1100). Right speech and action together partly resemble those sections of the Ten Commandments that pertain to relations to neighbors rather than to God. (In fact, the Buddha endorsed correlates of all seven of these commandments.) Moreover, each aspect of right speech and action is explained by means of a role-reversal test rather similar to the Golden Rule: 'What is displeasing and disagreeable to me is displeasing and disagreeable to the other too. How

176

can I inflict upon another what is displeasing and disagreeable to me?' (C II 1797–8).

But there are also important differences from the Ten Commandments. What is striking about right speech is that it does much more than prohibit lying. All speech that is in any way harmful is condemned (malicious and harsh speech), and even speech that fails to be productive is considered wrong (idle chatter). The Buddha said he taught the *Dhamma* because it is both true and useful, and his general attitude towards speech is that we should try to speak not only truthfully, but also in ways that are beneficial. We should engage in verbal conduct, he said, that 'causes unwholesome states to diminish and wholesome states to increase.' For example, a person should 'not repeat elsewhere what he has heard here in order to divide (those people) from these ... thus he is one who reunites those who are divided, a promoter of friendships, who enjoys concord.' Again, someone should speak 'such words as are ... courteous, desired by many, and agreeable to many' and 'as are worth recording, reasonable, moderate, and beneficial' (M 916). The Buddha plainly thought speech is a powerful force in human life. He believed we should always speak in ways that are both truthful and helpful, and he especially warned against speech that was in any way divisive.

With respect to right action, the Buddha said we are prohibited from killing not only human beings, but all living beings. More broadly, we are to show compassion towards living beings: 'With rod and weapon laid aside, gently and kindly, he abides compassionate to all living beings' (M 914). It is easy to see a rationale for the Buddha's concern for all living beings, or at least all animals. He believed human beings are part of a cosmic cycle of rebirth that includes animals, human beings, and gods. Hence, to kill an animal is to kill a being that may have been or may become a human being. In this respect, the Buddha's outlook contrasts sharply with the predominant viewpoint in Western traditions. Western philosophers such as Aristotle and Kant have typically emphasized the ways in which human beings differ from other animals, primarily in terms of our rationality, and they have taken this to mean there is a fundamental moral difference between killing a human being and killing an animal. The Buddha does not deny that there are differences between human beings and other animals: we are higher in the cosmic hierarchy than animals. Nor does he deny that these differences have moral implications: it is worse to kill a human being than an animal. Nonetheless, there is not a deep divide here. Human beings and animals are part of the same cycle of rebirth, and we should show compassion towards both, first and foremost by not killing them.

The other two forms of right action are fairly straightforward. We are to abstain from 'taking what is not given.' Stealing typically focuses on the fulfillment of one's own desires and expresses ill will towards other persons. In addition, we are not to engage in 'misconduct in sensual pleasures.' Right intention already included renunciation of sensual desires. These refer to all pleasures and desires of the body, but especially those that are sexual. According to the Buddha, speaking about lay men, a person should 'not have intercourse with such women as are protected by their mother, father, mother and father, brother, sister, or relatives, who have a husband, who are protected by law, or with those who are garlanded in token of betrothal' (M 914–15). Moreover, he prohibited *bhikkhus* and *bhikkhunīs* from having sexual intercourse at all. As we have seen, the Buddha thought sexual desire was a serious obstacle to attaining *Nibbāna*, and he held that the highest levels of enlightenment required celibacy.

The Buddha had rather little to say about right livelihood. He did offer as examples of wrong livelihood such things as scheming and earning one's living by trading in weapons, human beings, meat, intoxicants, and poisons (see M 938 and G III 153). He also warned against earning a living by engaging in a wide array of superstitious (and hence fraudulent) practices such as palmistry, divining by signs, and fortune telling (see L 71–3). In general, we are not to earn our living in ways that violate the other moral precepts. Hence, any occupation that involves wrongful speech, killing living beings, stealing, or illicit sexual relations would violate the right livelihood principle. The spirit of this principle is that we are not to earn a living in ways that are incompatible with the pursuit of enlightenment/This might have significant implications for lay persons in the contemporary world. For example, insofar as corporations, through their advertising, promote a preoccupation with fulfillment of desires that is a serious obstacle to enlightenment, questions may be raised whether followers of the Buddha should depend upon them for their livelihood/

2 Further aspects of the Buddha's moral teaching

There are several respects in which the virtue section of the Eightfold Path is an incomplete expression of the Buddha's overall moral teaching. First, the Buddha sometimes said there were five basic ethical precepts. These include four we have already considered plus abstention from intoxicants. According to the Buddha, if 'a lay follower abstains from the destruction of life, from taking what is not given, from sexual misconduct, from false speech and from wines, liquor and intoxicants which are a basis for negligence, the lay follower is virtuous' (N 207). By way of rationale for the last, the Buddha said that 'addiction to strong drink and sloth-producing drugs is one way of wasting one's substance,' and he warned that this has various dangers such as 'increased quarrelling' and 'weakening the intellect' (L 462). Moreover, the emphasis he placed on mindfulness, a form of mental alertness, is incompatible with a permissive attitude towards intoxication.

The Buddha also discussed numerous states of mind or character traits that go beyond right speech, action, and livelihood. For example, covetousness received special attention: a person should 'not covet the wealth and property of others thus: "Oh, may what belongs to another be mine!"' (M 383). In addition, all of the following were said to hinder the path to enlightenment: ill will, anger, revenge, spitefulness, contempt, domineering attitude, envy, avarice, fraud, obstinacy, presumption, tenacity, conceit, arrogance, vanity, negligence, sloth, torpor, laziness, restlessness, remorse, shamelessness, and despair (for example, see M 118). On the other hand, the Buddha endorsed many positive character traits such as compassion, loving-kindness, and generosity. In general, he took the roots of unwholesome action to be greed, hatred, and delusion, and the roots of wholesome action to be the opposite of these (see N 49–50).

Finally, the Buddha distinguished between the moral code for *bhikkhus* and *bhikkhunīs* and the moral code for laypersons (though there was considerable overlap). We have already seen that members of the *Sangha* were to be celibate. Their life was to be quite ascetic in other respects as well. For example, they were not to sing and dance, wear garlands or scents, use couches, or accept gold, silver and raw grain (see M 449). Lay followers were also encouraged to follow some of these ascetic practices on a temporary basis, but they were a way of life for members of the *Sangha*. The *bhikkhus* and *bhikkhunīs* were governed by more than 200 rules.

Speaking directly to laypersons, the Buddha warned against being out at unfitting times, attending fairs, being addicted to gambling, keeping bad company, and being habitually idle (see L 462). In addition, he described proper ways of behaving towards one's mother and father, teachers, husband or wife, friends and companions, masters or servants, and ascetics and brahmins. For example, a husband should be considerate to his wife 'by honouring her, by not disparaging her, by not being unfaithful to her, by giving authority to her, by providing her with adornments.' Likewise, a wife should reciprocate her husband 'by properly organizing her work, by being kind to the servants, by not being unfaithful, by protecting stores, and by being skillful and diligent in all she has to do.' Again, a person should serve friends and companions 'by gifts, by kindly words, by looking after their welfare, by treating them like himself, and by keeping his word.' His friend should reciprocate 'by looking after him when he is inattentive, by looking after his property when he is inattentive, by being a refuge when he is afraid, by not deserting him when he is in trouble, and by showing concern for his children' (L 467–8). Though the Buddha spoke primarily to *bhikkhus*, and to a lesser extent to *bhikkhunīs*, these comments show that he did have something specific to say about the moral lives of his lay followers. On the other hand, the basis of these responsibilities is not explained, and we are not told in what ways they are conducive to progress towards enlightenment or a better rebirth. They should probably be interpreted primarily as exemplifications of general virtues such as compassion and loving-kindness, but this is not articulated.

3 The Buddha's moral outlook and some Western moral philosophies

The Buddha's conception of morality contains many familiar features, but these must be understood in relationship to the endeavor to attain *Nibbāna*. Insofar as morality is a means to attain this end, its underlying purpose is to counter the various ways in which we give priority to ourselves at the expense of others. These self-enhancing activities reinforce the idea that human beings are distinct selves with independent interests that are often in competition with one another. As long as we are consumed by such activities, we will find it difficult to realize the truth of the Buddha's not-self doctrine. Conversely, if we were to begin living our lives in accordance with the Buddha's moral values, we would be living as if the distinction between selves were less important, and this would make it easier to grasp his not-self teaching. Once a person attains *Nibbāna*, he or she lives a fully selfless life that is in no way shaped by the idea that we are distinct selves. The Buddha's moral values are all shaped by this ideal; they are intended to help us understand and achieve a truly selfless life.

If we keep this perspective in mind, it will be illuminating to compare briefly the Buddha's moral outlook to some concerns and viewpoints that are common in Western philosophical traditions. An important issue in these traditions is whether or not moral values are objective. If moral objectivity means there are moral judgments that can be known to be true or false in an absolute sense, and not merely relative to a particular culture, then the Buddha was a moral objectivist. He would have rejected noncognitivist, skeptical, and relativist views that deny morality is objective in this respect. The Buddha believed the moral values he taught applied to all persons and, in principle, could be known by all persons on the basis of an understanding of human nature. If we ask how he thinks objective moral knowledge is acquired, his position is more difficult to classify in Western philosophical terms. The Buddha did not suggest that there is a straightforward argument that would justify morality. It might be said that morality would be self-evident to a fully enlightened person. But this means moral knowledge is gained by progressing on the many dimensions of the Eightfold Path. There is a role for rational understanding here. Yet there are moral preconditions for acquiring moral knowledge: a person who is morally corrupt is not in a position to obtain true moral understanding. Hence, it would be difficult to justify morality to such a person. On the other hand, this person could be given reasons to undergo a transformation that would put him or her in a state where moral understanding is possible. In the end, what is crucial for the Buddha are the meditative disciplines. Without these, the highest form of moral knowledge cannot be obtained, and these disciplines are outside the scope of standard Western epistemological perspectives.

Contemporary Western philosophers sometimes draw a distinction between moral philosophies that emphasize *rules* that prescribe or proscribe certain classes of morally significant actions, such as that we should keep our promises or not lie, and moral philosophies that stress *virtues* or character traits that are thought to be essential to living a morally good life, such as courage or generosity (for example, see MacIntyre 1984: 150–4 and 169–70). The distinction may not be a sharp one, but in any case it should be clear that the Buddha assigned importance to both rules and virtues. The moral values we have just considered include numerous rules that prescribe and proscribe classes of actions. But the Buddha also spoke a great deal about virtues such as loving-kindness and compassion that are better understood as morally valuable dispositions than as requirements to follow moral rules. Hence, it would be misleading to say that either rules or virtues had priority for the Buddha. Both are essential in achieving enlightenment. On the other hand, rule-oriented moral philosophies are sometimes taken to emphasize the question 'What actions should a person perform?' while virtue-oriented moral philosophies are understood to focus on the broader question 'What kind of person should one be?' In terms of this characterization, the Buddha has more in common with virtue moralities than rule moralities.

Insofar as the Buddha emphasized rules, we might wonder how rigorously he thought they should be applied. For example, did he think killing was never justified no matter what the circumstances or did he think in some cases there could be a compelling reason to take someone's life (for example, if that was the only way to prevent the person from killing many innocent people)? For the most part, the Buddha was not concerned to answer questions such as this. In general, his attitude appears rather demanding and this might lead us to suspect that he believed the rules were to be applied scrupulously with no exceptions. In the case of the prohibition of killing, this would commit him to pacifism. Though the Buddha is sometimes interpreted this way nowadays, it is not clear that he intended this strict position. For example, when an admirer of the Buddha, King Pasenadi, made a speech in which he declared himself 'able to have executed those who should be executed,' the Buddha praised his words as 'monuments to the *Dhamma*' (M 731–3). Again, when Channa, a disciple of the Buddha, committed suicide because he was in great pain, the Buddha said he 'used the knife blamelessly' (M 1116). With respect to animals, the Buddha declared that a *bhikkhu* may eat meat 'when it is not seen, not heard, and not suspected (that the living being has been slaughtered for the *bhikkhu*)' (M 474). These remarks suggest some flexibility in applying the rules. We might also recall that one of the fetters to enlightenment is having 'a mind obsessed and enslaved . . . by adherence to rules and observances' (M 538). On the other hand, it could be argued that the Buddha's deepest moral convictions imply, if not strict pacifism, at least a near-total opposition to killing that would preclude the massive destruction of contemporary warfare under virtually any circumstance.

In Western philosophy, an emphasis on moral rules is often thought to be a feature of modern theories such as Kantianism and utilitarianism. There are respects in which the Buddha's moral outlook appears to resemble these theories, but in the end the differences are more significant. Kant's insistence that the will is the locus of moral value is reflected in the Buddha's belief that the moral quality of our intentions is what is primarily important in determining the morality of our actions. Moreover, Kant's ideal of a kingdom of ends in which each person is respected as an end in himself may be affirmed to some extent in the importance the Buddha assigned to harmonious relations among people.

However, Kant thought morality was rooted in the fact that we are rational beings: each person is to be respected as a rational being, and we are to think about morality on the basis of a principle, the Categorical Imperative, that is justified from the standpoint of pure practical reason. This rationalist framework is foreign to the sensibility of the Buddha, and the assumption of Kant's moral philosophy that each person is a distinct free and rational will appears to conflict with the Buddha's not-self teaching. Moreover, Kant believed that morality and happiness are distinct goods and that a person's ultimate commitment ought to be to morality first and his own happiness second. The Buddha did not emphasize this distinction: a person who attains *Nibbāna* simultaneously achieves the greatest happiness and the highest morality. For Kant, morality is acting out of respect for the moral law and happiness is the fulfillment of our desires. God ensures that in the afterlife each person is happy in proportion to his or her morality. (In this there is an analogue to the ideas of *kamma* and rebirth, though the Buddha did not think this proportion was brought about by God.) For the Buddha, morality is centrally compassion and loving-kindness, and happiness is non-attachment with respect to our desires. Both are achieved by living selflessly.

According to utilitarianism, in its simplest form, an action is right if and only if, among available alternatives, it maximizes the happiness of all persons. Happiness is usually understood in terms of pleasure and pain or, in more complex theories, the desires and aversions of fully informed and rational persons. The idea of maximizing happiness has some affinity with the Buddha's moral outlook, though he described this in the language of compassion. Moreover, it is often said that, in emphasizing the maximization of overall happiness, utilitarianism does not recognize or stress the 'separateness of persons' (Parfit 1984: 329–30), and this might he thought to resemble the Buddha's not-self teaching. In addition, insofar as utilitarianism sometimes requires us to maximize the happiness of all sentient beings, it connects with the Buddha's belief that we should bring animals into the scope of our moral concerns. These are not insignificant similarities, and the Buddha's moral teaching has sometimes been interpreted as a form of utilitarianism.

Nonetheless, there are fundamental differences. Utilitarianism tends to take the common sense understanding of happiness largely for granted. It is happiness in this sense, with at most minor modification, that is to be maximized. But the Buddha thought this conception is flawed. Real happiness does not consist of fulfilling our desires (not even those of fully informed and rational beings, as utilitarians understand this). Happiness is achieved through non-attachment to our desires. Hence, the Buddha's compassion for all beings is rather different than the utilitarian's concern for the maximization of happiness. This difference is also reflected in the fact that the Buddha believed a radical transformation of persons is required to bring us to the correct moral stance. Though utilitarianism is sometimes interpreted as demanding a comparable transformation, its proponents are usually more interested in showing that utilitarianism mostly sustains the moral beliefs people already have (hence, the prominence of rule and two-level versions that justify everyday moral rules as maximizing happiness). There is one final difference. Utilitarianism is closely linked to a naturalistic or scientific conception of the world. It is often thought to be a moral outlook that may be justified or at least understood from that perspective, in contrast to explicit religious conceptions and metaphysically more adventuresome positions such as Kantianism (with its noumenal conception of free will) or Aristotelianism (with its teleological conception of human nature). Though the Buddha has sometimes —(a) been interpreted in more naturalistic terms, his overall teaching places him on the opposite side from utilitarianism in this divide.

The most prominent Western moral theory that stresses virtues is the eudaimonism of the ancient philosophers, especially Aristotle. Eudaimonism begins with a conception of a good human life as *eudaimonia* – usually translated as happiness, well-being, or flourishing – and it understands virtues such as courage, temperance, and justice as character traits that are conducive to or constitutive of such a life. Aristotle's emphasis on virtue, and his conviction that a life of virtue and a happy life are closely connected, suggests some common ground with the Buddha's moral outlook. In fact, it has been claimed that Aristotle's moral philosophy is the closest parallel in the Western traditions to the Buddha's moral perspective. Moreover, what they share has been the source of an accusation, directed to each, that it is really a form of egoism: the focus is on achieving *my* happiness or overcoming *my* suffering, and moral virtue seems only a fortunate by-product of this endeavor. This charge is misleading in both cases. The person of Aristotelian virtue has considerable concern for the good of others for their own sake. His aim is not to fulfill selfish desires. Likewise, though the initial motivation for undertaking the Eightfold Path may emphasize one's own suffering, the fully enlightened person has selfless compassion for all beings.

Aristotle and the Buddha both advocated a moral perfection of the person that involves intellectual, moral, and emotional training. Nonetheless, as we saw in the discussion of the doctrine of the mean and the middle way (chapter 14, section 1), the similarities between them are limited. Aristotle placed great importance on our nature as rational beings. This determines our ultimate well-being and the virtues that contribute to it. For Aristotle, the basic model is the regulation of desires and emotions by reason. For the Buddha, desires

183

and emotions are also regulated, but not in the manner of Aristotle's man of practical reason. Rather, they are reshaped from the perspective of the realization of selflessness, a realization that depends more on the meditative disciplines than on rational inquiry. This is why the Buddha envisioned a more fundamental transformation of the person than Aristotle did. Neither of the two ideal lives featured by Aristotle – the political and military life, and the life of theoretical study or contemplation – bears much similarity to the life of the *arahant*. The contemplative life may be the closer of the two, but its stress on rational inquiry and its lack of emphasis on compassion for all beings sets it apart from the Buddha's ideal. Moreover, specific Aristotelian virtues such as courage (properly facing the threat of death in war) and magnanimity (having a correct sense of one's own worth and honor) play no role in the Buddha's account. Likewise, the notion of non-attachment has no correlate in Aristotle.

A somewhat closer comparison may be found in the eudaimonism of the Stoics (one of the Hellenistic philosophies discussed in chapter 4). The Stoics believed that virtue is the only good and is sufficient for happiness. They thought anything outside one's virtue – that is, anything outside one's control – could not affect one's real happiness. Hence, they said a person should be concerned only with his or her own virtue and should be indifferent to such things as health, wealth, power, the death of friends and relations, and so on. This idea of indifference bears some resemblance to the Buddha's concept of non-attachment, and consequently the Stoics advocated a transformation of the person that is in some respects as extraordinary as that urged by the Buddha. As a result, the *arahant* may sometimes strike us as something of a stoic.

The difference, once again, is that the Stoics believed that human beings are essentially rational beings and that morality is the product of reason. Somewhat like Kant, they understood moral impartiality by reference to distinct, but morally equal, rational selves rather than in terms of the illusion of selfhood. Hence, though there is some moral overlap, there is a significant metaphysical and epistemological divide between the Stoics and the Buddha.

There is one final respect in which the Buddha's moral outlook invites comparison with Western moral perspectives. The Buddha proclaimed a universal doctrine: in principle, any person who undertakes the Eightfold Path can achieve enlightenment. But he also drew a sharp distinction between *bhikkhus* and *bhikkhunīs* on the one hand and laypersons on the other. The former were held to higher moral standards and were promised greater, or at least prompter, rewards. The idea that some persons are held to higher moral standards than others may seem at odds with the professed universalism of many Western moral theories in which it is said that everyone is held to the same standard. However, the notion that some persons have a higher moral calling than others, or that some actions are supererogatory in the sense of going beyond the ordinary demands of morality, is not unfamiliar in the West, especially in its religious traditions. The Buddha made systematic use of differential moral standards, but this should not be entirely foreign to Western stream-observers.

SUGGESTED READING

The Buddha's ethical teaching is emphasized in the *Sāleyyaka Sutta* ('The Brahmins of Sālā'), M #41. See also the *Sallekha Sutta* ('Effacement'), M # 8 and the *Potaliya Sutta* ('To Potaliya'), M #54. The ethical precepts for lay persons are expressed in the *Sigālaka Sutta* (To Sigālaka: Advice to Lay People'), L #31.

Buddhism and ethics are discussed in Danto (1972: chapter 4), Fu and Wawrytko (1991), Gruzalski (2001), Harvey (1995b and 2000), Kalupahana (1995), Katz (1992), Keown (1992 and 2000), W.L. King (2001), Kupperman (1999), Macy (1979), Saddhatissa (1997); Sizemore and Swearer (1990), and Whitehill (1994).

16

THE EIGHTFOLD PATH: CONCENTRATION

The third and final tier of the Eightfold Path is called 'Concentration.' It includes right effort, right mindfulness, and right concentration. The last two of these mental disciplines are usually described in English as forms of meditation, and they are of the utmost importance for the Buddha. He achieved his own enlightenment through meditation, and he believed meditation was essential for anyone else who sought enlightenment. The Buddha continued to meditate throughout his life, even after his enlightenment. This suggests that meditation is not only a means to enlightenment, but also a constitutive part of an enlightened life. Though the Buddha taught meditation primarily to the *bhikkhus* and *bhikkhunīs*, at least some laypersons also practiced it. He taught many different meditation techniques, and he stressed the importance of each person practicing the right techniques given his or her own specific circumstances, needs, and dispositions. The Buddha himself first learned meditation from his original teachers, especially Āḷāra Kālāma and Uddaka Rāmaputta. To some extent he borrowed their techniques, but he also developed his own approaches.

1 Right effort, mindfulness, and concentration

Right effort brings about a transition from virtue to meditation. It involves forms of striving that pertain to both moral preparation and the meditative disciplines of mindfulness and concentration. In the standard account, it is said that a person 'awakens zeal . . . makes effort, arouses energy, exerts his mind, and strives' for the following.

(1) The non-arising of unarisen evil unwholesome states.
(2) The abandoning of arisen evil unwholesome states.
(3) The arising of unarisen wholesome states.
(4) The continuance, non-disappearance, strengthening, increase, and fulfillment by development of arisen wholesome states (M 1100).

Unwholesome states are those that hinder the attainment of enlightenment, while wholesome states are those that foster enlightenment. The root of

186

unwholesome states is greed (*lobha*), hatred (*dosa*) and delusion (*moha*), while the root of wholesome states is non-greed, non-hatred, and non-delusion.

In an elaboration of these four forms of effort, the Buddha says, with respect to (1), that a person who sees 'an object with the eye, is not entranced by its general features or by its details.' Since evil, unwholesome states might arise from uncontrolled sight, he 'sets a guard over the eye-faculty, wins the restraint thereof,' and likewise for the other senses. As for (2), when a sensual, malign and cruel thought arises, the person 'abandons it, expels it, makes an end of it, [and] drives it out of renewed existence.' Regarding (3), the person strives to develop various enlightenment factors such as energy, tranquility, mindfulness, concentration, and the like. Finally, with respect to (4), the person focuses on a 'favourable concentration-mark' such as 'the idea of the skeleton' (we will see the significance of this shortly) (G II 15–16). In short, the first two forms of right effort involve moral development, while the remaining two anticipate types of meditation.

Right effort brings out the extent to which the Buddha believed a good deal of determination and striving were required to achieve enlightenment. Only when the mind is free of unwholesome states and possesses wholesome ones may *Nibbāna* be attained. The Buddha thought this demanded considerable exertion at the outset, and much of his teaching consisted of exhortations to his followers to make this effort.

Right concentration and right mindfulness refer to two rather different forms of meditation that are frequently described in the *Sutta Piṭaka*. There are questions about the relationship between them, whether they can always be separated, and whether they are fully compatible with one another. The Buddha also distinguished serenity meditation (*samatha-bhāvanā*) and insight meditation (*vipassanā-bhāvanā*). These bring about mental purity and wisdom respectively, and together they 'partake of supreme knowledge' (N 42). The Buddha suggested these may be related in different ways. In one of them, insight is preceded by serenity (see N 114). Following this, a common interpretation takes serenity meditation to be preliminary and mainly to concern right concentration, and insight meditation to be ultimate and primarily to pertain to right mindfulness. Despite their reverse order in the Eightfold Path, we will consider concentration and mindfulness from this perspective.

The purpose of serenity meditation is to cleanse the mind of various imperfections and obstacles that prevent the attainment of enlightenment. The Buddha thought the mind in its unenlightened state was in so much appetitive and emotional turmoil, primarily on account of its self-centered craving for and clinging to the permanent possession of impermanent things, that it could understand the reality of the human situation only after significant transformation. Serenity meditation is a form of mental discipline that aims to purify the mind by training it to focus completely and exclusively on some single meditation object (*kasiṇa*) such as a red clay disk or a bowl of water (see M 640). The Buddha often emphasized the importance of moral and intellectual preparation before meditation. For example, the meditator should have abandoned the 'five hindrances' of covetousness, ill will, sloth and torpor, restlessness and remorse, and doubt (M 451). Again, the meditator should have the 'seven good qualities' of faith, shame of misconduct, fear of wrongdoing, learning and memory, right effort, mindfulness, and wisdom (M 462–3).

The first step of serenity meditation proper is to find an appropriate location and assume the correct posture. The meditator 'resorts to a secluded resting place' and he 'sits down, folding his legs crosswise, setting his body erect, and establishing mindfulness before him' (M 876). By focusing fully and solely on the meditation object, the meditator may now ascend the four *jhānas* (meditative absorptions) of right concentration.

(1) Secluded from both 'sensual pleasures' and 'unwholesome states' one attains a *jhāna* 'accompanied by applied and sustained thought, with rapture and pleasure born of seclusion.'
(2) 'With the stilling of applied and sustained thought,' one attains a *jhāna* that 'has self-confidence and singleness of mind without applied and sustained thought, with rapture and pleasure born of concentration.'
(3) When rapture fades away, one 'abides in equanimity, and mindful and fully aware, still feeling pleasure with the body' attains a *jhāna* of which it may be said, 'He has a pleasant abiding who has equanimity and is mindful.'
(4) With the abandonment of 'pleasure and pain' and the 'disappearance of joy and grief,' one attains a *jhāna* that 'has neither-pain-nor-pleasure and purity of mindfulness due to equanimity.' (M 1101)

These four *jhānas* are said to concern the form realm and they correspond to planes of that realm in the Buddha's cosmology. The general direction of progress moves from pleasant intellectual thought to a highly focused state of mental concentration that results in an equanimity beyond pleasure and pain. The Buddha thought this purification was essential to achieving enlightenment, but he also warned against becoming attached to these meditative achievements. Someone who has attained these four *jhānas* 'neither lauds himself nor disparages others because of his attainment' (M 911).

According to the Buddha, once the fourth *jhāna* has been attained various things are possible. First, one could surmount 'the perceptions of form' and enter the four bases of formlessness: infinite space, infinite consciousness, nothingness, and neither-perception-nor-non-perception (M 267–8). These correspond to the formless realm, the highest level of the Buddha's cosmology. The last two are the meditation levels the Buddha attained with his teachers Kālāma and Rāmaputta. Beyond this, the Buddha said, a person could attain a final, ninth level, the 'cessation of perception and feeling'

(M 268). This appears to be a glimpse of *Nibbāna* as ultimate reality. Second, one could gain various 'supernormal powers' such as walking on water, hearing distant sounds, and directly knowing the minds of others (L 105). Finally, and very importantly, a person could achieve the three kinds of knowledge the Buddha himself gained at his enlightenment: knowledge of past lives, knowledge of rebirth, and knowledge of the Four Noble Truths (see M 369–70). This brings us to insight meditation.

The basics of serenity meditation – that is, the four *jhānas* – bring about a high level of tranquility and concentration. They purify the mind so that enlightenment is possible. But only with insight meditation can full enlightenment be achieved. The purpose of insight meditation is to directly know reality as it actually is, specifically the impermanence of all things, the suffering connected with this, the not-self teaching, the Four Noble Truths, and ultimately *Nibbāna*. Insight meditation is most thoroughly outlined in what the Buddha called 'the four foundations of mindfulness.' 'Ardent, fully aware, and mindful, having put away covetousness and grief for the world,' the Buddha said, a person abides contemplating:

(1) the body as a body,
(2) feelings as feelings,
(3) mind as mind, and
(4) mind-objects as mind-objects.

In a *sutta* devoted to the topic, the four foundations of mindfulness are described as 'the direct path for the purification of beings, for the surmounting of sorrow and lamentation, for the disappearance of pain and grief, for the attainment of the true way, for the realization of *Nibbāna*' (M 145). The Eightfold Path as a whole is also portrayed as 'the way leading to the development of the establishment of mindfulness' (C II 1660).

Mindfulness of the body as a body begins with a meditation on breathing, one of the central meditation techniques for the Buddha (breathing may also be an object of serenity meditation). The meditator is to find an appropriate location and assume the lotus position as described on page 188. Then:

> Ever mindful he breathes in, mindful he breaths out. Breathing in long, he understands: 'I breath in long'; or breathing out long, he understands: 'I breath out long'. Breathing in short, he understands: 'I breathe in short'; or breathing out short, he understands: 'I breathe out short'. He trains thus: 'I shall breath in experiencing the whole body (of breath)'; he trains thus: 'I shall breath out experiencing the whole body (of breath)'. He trains thus: 'I shall breathe in tranquillizing the bodily formation'; he trains thus: 'I shall breathe out tranquillizing the bodily formation.'
>
> (M 145–6)

The purpose here is not to breathe in any particular way, but to alertly observe in minute detail exactly how one is breathing. This is not an intellectual exercise, but neither is it mere passivity. Nothing is forced, no judgments are formed, no reactions are elicited. There is simply pure, unadulterated awareness. In the Buddha's teaching, the meditation on breathing has considerable significance. Breathing both instantiates and represents the features of impermanence and interdependence in all things. We breathe at every moment of our lives, ordinarily without taking notice of the fact. In meditation, we are to focus exclusive attention on this ever-present phenomenon in order to observe its true features. This is emphasized in the insight refrain that follows the passage above (and, with slight variation, follows each aspect of the mindfulness meditation):

> In this way he abides contemplating the body as a body internally, or he abides contemplating the body as a body externally, or he abides contemplating the body as a body both internally and externally. Or else he abides contemplating in the body its arising factors, or he abides contemplating in the body its vanishing factors, or he abides contemplating in the body both its arising and vanishing factors. Or else mindfulness that 'there is a body' is simply established in him to the extent necessary for bare knowledge and mindfulness. And he abides independent, not clinging to anything in the world.
>
> (M 146).

Pure mindful observation of breathing makes us aware of its constant change, of the process of arising and vanishing, and this awareness is said to bring about non-clinging or non-attachment to such impermanent phenomena.

The remaining meditations concerning mindfulness do not require the lotus position. Those pertaining to the body concern four postures (walking, standing, sitting, and lying down), awareness of various bodily activities (such as stretching, eating, falling asleep, and so on), the various parts of the body (such as the hair, teeth, blood, sweat and tears), the four elements of the body (earth, water, fire, and air), and the decomposition of the body after death. The last is meant to bring to clear awareness that our own body 'is not exempt from that fate' (M 148).

The contemplations of feelings as feelings include feelings that are pleasant, painful, or neither painful-nor-pleasant; in each case, these may be worldly or unworldly. The meditations of mind as mind pertain to a mind affected or unaffected by lust, hate, and delusion, or that may be contracted or distracted, surpassed or unsurpassed, concentrated or unconcentrated, and liberated or unliberated. The last contemplations concern a variety of mind-objects or phenomena (translations of the term '*dhammā*'). These include the five hindrances (sensual desire, ill will, sloth and torpor, restlessness and remorse, and doubt), the five aggregates (material form, feeling, perception, the formations, and consciousness), the six sense bases (the eye, ear, nose, tongue, body, and mind), the seven enlightenment factors (mindfulness, investigation of states, energy, rapture, tranquility, concentration, and equanimity), and the Four Noble Truths. In each case, a version of the insight refrain follows.

The purpose of the first three of the four foundations of mindfulness (body, feelings, and mind) is to carefully observe various aspects of one's person. This enables us to fully realize that they are characterized by impermanence, suffering, and the absence of any self. With this realization, we are liberated from 'clinging to anything in the world.' For example, regarding mindfulness of the earth element of the body, the Buddha says: 'That should be seen as it actually is with proper wisdom thus: "This is not mine, this I am not, this is not my self".' Seeing this 'makes the mind dispassionate towards the earth element' (M 528). Mindful awareness of aspects of one's person as impermanent, suffering, and not-self has a liberating capacity. It undermines the ground of clinging or attachment, the belief that there is an 'I' to which things may be attached, and it allows us to pierce through these ever-changing and conditioned matters to what is beyond all change and conditioning. Mindfulness brings about the 'realization of *Nibbāna*.' The fourth foundation (mind-objects) continues this theme, but in a more systematic fashion and with greater attention to the theoretical dimensions of the Buddha's teaching. The four forms of mindfulness together involve sustained awareness of the true nature of all phenomena, and this awareness enables us to grasp the indescribable 'deathless element' that transcends these phenomena and liberates us from suffering.

2 Assessing Buddhist meditation

The brief outline of right effort, concentration, and mindfulness we have just considered is not enough to teach a person how to undertake, much less perfect, the Buddha's meditation techniques. He made it clear that a good deal more detailed, individual instruction and training would be necessary to gain the ability to meditate properly and thereby gain enlightenment (just as a person could not become proficient in ballet or baseball merely by reading a book). Moreover, he described numerous other meditation techniques such as a meditation involving the four kinds of immeasurable deliverance of mind – loving-kindness, compassion, appreciative joy, and equanimity (see M 456–7). However, the outline in the last section may be enough for stream-observers to begin an assessment of the worth of Buddhist meditation. The Buddha assigned considerable epistemic significance to meditation. He believed it is necessary, though not sufficient, to obtain the knowledge that would enable us to attain *Nibbāna* and thereby overcome suffering. It is not sufficient because of the importance of moral training and intellectual understanding in the other aspects of the Eightfold Path. But it is necessary.

Without meditation, the Buddha thought, full understanding of his teaching is impossible. Nonetheless, skeptical stream-observers may question whether Buddhist meditation can give us the liberating knowledge the Buddha claims it provides.

Generally speaking, Buddhist meditation is said to bring about a special kind of knowledge-producing experience. It often involves sense-experience and it sometimes resembles sense-experience in making us aware of what is real. But meditation is intended to be a form of experience that is distinct from, and in some sense transcends, ordinary sense-experience. Moreover, though meditation requires intellectual preparation, it is not itself simply intellectual understanding (based, for example, solely on rational argumentation). Yet meditation does not result in a subjective or non-cognitive experience. It is supposed to provide objective knowledge, albeit knowledge that defies adequate linguistic description insofar as it pertains to *Nibbāna*. Let us assume that both the Buddha and many of his followers, during his lifetime and since, have sincerely reported to have gained enlightenment on the basis of meditation and other aspects of the Eightfold Path. How should stream-observers assess the epistemic worth of these reports?

It might be contended that, in order to answer this question, we first need to establish where the burden of proof lies. On the one hand, someone might say that the burden rests with Buddhists to prove to us stream-observers that meditation produces genuine knowledge. Against this, it may be said that stream-observers are not now in a position to directly confirm or disconfirm the reports of Buddhist meditators. What we now know or think we know, Buddhists might say, is not an adequate criterion for judging the worth of Buddhist meditation because we are caught up in craving and attachment to things of the world. On the other hand, someone else might say that the burden rests with skeptics to establish that meditation does not produce knowledge. Buddhism has a long and established tradition, and we should assume that the claim that meditation gives knowledge is correct unless there are sufficient reasons to doubt this. Against this, skeptics may reply that all sorts of bizarre claims to knowledge may be difficult to refute, but it does not follow that we should accept these claims.

It is unlikely that we can resolve this debate about the burden of proof. Both the Buddhists and the skeptics have a point. All we can do is consider some specific questions that might be raised about Buddhist meditation and reflect on what may be said in response to them. It will then be up to each of us to determine whether or not, in the context of his overall teaching, the Buddha's meditation techniques have enough prima facie credibility to make them worth pursuing. Of course, there are many different techniques and it is not entirely clear how they relate to one another. Nonetheless, the basic approach sketched on pages 187–91 is evident enough. We are first to bring purity and tranquility to the mind through sustained concentration on some meditation object, and we are then to bring mindful awareness to various aspects of our person. If we do this, it is maintained, we can eventually realize and be liberated by the basic teaching of the Buddha. It is easy to see how this could be right. We cannot understand now because the mind is impure, and we will be able to understand once the mind is purified. Still, questions may be raised about the epistemic value of this method.

There are two immediate respects in which it might be thought that there are substantial reasons to doubt the credibility of meditation. First, one of the claims made by the Buddha is that meditation makes it possible to acquire supernormal powers such as hearing distant sounds and reading the minds of others. It would be fairly easy to test for such powers, and if it turned out that no meditators actually possessed them, then this would be reason to doubt that meditation produces the ability to acquire this kind of knowledge. But perhaps the ability to gain these powers is not essential to the Buddha's teaching about the attainment of enlightenment. In any case, this claim is clearly not central.

Second, the Buddha says that meditation gives us knowledge of rebirth, both the general phenomenon and specifics of particular cases. Earlier it was suggested that the doctrine of rebirth appears to conflict with much that we know about the world (chapter 9, section 3). If this were true, it would provide a reason to question the contention that Buddhist meditation provides knowledge. Unlike the first case, it must be admitted that rebirth is a central part of the Buddha's teaching. Moreover, the equally central idea of *kamma* appears untenable in the absence of rebirth.

However, we could set these issues aside and ask whether it is plausible to suppose that any important elements of the Buddha's teaching could be known through Buddhist meditation. In particular, let us restrict attention to the key claims to knowledge concerning the Four Noble Truths, impermanence, interdependence, not-self, and *Nibbāna* (thereby precluding the supernormal powers, rebirth, and *kamma*). With respect to claims such as these, do we have reason to accept or reject the contention that they could be known through Buddhist meditation? One source of doubt is the series of philosophical questions concerning these claims that have been raised in the previous chapters. If the Buddha's claims were not philosophically cogent, that would be a basis for doubt. But let us assume for the sake of argument that this is not a problem, that the Buddha's teaching in these respects is philosophically coherent, or at least not incoherent. There remain several other possible sources of doubt about meditation that stream-observers need to consider.

We have an account of what the life of an *arahant* is supposed to be like. Suppose it turned out that purported *arahants* did not generally live in this way. For example, suppose they lacked compassion or were rather attached to material goods. Since the knowledge they are said to have is supposed to bring it about that they do not live this way, this would be a reason to doubt that they have this knowledge. Of course, there can always be fraudulent cases. However, it may be said on behalf of the Buddha that *arahants* – and

193

perhaps more generally persons who are especially accomplished in the teaching of the Buddha – do largely live the lives they are expected to live. If this were true, the objection would be answered. On the other hand, the fact that they live this way, though it might encourage our confidence, would not necessarily show that they have the knowledge claimed. There could be other explanations.

Similarly, if persons who report meditative knowledge were known to be unreliable in various ways (for example, by having a bad memory, being especially gullible, giving inconsistent reports, and so on), then this would be another ground for doubt. Once again, it may be said in support of the Buddha that this is not generally the case (not that no such person is unreliable, but that they are not typically so). If this were correct, we would have a response to the objection. Also, as before, reliability in these respects would not necessarily confirm meditative knowledge. In both this and the previous case, empirical research presumably could confirm or disconfirm the claims made on behalf of the Buddha.

Another source of doubt might be found in the apparent disanalogies between sense-experience and meditative experience. To a very great extent, sense-experience is a common possession of all human beings, but nothing close to this can be said of meditative experience. On account of this, reports based on sense-experience can be checked by numerous persons, but reports about *Nibbāna* as ultimate reality, or about the attainment of *Nibbāna*-after-death, for example, cannot similarly be checked. In response, it may be said in defense of the Buddha that there are forms of knowledge based on sense-experience that are possessed by only a few persons – for instance, knowledge of coffee or wine based on its taste, or knowledge of the medical significance of an X-ray. These are cases of genuine knowledge based on sense-experience, but they require special abilities and training to acquire. Something similar might be said about Buddhist meditation. Moreover, it may be said that to a large extent reports based on Buddhist meditation can be checked by others, but only those who have undertaken the Eightfold Path. Hence, there is a significant role for intersubjective verification of these reports. Finally, it may also be noted that there are some kinds of reports we accept as generally authoritative even though they cannot be verified by other persons – for example, introspective reports about whether a person has a headache. Perhaps intersubjective verification is not essential for knowledge.

Suspicion may also be raised by the claim that the knowledge meditators are said to acquire is so heavily influenced by their expectations, given their Buddhist beliefs, that it is not reliable. In effect, meditators experience in meditation what they expect to experience, not what is objectively there to be experienced. Of course, it is often the case that our expectations influence what we think we observe. But from this fact we ordinarily conclude not that all beliefs where this can happen are doubtful, but that particular ones are doubtful that we have reason to suspect are adversely influenced by expectations. By parity of reasoning, it may be said on the Buddha's behalf, this cannot be a basis for casting doubt on all reports based on meditation unless it can be shown that all or nearly all meditators are unduly influenced in this way. And it seems unlikely that this could be shown. Just as there are persons who are capable of an objective assessment of their own team's chances in the championship game, so there may be meditators who are capable of an objective assessment of what meditation reveals.

It might also be said that the beliefs of meditators can be explained in purely naturalistic terms on the basis of psychology or physiology. For example, it might be claimed that serenity meditation puts the brain in a highly unusual state, and that the supposed knowledge that meditators gain is nothing more than an effect of this state. One difficulty with this critique is that all beliefs have a naturalistic explanation. Whether a particular naturalistic explanation supplies a basis for skepticism about some class of beliefs depends on whether we have grounds for thinking the explanation undermines the reliability of the beliefs. For example, we might think that a particular kind of drug-induced state was unreliable if persons in that state made reports we could show on independent grounds to be false (say, if they always forgot their address). Conversely, we might believe that another kind of drug-induced state was especially reliable if persons in that state performed much better intellectually (say, if they could do more complex mathematical calculations). A Buddhist might respond that meditation may well alter the state of the brain. What must be shown, but cannot be, is that there are independent grounds for supposing the reports of Buddhist meditation are unreliable. In any case, it seems clear that the issue of reliability would have to be brought into this discussion.

Finally, it might be argued that reports based on Buddhist meditation are part of a larger class of reports based on religious experience in many different *James* traditions (Hindu, Jewish, Christian, Muslim, and so on), and that the reports in this larger class often contradict one another. Therefore, there is reason to question all these reports, including the Buddhist ones. The Buddhist might respond that it is not evident why Buddhist meditation should be considered part of the larger class of religious experiences. Buddhist meditation is a highly specific set of techniques that are quite different from anything found in other religious traditions. Why should the fact that persons in those other traditions who rely on different approaches and give reports incompatible with Buddhism count against the authority of the reports based on Buddhist meditation? Since the reports from other traditions are not based on Buddhist techniques, there is no reason to expect that they would be consistent with the teachings of the Buddha.

In response, a modification of this objection may be given that does not depend on classifying Buddhist meditation as one form of religious experience. It contends that the conflicting experience-based reports of other religious traditions could be justified to the same extent as the reports based on Buddhist meditation. That is, analogous and equally plausible responses to the objections already given could be made on behalf of the reports in these different traditions, and since these reports cannot all be true, we have reason to question all of them, including the Buddhist ones. This is a more serious objection. However, in order to be established, it would have to be shown that equally plausible responses could be made in all the traditions, and this is a large agenda. There are several possibilities here. Perhaps a close look at reports that genuinely could be said to be equally plausible do not conflict to the extent supposed. Or perhaps the respects in which these religious traditions do conflict are not directly based on religious experiences. Or perhaps we do not know enough about these issues to adequately assess this objection. The defender of the Buddha would probably say that, insofar as there is real conflict, the reports based on Buddhist meditation are better justified. It would be difficult to prove this, but it may be just as difficult to refute it.

In short, there are a number of grounds for challenging the epistemic credentials of Buddhist meditation, but Buddhists are not without resources for answering these challenges. Stream-observers can determine for themselves whether these responses are adequate. However, even if they were adequate, this would only show that there are no grounds for doubt, not that Buddhist meditation actually provides the knowledge claimed. To establish that it does, the Buddha has much to say, as we have seen in the explanations throughout this book. Beyond these, he has only one thing to say: follow the Eightfold Path, and in particular meditate, and you will find out for yourself.

SUGGESTED READING

A key presentation of Buddhist meditation is the *Satipaṭṭhāna Sutta* ('The Foundations of Mindfulness'), M #10. See also the *Ānāpānasati Sutta* ('Mindfulness of Breathing'), M #118, the *Kāyagatāsati Sutta* ('Mindfulness of the Body'), M #119, and the *Mahāsatipaṭṭhāna Sutta* ('The Greater Discourse on the Foundations of Mindfulness'), L #22.

For discussions of Buddhist meditation, see Conze (1997), Griffiths (1986: chapter 1), W.L. King (1980), Strenski (1980), and Swearer (1973). Contemporary guides to Buddhist meditation rooted in the approaches described in this chapter can be found in Goldstein and Kornfield (2001) and Gunaratana (1992). There has been much discussion of the epistemic evaluation of religious experience, typically within the Christian context. For a critique, see Mackie (1982: chapter 10). For defenses, see Alston (1991), Davis (1989), Swinburne (1979: chapter 13), and Yandell (1993).

17

A MESSAGE OF HOPE: THE BUDDHA'S INVITATION TO LIVE SELFLESSLY

No doubt stream-observers have a variety of responses to the teaching of the Buddha. A few may embrace it as a whole, more than a few will probably reject it entirely, and many are likely to be attracted to some aspects, while remaining skeptical of others. The Buddha's teaching is first and foremost a message of hope: he promises that a reorientation of our lives will bring about the happiness we seek but may find difficult to achieve, the compassion we admire but may feel challenged to sustain, and the peace we yearn for but may discover often eludes us. To focus reflection on some central issues, it may be helpful to bring this inquiry to a close by briefly restating the Buddha's teaching as a series of invitations to think about some important questions in our lives, and suggestions about some beneficial ways of doing this. Our responses to these invitations and suggestions will say a great deal about how far and in what respects we are, or are not, prepared to follow the Buddha.

The first invitation asks us to think about the quality of our life as a whole in a fundamental and sustained way. Human lives vary tremendously: some persons are rather fortunate, some are far less so. The Buddha does not deny this, but he focuses on what we all have in common. We might call this our frailty or fragility. In a number of respects, human beings are extraordinary creatures, capable of astonishing accomplishments. But we are all subject to disease and injury, to the decline of old age, and eventually to death. Not only that, everything we cherish is equally frail: our friends and loved ones, our job, our favorite activities, our treasured places, and our prized possessions. All of these things will eventually decline in value or disappear. When we reflect on this, the Buddha suggests, we will realize that, though life has many positive dimensions, there is something deeply unsatisfactory in the fact that everything we value is so frail. We live in the shadow of loss, of regrets over the past and anxieties for the future. Most of us do not dwell on this much of the time. It usually requires an unexpected setback – a death, an accident, a failure, a disappointment – to remind us how fragile our lives are. These are the moments, perhaps, when the Buddha's first suggestion may ring true.

The second invitation asks us to consider why the fragility of our lives is a source of dissatisfaction. An initial answer is obvious: all that we value will not last. The Buddha urges that we press beyond this answer. Dissatisfaction arises, he suggests, because of a discrepancy between what we desire and the way the world works. We desire to possess what we think are good things, and to avoid what appear to be bad things, not just for a few minutes, or hours, or days, but for a very long time, in some cases forever. Unfortunately, the world is in constant change and persistently thwarts this desire. The gulf between our desire for certain kinds of stability and the unrelenting instability of the world is the general explanation of the dissatisfaction that always tacitly accompanies us.

The third invitation brings us to a crucial juncture. What, the Buddha asks us, can be done to overcome this dissatisfaction? One answer is 'Nothing.' The gap between the desire for permanence and the impermanence of the world cannot be bridged, and hence life is inevitably dissatisfying. This is the answer of despair. Many of us are probably tempted by this at one time or another. But the Buddha thinks we are usually sustained by a different answer: despite the instability of the world, we suppose that if we exert ourselves enough, we can control the world sufficiently to bring it into substantial accord with our desires. This works to an extent, though some people are more successful at it than others. The Buddha agrees that this may bring a measure of happiness. In the end, however, he believes it is a recipe for frustration. We can swim upriver for a time, but not for long. Sooner or later the forces of change will overcome us. Much can go wrong: our spouse may leave us, our job may be taken from us, our house may burn down. If nothing else, eventually each of us and all those we love will grow old, get sick, and die. If these were the only two answers, our prospects might seem bleak. However, the Buddha believes there is a third answer, an answer of hope: we could come to realize that our happiness need not depend on the fulfillment of our desires. The Buddha realizes this is not an easy suggestion to accept, but he thinks if we follow him further we can see for ourselves that it is true.

The Buddha's next invitation asks us to reflect on why fulfillment of desires is so important to us. The answer may seem obvious: these are my desires and my happiness depends on fulfilling them. The Buddha agrees that this is what we ordinarily think. He then makes an extraordinary suggestion: though there is some sense in which the thought that these are my desires is true, perhaps this truth is more contingent and superficial than I have supposed, and it does not represent the deepest and most important reality about who or what human beings are. We find it overwhelmingly natural to think in terms of personal ownership: 'This is my mind and my body, and these are my thoughts, my feelings, and my desires.' We then try to extend this sense of ownership further: 'These are my accomplishments, my children, my possessions, and so on.' But is there really something – myself – that can truly be said to own these things? We think it is obvious that there is. The Buddha asks us to reconsider this idea. The notion that I am a self means that I am a distinct thing in the world with identity through time. There is something, me, that is clearly different from other things and is always present. But if we attend very closely to everything associated with our person, the Buddha proposes, we will find that there is no such self. There is only a collection of interdependent and ever-changing processes: thinking, feeling, wanting, hoping – but no self who owns these.

We feel threatened by this suggestion. 'Myself is the most important thing about me,' each of us is inclined to say 'If I lose that, there will be nothing left.' The Buddha recognizes that we feel threatened, but he thinks this feeling is rooted in a misunderstanding. His next invitation, perhaps the hardest to accept, is to consider whether piercing through the illusion of selfhood might reveal not nothing, but, so to speak, everything. Liberation from the belief in selfhood, the Buddha suggests, will bring the unsatisfactory dimensions of life to an end. Liberated from the thought of ownership, there will no longer be a deep sense of identification with 'my desires' as things that must be fulfilled for 'me' to be happy. Liberated from the thought of being distinct from other beings, there will be compassion and loving-kindness for all creatures. Liberated from the thought of having identity, there will no longer be a preoccupation with regrets about the past and anxieties for the future. The result will be tranquility, happiness, freedom from the unsatisfying scenario of constantly striving to find some stable good to attach myself to in a relentlessly frail and fragile world. The Buddha endeavors to explain why this makes sense. However, in the end, there is not so much a strict argument from premise to conclusion here as a promise that the realization of selflessness will have some powerful and positive effects.

All this probably seems a rather remote prospect. So much of life revolves around being myself that it is hard to imagine living on any other terms. The fear persists that without me there is nothing: annihilation, not the highest happiness. The Buddha's next invitation is put forward with great hesitation. He asks each of us to consider the possibility that, though I think I am really a self, there is, it might be said, much more to being a human being than that. The Buddha believes dissolving the illusion of selfhood enables us to realize we are already in touch with an indescribable reality he tries to gesture toward with the word 'Nibbāna.' This is not our true self. It is not a thing or substance at all. Nor is it a process. It utterly transcends the frailness and fragility, the impermanence and interdependence, of the world of everyday experience. Finding ordinary language inadequate, the Buddha tries to evoke Nibbāna through the terminology of absence: it is 'deathless,' 'not-conditioned,' and the like. But Nibbāna can be understood truly only through direct experience. The Buddha's own experience of Nibbāna convinced him that uncovering the illusion of selfhood brought liberation, not annihilation. He can only hint at what this might be like and point the way to perceiving it for ourselves.

The Buddha's final and most important invitation asks us to discover on our own whether there is any truth in what he says. 'When you know for yourselves,' he states, that 'these things, if undertaken and practiced, lead to

199

welfare and happiness,' only then should you 'engage in them' (N 66). He does not think this knowledge will come easily. We are too enmeshed in the idea of ourselves and in finding happiness by attaching ourselves to things in this fragile world to quickly overcome the illusion of selfhood. So he provides some signposts to guide us on the path to enlightenment. In part, these consist of a group of ideas, what we have been exploring throughout this book. Think about whether these make sense, he says. In part, they suggest we will probably need to live differently, in a manner that more closely approximates selfless living, if we are to see aright. All this is important, but still preliminary. The Buddha thinks our mind is like a pool of murky water, muddied by cravings and attachments. To really see for ourselves, we need to purify the mind. He believes this can be done by training the mind to concentrate all its attention on a single object. A good starting place is one's own breathing. Once the mind is purified, he says, we should direct it to all that we associate with ourselves. When we do this, the mind gradually becomes fully aware: everything previously taken to be oneself dissolves and *Nibbāna* remains.

The Buddha's invitation to live selflessly is a unique, powerful, and hopeful message, hard to comprehend, difficult to embrace, strenuous to practice. It is a remarkable vision that has been found deeply attractive and extraordinarily perplexing, sometimes both at once.

SUGGESTED READING

The suggestions here will take the reader into Buddhist traditions that developed after the life of the Buddha. For introductions to Buddhism, see Lopez (2001) and Strong (2002). General accounts of Buddhist philosophy may be found in Gethin (1998), Harvey (1990), Kalupahana (1976 and 1992), and Mitchell (2002). Indian Buddhism is discussed in Akira (1990), Ling (1976), Warder (1970), and Williams and Tribe (2000). Kapstein (2001) considers Indian and Tibetan Buddhism. *Mahāyāna* Buddhism is examined in Williams (1989). Buddhism has been compared to the work of a number of Western philosophers. For example, in addition to studies suggested earlier, there are comparisons with James in Kalupahana (1987), with Nietzsche in Morrison (1997), and with Wittgenstein in Gudmunsen (1977). Additional avenues to learning about the teaching of the Buddha may be found by consulting the Buddhist resources on the Internet that follow on page 201.

BUDDHIST RESOURCES
ON THE INTERNET

(all sites accessed 15 March 2003)

Access to Insight: Readings in Theravada Buddhism
  Online. Available HTTP: http://www.accesstoinsight.org

Buddhist Information and Education Network
  Online. Available HTTP: http://www.buddhanet.net

Buddhist Studies – Texts Input/Translation Projects
  Online. Available HTTP: http://villa.lakes.com/cdpatton/ETexts.html

Buddhist Studies WWW Virtual Library
  Online. Available HTTP: http://www.ciolek.com/WWWVL-Buddhism.html

Buddhist Sutras on the Internet
  Online. Available HTTP: http://home.att.net/~edwardchang/sutraindex/english.htm

DharmaNet InterLinks: Buddhist Studies
  Online. Available HTTP: http://www.dharmanet.org/buddstdy.html

Digital Buddhist Library and Museum
  Online. Available HTTP: http://sino-sv3.sino.uni-heidelberg.de

Digital Dictionary of Buddhism
  Online. Available HTTP: http://www.acmuller.net/ddb/ddb-intro.htm

Electronic Resources for the Study of Buddhist Texts
  Online. Available HTTP: http://www.geocities.com/manjushri_2000/buddhisttexts.
  html

Journal of Buddhist Ethics
  Online. Available HTTP: http://jbe.gold.ac.uk

LinksPitaka: Academic Buddhist Resources
  Online. Available HTTP: http://www.pitaka.ch/academ.htm

Resources for the Study of Buddhism
  Online. Available HTTP: http://online.sfsu.edu/~rone/Buddhism/Buddhism.htm

Urban Dharma
  Online. Available HTTP: http://www.urbandharma.org

GLOSSARY OF IMPORTANT
PĀLI TERMS

(in English alphabetical order)

Abhidhamma Piṭaka   one of the 'Three Baskets' of texts that make up the
  Pāli canon
ājīva   livelihood; right livelihood is one of the steps in the Eightfold Path
akusala   unwholesome; unwholesome volitions are ordinarily accompanied
  by greed, hatred, or delusion; they bring about unhappiness for the person
anāgāmin   non-returner; someone at the third of the four stages of enlightenment
anattā   not-self
anicca   impermanent
anupādisesa-nibbānadhātu   *Nibbāna*-element with no residue left; *Nibbāna*-
  after-death
arahant   liberated or accomplished person; someone at the highest of the
  four stages of enlightenment
ariya aṭṭhangika magga   Noble Eightfold Path
ariya sacca   noble truths; the Four Noble Truths summarize the Buddha's
  teaching
āsava   taints, cankers, corruptions
asmi māna   ego-conceit, the conceit 'I am'
attā   self
avijjā   ignorance; the first link in the twelvefold formula, what conditions
  formations
bhava   being, existence, becoming; a link in the twelvefold formula, what
  conditions birth
bhāvanā   (mental) development, meditation
bhikkhu   Buddhist monk
bhikkhunī   Buddhist nun
buddha   enlightened one; one who rediscovers the *Dhamma* and proclaims
  it to the world
dāna   gift, giving, liberality, generosity
deva   god, deity, heavenly being; these beings are part of the cycle of rebirth

Dhammā   the teaching of the Buddha

dhammā   things, phenomena, mind-objects, states, qualities

diṭṭhi   view, belief; right view is one of the steps in the Eightfold Path

dosa   hatred, anger; one of the three unwholesome roots, destroyed in an *arahant*

dukkha   suffering, unsatisfactoriness, pain; the subject of the Four Noble Truths

jarāmaraṇa   aging and death; the last link in the twelvefold formula, conditioned by birth

jāti   birth; a link in the twelvefold formula, what conditions aging and death

jhāna   meditative absorption, meditation

jīva   soul

kamma   action; morally wholesome actions improve a person's future well-being, and morally unwholesome actions have the opposite effect

kammanta   action; right action is one of the steps in the Eightfold Path

karuṇā   compassion; one of the four immeasurable deliverances of mind

kasiṇa   meditation device

khandha   aggregate, mass; the five aggregates that make up a person are material form, feelings, perceptions, formations, and consciousness.

kusala   wholesome; wholesome volitions are ordinarily accompanied by the absence of greed, hatred, and delusion; they bring about well-being for the person

lobha   greed; one of the three unwholesome roots

majjhimā paṭipadā   middle way; the Noble Eightfold Path is a middle way between indulgence in the senses and self-mortification

mettā   loving-kindness; one of the four immeasurable deliverances of mind

moha   delusion; one of the three unwholesome roots, destroyed in an *arahant*

muditā   appreciative joy; one of the four immeasurable deliverances of mind

nāma   mentality

nāmarūpa   mentality-materiality; a link in the twelvefold formula, what conditions the sixfold base

ñāṇa   knowledge; right knowledge is sometimes added to the Eightfold Path

Nibbāna   extinction; final deliverance from suffering

Nikāya   a division of the *Sutta Piṭaka*

nīvaraṇa   hindrances; the five hindrances to meditation are usually said to be sensual desire, ill will, sloth and torpor, restlessness and remorse, and doubt

paccaya   condition; the term used in the twelvefold formula

paññā   wisdom, knowledge; one of the three divisions of the Eightfold Path

paramattha sacca   ultimate truth; contrasted with conventional truth in early Buddhist history

paṭicca samuppāda   dependent origination; this is elaborated by the twelvefold formula

phassa   contact, sense-impression; a link in the twelvefold formula, what conditions feeling *rāga* lust; destroyed in an *arahant*

rūpa form, material form, materiality; the first of the five aggregates

sacca truth

saddhā faith, confidence

sakadāgāmin once-returner; someone at the second of the four stages of enlightenment

saḷāyatana the sixfold base (the senses and the mind); a link in the twelvefold formula, what conditions contact

samādhi concentration; right concentration is one of the steps in the Eightfold Path, and one of the three divisions of the Path

samaṇa recluse, ascetic, spiritual striver

samatha serenity, tranquility; a form of meditation

sammā right, correct, rightly, completely; the term used in each step of the Eightfold Path

sammuti sacca conventional truth; contrasted with ultimate truth in early Buddhist history

saṁsāra perpetual wondering; round of rebirths

saṁyojana fetters

Sangha the Buddhist monastic order

sankappa intention; right intention is one of the steps in the Eightfold Path

sankhāra formation; volitional activity; the fourth of the five aggregates; a link in the twelvefold formula, what conditions consciousness

saññā perception; the third of the five aggregates

sassatavāda eternalism

sati mindfulness; right mindfulness is one of the steps in the Eightfold Path

sa-upādisesa-nibbānadhātu *Nibbāna*-element with residue left; *Nibbāna*-in-life

sīla virtue, morality; one of the three divisions of the Eightfold Path

sotāpanna stream-enterer; someone at the first of the four stages of enlightenment

sukha happiness, pleasure, happy, pleasant

suññatā voidness, emptiness

sutta discourse of the Buddha

Sutta Piṭaka one of the 'Three Baskets' of texts that make up the *Pāli* canon

taṇhā craving; a link in the twelvefold formula, what conditions clinging

Tathāgata Thus Come One, Thus Gone One; epithet of the Buddha

Tipiṭaka the 'Three Baskets' that make up the *Pāli* canon

ucchedavāda annihilationism

upādāna clinging, grasping, attaching; a link in the twelvefold formula, what conditions being

upāsaka male lay follower

upāsikā female lay follower

upekkhā equanimity; one of the four immeasurable deliverances of mind

vācā speech; right speech is one of the steps in the Eightfold Path *vāyāma*   effort; right effort is one of the steps in the Eightfold Path

vedanā   feeling, sensation; the second of the five aggregates; a link in the twelvefold formula, what conditions craving

vibhava   extermination, non-existence

vimutti   deliverance; right deliverance is sometimes added to the Eightfold Path

Vinaya Piṭaka   one of the 'Three Baskets' of texts that make up the *Pāli* canon

viññāṇa   consciousness; the last of the five aggregates; a link in the twelvefold formula, what conditions mentality-materiality

vipassanā   insight; a form of meditation

BIBLIOGRAPHY

Selected translations of the *Sutta Piṭaka* of the *Pāli* canon

Dīgha Nikāya

    Dialogues of the Buddha, 3 vols, translated by T.W. and C.A.F. Rhys Davids, 1899–1921, Reprint, London: Pali Text Society, 1977.

    The Long Discourses of the Buddha, translated by M. Walshe, Boston: Wisdom Publications, 1987.

Majjhima Nikāya

    Middle Length Sayings, 3 vols, translated by I.B. Horner, 1954–1959, Reprint, London: Pali Text Society, 1975–1977.

    The Middle Length Discourses of the Buddha, translated by Bhikkhu Ñāṇamoli and Bhikkhu Bodhi, Boston: Wisdom Publications, 1995.

Saṃyutta Nikāya

    The Book of Kindred Sayings, 5 vols, translated by C.A.F. Rhys Davids and F.L. Woodward, 1917–1930, Reprint, London: Pali Text Society, 1973–1979.

    The Connected Discourses of the Buddha, 2 vols, translated by Bhikkhu Bodhi, Boston: Wisdom Publications, 2000.

Aṅguttara Nikāya

    The Book of the Gradual Sayings, 5 vols, translated by F.L. Woodward, 1932–1936, Reprint, London: Pali Text Society, 1972–1979.

    Numerical Discourses of the Buddha: An Anthology of Suttas from the Aṅguttara Nikāya, translated by N. Thera and Bhikkhu Bodhi, Walnut Creek, CA: AltaMira Press, 1999.

Dhammapada (part of the *Khuddaka Nikāya*)

    The Dhammapada, translated by S. Radhakrishnan, London: Oxford University Press, 1966.

    The Dhammapada: The Buddha's Path of Wisdom, translated by A. Buddharakkhita, Kandy, Sri Lanka: Buddhist Publication Society, 1985.

Udāna and Itivuttaka (parts of the *Khuddaka Nikāya*)

    The Minor Anthologies of the Pali Canon, Part II: Udāna: Verses of Uplift and Itivuttaka: As it Was Said, translated by F.L. Woodward, London: Geoffrey Cumberlege, Oxford University Press, 1948.

    The Udāna: Inspired Utterances of the Buddha and The Itivuttaka: The Buddha's Sayings, translated by J.D. Ireland, Kandy, Sri Lanka: Buddhist Publication Society, 1997.

Therīgāthā (**part of the** *Khuddaka Nikāya*)
   The First Buddhist Women: Translations and Commentary on the Therigatha, translated by S. Murcott, Berkeley, CA: Parallax Press, 1991.
   Poems of Early Buddhist Nuns (Therīgāthā), translated by C.A.F. Rhys Davids and K.R. Norman, 1909, Reprint, Oxford: Pali Text Society, 1997.

Secondary sources

Akira, H. (1990) *A History of Indian Buddhism: From Śākyamuni to Early Mahāyāna*, translated by P. Groner, Honolulu: University of Hawaii Press.
Alston, W.P. (1991) *Perceiving God: The Epistemology of Religious Experience*, Ithaca, NY: Cornell University Press.
Alt, W. (1980) 'There Is No Paradox of Desire in Buddhism,' *Philosophy East and West* 30: 521–8.
Anderson, C.S. (1999) *Pain and Its Ending: The Four Noble Truths in the Theravāda Buddhist Canon*, Richmond, Surrey: Curzon Press.
Anderson, S.L. (1978) 'The Substantive Center Theory versus the Bundle Theory,' *The Monist* 61: 96–108.
Annas, J. (1993) *The Morality of Happiness*, New York: Oxford University Press.
Aristotle (1999) *Nicomachean Ethics*, Second Edition, translated by T. Irwin, Indianapolis, IN: Hackett Publishing Company.
Armstrong, K. (2001) *Buddha*, New York: Penguin Putnam.
Aronson, H.B. (1979) 'The Relationship of the Karmic to the Nirvanic in Theravāda Buddhism,' *Journal of Religious Ethics* 7: 28–36.
Bastow, D. (1969) 'Buddhist Ethics,' *Religious Studies* 5: 195–206.
—— (1986) 'Self-Construction in Buddhism,' *Ratio* 28: 97–113.
—— (1988) 'An Example of Self-Change: The Buddhist Path,' *Religious Studies* 24: 157–72.
Basu, A. (1997) 'Reducing Concern with Self: Parfit and the Ancient Buddhist Schools,' in D. Allen (ed.) *Culture and Self: Philosophical and Religious Perspectives, East and West*, Boulder, CO: Westview Press.
Batchelor, S. (1994) *The Awakening of the West: The Encounter of Buddhism and Western Culture*, Berkeley, CA: Parallax Press.
Bond, G.D. (1996) 'Theravāda Buddhism's Two Formulations of the *Dasa Sīla* and the Ethics of the Gradual Path,' in F.J. Hoffman and D. Mahinda (eds) *Pāli Buddhism*, Richmond, Surrey: Curzon Press.
Bouquet, A.C. (1961) 'Stoics and Buddhists,' *Philosophical Quarterly* (India) 33: 205–221.
Brennan, A. (1994) 'The Disunity of the Self,' in J.J. MacIntosh and H.A. Meynall (eds) *Faith, Scepticism and Personal Identity: A Festschrift for Terence Penelhum*, Calgary: University of Calgary Press.
Buddhaghosa, B. (1999) *The Path of Purification*, translated by Bhikkhu Ñāṇamoli, Seattle, WA: Buddhist Publication Society Pariyatti Editions.
Carrithers, M. (1983) *The Buddha*, Oxford: Oxford University Press.
Chappell, D.W. (ed.) (1999) *Buddhist Peacework: Creating Cultures of Peace*, Boston: Wisdom Publications.
Chatalian, G. (1983) 'Early Indian Buddhism and the Nature of Philosophy: A Philosophical Investigation,' *Journal of Indian Philosophy* 11: 167–222.

Chisholm, R.M. (1976) *Person and Object: A Metaphysical Study*, La Salle, IL: Open Court Publishing Company.

Collins, S. (1982) *Selfless Persons: Imagery and Thought in* Theravāda *Buddhism*, Cambridge: Cambridge University Press.

—— (1985) 'Buddhism in Recent British Philosophy and Theology,' *Religious Studies* 21: 475–93.

—— (1994) 'What Are Buddhists *Doing* When They Deny the Self?,' in F.E. Reynolds and D. Tracy (eds) *Religion and Practical Reason: New Essays in the Comparative Philosophy of Religions*, Albany, NY: State University of New York Press.

—— (1997) 'A Buddhist Debate about the Self; and Remarks on Buddhism in the Work of Derek Parfit and Galen Strawson,' *Journal of Indian Philosophy* 25: 467–93.

—— (1998) *Nirvana and Other Buddhist Felicities: Utopias of the Pali Imaginaire*, Cambridge: Cambridge University Press.

Conze, E. (1963a) 'Buddhist Philosophy and Its European Parallels,' *Philosophy East and West* 13: 9–23.

—— (1963b) 'Spurious Parallels to Buddhist Philosophy,' *Philosophy East and West* 13: 105–15.

—— (1967) *Buddhist Thought in India: Three Phases of Buddhist Philosophy*, Ann Arbor, MI: University of Michigan Press.

—— (1997) *Buddhist Meditation*, New Dehli: Munshiram Manoharlal Publishers.

Cruise, H. (1983) 'Early Buddhism: Some Recent Misconceptions,' *Philosophy East and West* 33: 149–66.

Dalmiya, V. (2001) 'Particularizing the Moral Self: A Feminist Buddhist Exchange,' *Sophia* 40: 61–72.

Danto, A.C. (1972) *Mysticism and Morality: Oriental Thought and Moral Philosophy*, New York: Harper & Row.

Davis, C.F. (1989) *The Evidential Force of Religious Experience*, Oxford: Clarendon Press.

Descartes, R. (1984) 'Meditations on First Philosophy,' in J. Cottingham, R. Stoothoff, and D. Murdoch (trs) *The Philosophical Writings of Descartes*, vol. II, Cambridge: Cambridge University Press.

—— (1985) 'Discourse and Essays,' in J. Cottingham, R. Stoothoff, and D. Murdoch (trs) *The Philosophical Writings of Descartes*, vol. I, Cambridge: Cambridge University Press.

Dhamma, R. (1997) *The First Discourse of the Buddha: Turning the Wheel of Dhamma*, Boston: Wisdom Publications.

Dillon, M. (2000) 'Dialogues with Death: The Last Days of Socrates and the Buddha,' *Philosophy East and West* 50: 525–58.

Dissanayake, W. (1993) 'Self and Body in Theravada Buddhism: A Tropological Analysis of the "Dhammapada",' in T.P. Kasulis, R.T. Ames, and W. Dissanayake (eds) *Self as Body in Asian Theory and Practice*, Albany, NY: State University of New York Press.

Doore, G. (1979) 'The "Radically Empiricist" Interpretation of Early Buddhist *Nirvāṇa*,' *Religious Studies* 15: 65–70.

Edwards, P. (1996) *Reincarnation: A Critical Examination*, Amherst, NY: Prometheus Books.

—— (ed.) (1997) *Immortality*, Amherst, NY: Prometheus Books.

Epstein, M. (1995) *Thoughts Without a Thinker: Psychotheraphy from a Buddhist Perspective*, New York: Basic Books.

Eppsteiner, F. (ed.) (1988) *The Path of Compassion: Writings on Socially Engaged Buddhism*, Revised Second Edition, Berkeley, CA: Parallax Press.

Fields, R. (1992) *How the Swans Came to the Lake: A Narrative History of Buddhism in America*, Third Edition, revised and updated, Boston: Shambhala.

Flintoff, E. (1980) 'Pyrrho and India,' *Phronesis* 25: 88–108.

Fu, C.W-H. and Wawrytko, S. (eds) (1991) *Buddhist Ethics and Modern Society: A Symposium*, Westport, CT: Greenwood Press.

Garfield, J.L. (2002) *Empty Words: Buddhist Philosophy and Cross-Cultural Interpretation*, New York: Oxford University Press.

Geertz, C. (1973) *The Interpretation of Cultures*, New York: Basic Books.

—— (1983) *Local Knowledge: Further Essays in Interpretive Anthropology*, New York: Basic Books.

Gethin, R. (1986) 'The Five *Khandhas*: Their Treatment in the *Nikāyas* and Early *Abhidhamma*,' *Journal of Indian Philosophy* 14: 35–53.

—— (1998) *The Foundations of Buddhism*, New York: Oxford University Press.

Giles, J. (1993) 'The No-self Theory: Hume, Buddhism, and Personal Identity,' *Philosophy East and West* 43: 175–200.

—— (1997) *No Self to Be Found: The Search for Personal Identity*, Lanham, MD: University Press of America.

Gilligan, C. (1987) 'Moral Orientation and Moral Development,' in E.F. Kittay and D. Meyers (eds) *Women and Moral Theory*, Totowa, NJ: Rowman & Littlefield.

Goldstein, J. and Kornfield, J. (2001) *Seeking the Heart of Wisdom: The Path of Insight Meditation*, Boston: Shambhala Publications.

Gómez, L.O. (1975) 'Some Aspects of the Free-will Question in the *Nikāyas*,' *Philosophy East and West* 25: 81–90.

Greene, B. (2000) *The Elegant Universe: Superstrings, Hidden Dimensions, and the Quest for the Ultimate Theory*, New York: Vintage Books.

Griffiths, P.J. (1982) 'Notes Towards a Critique of Buddhist Karmic Theory,' *Religious Studies* 18: 277–91.

—— (1984) 'Karma and Personal Identity: A Response to Professor White,' *Religious Studies* 20: 481–5.

—— (1986) *On Being Mindless: Buddhist Meditation and the Mind-Body Problem*, La Salle, IL: Open Court.

Gross, R.M. (1993) *Buddhism after Patriarchy: A Feminist History, Analysis, and Reconstruction of Buddhism*, Albany, NY: State University of New York Press.

—— (1999) 'Strategies for a Feminist Revalorization of Buddhism,' in A. Sharma and K.K. Young (eds) *Feminism and World Religions*, Albany, NY: State University of New York Press.

Gruzalski, B. (1996) 'The Possibility of Nonattachment,' in R. Puligandla and D.L. Miller (eds) *Buddhism and the Emerging World Civilization: Essays in Honor of Nolan Pliny Jacobson*, Carbondale, IL: Southern Illinois University Press.

—— (2000) *On the Buddha*, Belmont, CA: Wadsworth.

—— (2001) 'Four Aspects of Buddhist Ethics Unfamiliar in the West,' in N. Smart and B.S. Murthy (eds) *East-West Encounters in Philosophy and Religion*, Long Beach, CA: Long Beach Publications.

Gudmunsen, C. (1972) 'Ethics Gets in the Way: A Reply to David Bastow,' *Religious Ethics* 8: 311–18.

—— (1977) *Wittgenstein and Buddhism*, London: Macmillan Press.

Gunaratana, H. (1992) *Mindfulness in Plain English*, Boston: Wisdom Publications.

Gunaratna, V.F. (1980) *Rebirth Explained*, Kandy, Sri Lanka: Buddhist Publication Society.

Gupta, B. (1978) 'Another Look at the Buddha-Hume "Connection",' *Indian Philosophical Quarterly* 5 (new series): 371–86.

Gupta, R. (1977) '"Twelve-membered Dependent Origination": An Attempted Reappraisal,' *Journal of Indian Philosophy* 5: 163–86.

Habito, R.L.F., S.J. (1988) 'Buddhist Philosophy as Experiential Path: A Journey Through the *Sutta Nipāta*,' *International Philosophical Quarterly* 28: 125–39.

Hadot, P. (1995) *Philosophy as a Way of Life: Spiritual Exercises from Socrates to Foucault*, translated by Michael Chase, Oxford: Blackwell Publishers.

—— (2002) *What is Ancient Philosophy?*, translated by Michael Chase, Cambridge, MA: Harvard University Press.

Hamilton, S. (1996) *Identity and Experience: The Constitution of the Human Being According to Early Buddhism*, London: Luzac Oriental.

—— (2000) *Early Buddhism: A New Approach – The I of the Beholder*, Richmond, Surrey: Curzon Press.

—— (2001) *Indian Philosophy: A Very Short Introduction*, Oxford: Oxford University Press.

Hartshorne, C. (1960) 'The Buddhist-Whiteheadian View of the Self and the Religious Traditions,' *Proceedings of the IXth International Congress for the History of Religions*, Tokyo: Maruzen.

Harvey, P. (1990) *An Introduction to Buddhism: Teachings, History, and Practices*, Cambridge: Cambridge University Press.

—— (1993) 'The Mind–Body Relationship in *Pāli* Buddhism: A Philosophical Investigation,' *Asian Philosophy* 3: 29–41.

—— (1995a) *The Selfless Mind: Personality, Consciousness and Nirvāṇa in Early Buddhism*, Richmond, Surrey: Curzon Press.

—— (1995b) 'Criteria for Judging the Unwholesomeness of Actions in the Texts of Theravaada Buddhism,' *Journal of Buddhist Ethics* 2: 140–51. Online. Available HTTP: http://jbe.gold.ac.uk (accessed 15 March 2003).

—— (2000) *An Introduction to Buddhist Ethics: Foundations, Values and Issues*, Cambridge: Cambridge University Press.

Herman, A.L. (1979) 'A Solution to the Paradox of Desire in Buddhism,' *Philosophy East and West* 29: 91–4.

—— (1980) 'Ah, But There Is a Paradox of Desire in Buddhism – A Reply to Wayne Alt,' *Philosophy East and West* 30: 529–32.

—— (1996) 'Two Dogmas of Buddhism,' in F.J. Hoffman and D. Mahinda (eds) *Pāli Buddhism*, Richmond, Surrey: Curzon Press.

Hershock, P.D. (2000) 'Family Matters: Dramatic Interdependence and the Intimate Realization of Buddhist Liberation,' *Journal of Buddhist Ethics* 7: 86–104. Online. Available HTTP: http://jbe.gold.ac.uk (accessed 15 March 2003).

Hick, J. (1989) *An Interpretation of Religion: Human Responses to the Transcendent*, New Haven, CT: Yale University Press.

—— (1994) *Death and Eternal Life*, Louisville, KY: Westminster/John Knox Press.

Hoffman, F.J. (1982) 'The Buddhist Empiricism Thesis,' *Religious Studies* 18: 151–8.
—— (1985) 'Buddhist Belief "In",' *Religious Studies* 21: 381–7.
—— (1987) *Rationality and Mind in Early Buddhism*, Delhi: Motilal Banarsidass.
—— (1991) 'Towards a Philosophy of Buddhist Religion,' *Asian Philosophy* 1: 21–8.
Holder, J.J. (1996) 'The Early Buddhist Theory of Truth: A Contextualist Pragmatic Interpretation,' *International Philosophical Quarterly* 36: 443–59.
Hume, D. (1967) *A Treatise of Human Understanding*, Oxford: Clarendon Press.
Inada, K.K. (1969) 'Some Basic Misconceptions of Buddhism,' *International Philosophical Quarterly* 19: 101–19.
—— (1970) 'Buddhist Naturalism and the Myth of Rebirth,' *International Journal for Philosophy of Religion* 1: 46–53.
—— (1975) 'The Metaphysics of Buddhist Experience and the Whiteheadian Encounter,' *Philosophy East and West* 25: 465–88.
—— (1979) 'Problematics of the Buddhist Nature of the Self,' *Philosophy East and West* 29: 141–58.
—— (1985) 'Two Strains in Buddhist Causality,' *Journal of Chinese Philosophy* 12: 49–56.
Jacobson, N.P. (1969) 'The Possibility of Oriental Influence in Hume's Philosophy,' *Philosophy East and West* 19: 17–37.
Jayatilleke, K.N. (1963) *Early Buddhist Theory of Knowledge*, London: George Allen & Unwin.
—— (1974) *The Message of the Buddha*, New York: The Free Press.
Johansson, R.E.A. (1969) *The Psychology of Nirvana*, London: George Allen and Unwin.
Kalansuriya, A.D.P. (1979) 'Two Modern Sinhalese Views of *Nibbāna*,' *Religion* 9: 1–12.
Kalupahana, D.J. (1975) *Causality: The Central Philosophy of Buddhism*, Honolulu: University Press of Hawaii.
—— (1976) *Buddhist Philosophy: A Historical Analysis*, Honolulu: University of Hawaii Press.
—— (1987) *The Principles of Buddhist Psychology*, Albany, NY: State University of New York Press.
—— (1992) *A History of Buddhist Philosophy: Continuities and Discontinuities*, Honolulu: University of Hawaii Press.
—— (1995) *Ethics in Early Buddhism*, Honolulu: University of Hawaii Press.
Kant, I. (1978) *Anthropology from a Pragmatic Point of View*, translated by V.L. Dowdell, revised and edited by H.H. Rudnick, Carbondale, IL: Southern Illinois University Press.
—— (1997) *Critique of Pure Reason*, translated by P. Guyer and A.W. Wood, Cambridge: Cambridge University Press.
Kapstein, M.T. (2001) *Reason's Traces: Identity and Interpretation in Indian and Tibetan Buddhist Thought*, Boston: Wisdom Publications.
Katz, S.T. (1992) 'Ethics and Mysticism in Eastern Mystical Traditions,' *Religious Studies* 28: 253–67.
Keown, D. (1992) *The Nature of Buddhist Ethics*, New York: St. Martin's Press.
—— (1996) *Buddhism: A Very Short Introduction*, Oxford: Oxford University Press.
—— (ed.) (2000) *Contemporary Buddhist Ethics*, London: Curzon Press.

King, R. (1999) *Indian Philosophy: An Introduction to Hindu and Buddhist Thought*, Washington, DC: Georgetown University Press.

King, W.L. (1980) *Theravāda Meditation: The Buddhist Transformation of Yoga*, University Park, PA: The Pennsylvania State University Press.

—— (1983) 'The Existential Nature of Buddhist Ultimates,' *Philosophy East and West* 33: 263–71.

—— (1994) 'A Buddhist Ethic without Karmic Rebirth?,' *Journal of Buddhist Ethics* 1: 33–44. Online. Available HTTP: http://jbe.gold.ac.uk (accessed 15 March 2003).

—— (2001) *In the Hope of Nibbāna: The Ethics of Theravāda Buddhism*, Seattle: Pariyatti Press.

Kupperman, J.J. (1984) 'Investigations of the Self,' *Philosophy East and West* 34: 37–51.

—— (1999) *Learning From Asian Philosophy*, New York: Oxford University Press.

—— (2001) 'The Dhammapada,' *Classic Asian Philosophy: A Guide to the Essential Texts*, New York: Oxford University Press.

Larson, G.J. and Deutsch, E. (eds) (1988) *Interpreting Across Boundaries: New Essays in Comparative Philosophy*, Princeton, NJ: Princeton University Press.

Lesser, A.H. (1979) 'Eastern and Western Empiricism and the "No-Self" Theory,' *Religious Studies* 15: 55–64.

Ling, T. (1965) 'Buddhist Mysticism,' *Religious Studies* 1: 163–75.

—— (1976) *The Buddha: Buddhist Civilization in India and Ceylon*, Harmondsworth: Penguin Books.

Long, A.A. (1986) *Hellenistic Philosophy: Stoics, Epicureans, and Sceptics*, Second Edition, Berkeley, CA: University of California Press.

Long, A.A., and Sedley, D.N. (eds) (1987) *The Hellenistic Philosophers*, vol. 1: *Translations of the Principal Sources, with Philosophical Commentary*, Cambridge: Cambridge University Press.

Lopez, D.S. Jr. (ed.) (1988) *Buddhist Hermeneutics*, Honolulu: University of Hawaii Press.

—— (2001) *The Story of Buddhism: A Concise Guide to its History and Teachings*, New York: HarperCollins Publishers.

Lowe, E.J. (1991) 'Substance and Selfhood,' *Philosophy* 66: 81–99.

MacIntyre, A. (1984) *After Virtue: A Study in Moral Theory*, Second Edition, Notre Dame, IN: University of Notre Dame Press.

McTaggart, J.M.E. (1927) *The Nature of Existence*, vol. 2, Cambridge: Cambridge University Press.

Mackie, J.L. (1982) *The Miracle of Theism: Arguments for and against the Existence of God*, Oxford: Clarendon Press.

Macy, J.R. (1979) 'Dependent Co-arising: The Distinctiveness of Buddhist Ethics,' *Journal of Religious Ethics* 7: 38–52.

Magee, B. (1997) *The Philosophy of Schopenhauer*, Revised Edition, Oxford: Clarendon Press.

Mahinda, D. (1996) 'The Moral Significance of Buddhist *Nirvāṇa*: The Early Buddhist Model of Perfection,' in F.J. Hoffman and D. Mahinda (eds) *Pāli Buddhism*, Richmond, Surrey: Curzon Press.

Malalasekera, G.P. (1964) 'The Status of the Individual in Theravāda Buddhism,' *Philosophy East and West* 14: 145–56.

Maraldo, J.C. (1986) 'Hermeneutics and Historicity in the Study of Buddhism,' *Eastern Buddhist* 19 (new series): 17–43.

Mathur, D.C. (1978) 'The Historical Buddha (Gotama), Hume, and James on the Self: Comparisons and Evaluations,' *Philosophy East and West* 28: 253–69.

Matilal, B.K. (1989) '*Nyāya* Critique of the Buddhist Doctrine of Non-Soul,' *Journal of Indian Philosophy* 17: 61–79.

Mendis, N.K.G. (ed.) (1993) *The Questions of King Milinda: An Abridgement of the Milindapañha*, Kandy, Sri Lanka: Buddhist Publication Society.

Mitchell, D.W. (1975) 'Buddhist Theories of Causation – Commentary,' *Philosophy East and West* 25: 101–6.

—— (2002) *Buddhism: Introducing the Buddhist Experience*, New York: Oxford University Press.

Montalvo, D. (1999) 'The Buddhist Empiricism Thesis: An Extensive Critique,' *Asian Philosophy* 9: 51–70.

Morrison, R.G. (1997) *Nietzsche and Buddhism: A Study in Nihilism and Ironic Affinities*, New York: Oxford University Press.

Mueller-Vollmer, K. (ed.) (1985) *The Hermeneutics Reader: Texts of the German Tradition from the Enlightenment to the Present*, New York: Continuum.

Nagel, T. (1986) *The View from Nowhere*, New York: Oxford University Press.

Nakamura, H. (2000) *Gotama Buddha: A Biography Based on the Most Reliable Texts*, vol. 1, translated by Gaynor Sekimori, Tokyo: Kosei Publishing Co.

Ñāṇamoli, Bhikkhu (2001) *The Life of the Buddha According to the Pali Canon*, Seattle: BPS Pariyatti Editions.

Nicholls, M. (1999) 'The Influences of Eastern Thought on Schopenhauer's Doctrine of the Thing-in-Itself,' in C. Janaway (ed.) *The Cambridge Companion to Schopenhauer*, Cambridge: Cambridge University Press.

Nozick, R. (1989) *The Examined Life: Philosophical Meditations*, New York: Simon and Schuster.

Nussbaum, M.C. (1994) *The Therapy of Desire: Theory and Practice in Hellenistic Ethics*, Princeton, NJ: Princeton University Press.

—— (1997) *Cultivating Humanity: A Classical Defense of Reform in Liberal Education*, Cambridge, MA: Harvard University Press.

Nyanatiloka (ed.) (1988) *Buddhist Dictionary: Manual of Buddhist Terms and Doctrines*, Fourth Revised Edition, Kandy, Sri Lanka: Buddhist Publication Society.

Organ, T.W. (1954) 'The Silence of the Buddha,' *Philosophy East and West* 4: 125–40.

Parfit, D. (1984) *Reasons and Persons*, Oxford: Oxford University Press.

—— (1987) 'Divided Minds and the Nature of Persons,' in C. Blakemore and S. Greenfield (eds) *Mindwaves: Thoughts on Intelligence, Identity and Consciousness*, Oxford: Basil Blackwell.

—— (1995) 'The Unimportance of Identity,' in H. Harris (ed.) *Identity: Essays Based on Herbert Spencer Lectures Given in the University of Oxford*, Oxford: Oxford University Press.

Pascal, B. (1966) *Pensées*, trans. A.J. Krailshwimer, Harmondsworth: Penguin Books.

Paul, D.Y. (1979) *Women in Buddhism: Images of the Feminine in Mahayana Tradition*, Berkeley, CA: Asian Humanities Press.

Pérez-Remón, J. (1980) *Self and Non-Self in Early Buddhism*, The Hague: Mouton Publishers.

Perry, J. (ed.) (1975) *Personal Identity*, Berkeley, CA: University of California Press.

Pickering, J. (ed.) (1997) *The Authority of Experience: Essays on Buddhism and Psychology*, Richmond, Surrey: Curzon Press.

Powers, J. and Curtin, D. (1994) 'Mothering: Moral Cultivation in Buddhist and Feminist Ethics,' *Philosophy East and West* 44: 1–18.

Queen, C.S. (ed.) (2000) *Engaged Buddhism in the West*, Boston: Wisdom Publications.

Rahula, W. (1974) *What the Buddha Taught*, Revised Edition, New York: Grove Press.

Rajapakse, R. (1986) 'Buddhism as Religion and Philosophy,' *Religion* 16: 51–5.

Rajapakse, V. (1992) 'An Inquiry into Gender Considerations and Gender Conscious Reflectivity in Early Buddhism,' *International Studies in Philosophy* 24: 65–91.

Rescher, N. (1996) *Process Metaphysics: An Introduction to Process Philosophy*, Albany, NY: State University of New York Press.

Revel, J-F. and Ricard, M. (1998) *The Monk and the Philosopher: A Father and Son Discuss the Meaning of Life*, translated by J. Canti, New York: Schocken Books.

Reynolds, F.E. (1979) 'Four Modes of Theravāda Action,' *Journal of Religious Ethics* 7: 12–26.

Richards, G. (1978) 'Conceptions of the Self in Wittgenstein, Hume, and Buddhism: An Analysis and Comparison,' *Monist* 61: 42–55.

Rorty, A.M. (ed.) (1976) *The Identities of Persons*, Berkeley, CA: University of California Press.

Rubin, J.B. (1996) *Psychotheraphy and Buddhism: Toward an Integration*, New York: Plenum Press.

Rupp, G. (1971) 'The Relationship between *Nirvāṇa* and *Saṁsāra*: An Essay on the Evolution of Buddhist Ethics,' *Philosophy East and West* 21: 55–67.

Saddhatissa, H. (1997) *Buddhist Ethics*, Boston: Wisdom Publications.

Sessions, W.L. (1994) *The Concept of Faith: A Philosophical Investigation*, Ithaca, NY: Cornell University Press.

Sharples, R.W. (1996) *Stoics, Epicureans, and Sceptics: An Introduction to Hellenistic Philosophy*, London: Routledge.

Siderits, M. (1979) 'A Note on the Early Buddhist Theory of Truth,' *Philosophy East and West* 29: 491–99.

—— (1987) 'Beyond Compatibilism: A Buddhist Approach to Freedom and Determinism', *American Philosophical Quarterly*, 24: 149–59.

—— (1997) 'Buddhist Reductionism,' *Philosophy East and West* 47: 455–78.

—— (2001) 'Buddhism and Techno-Physicalism: Is the Eightfold Path a Program?,' *Philosophy East and West* 51: 307–14.

Sizemore, R.F. and Swearer, D.K. (eds) (1990) *Ethics, Wealth, and Salvation: A Study in Buddhist Social Ethics*, Columbia, SC: University of South Carolina Press.

Smart, N. (1984) 'Action and Suffering in the Theravadin Tradition,' *Philosophy East and West* 34: 371–8.

—— (1998) *The World's Religions*, Second Edition, Cambridge: Cambridge University Press.

Stevenson, I. (1987) *Children Who Remember Previous Lives*, Charlottesville, VA: The University Press of Virginia.

Stewart, H. (tr.) (1993) *A Net of Fireflies: Japanese Haiku and Haiku Paintings*, Rutland, VT: Charles E. Tuttle Company.

Stone, J. (1988) 'Parfit and the Buddha: Why There are No People,' *Philosophy and Phenomenological Research* 48: 519–32.

Strawson, G. (1999) 'The Sense of Self,' in M.J.C. Crabbe (ed.) *From Soul to Self*, London: Routledge.

Strawson, P.F. (1963) *Individuals: An Essay in Descriptive Metaphysics*, Garden City, NY: Anchor Books.

Streng, F. (1975) 'Reflections on the Attention Given to Mental Construction in the Indian Buddhist Analysis of Causality,' *Philosophy East and West* 25: 71–80.

Strenski, I. (1980) 'Gradual Enlightenment, Sudden Enlightenment and Empiricism,' *Philosophy East and West* 30: 3–20.

Strong, J.S. (2002) *The Experience of Buddhism: Sources and Interpretations*, Second Edition, Belmont, CA: Wadsworth Publishing Company.

Suzuki, D.T. (1999) *Manual of Zen Buddhism*, New York: Grove Press.

Swearer, D.K. (1972) 'Two Types of Saving Knowledge in the *Pāli Suttas*,' *Philosophy East and West* 22: 355–71.

—— (1973) 'Control and Freedom: The Structure of Buddhist Meditation in the *Pāli Suttas*,' *Philosophy East and West* 23: 435–55.

Swinburne, R. (1979) *The Existence of God*, Oxford: Clarendon Press.

Varma, V.P. (1963) 'The Origins and Sociology of the Early Buddhist Philosophy of Moral Determinism,' *Philosophy East and West* 13: 25–47.

Visvader, J. (1978) 'The Use of Paradox in Uroboric Philosophies,' *Philosophy East and West* 28: 455–67.

—— (1980) 'Reply to Wayne Alt's "There Is No Paradox of Desire in Buddhism",' *Philosophy East and West* 30: 533–4.

Warder, A.K. (1970) *Indian Buddhism*, Delhi: Motilal Banarsidass.

Watson, Burton (ed.) (1997) *The Vimalakirti Sutra*, New York: Columbia University Press.

Watts, J.D. (1982) 'Necessity and Sufficiency in the Buddha's Causal Scheme,' *Philosophy East and West* 32: 407–23.

Welbon, G.R. (1968) *The Buddhist Nirvāṇa and its Western Interpreters*, Chicago: University of Chicago Press.

White, J.E. (1983) 'Is Buddhist Karmic Theory False?,' *Religious Studies* 19: 223–8.

Whitehead, A.N. (1925) *Science and the Modern World*, New York: Free Press.

—— (1929) *Process and Reality: An Essay in Cosmology*, New York: Macmillan Company.

Whitehill, J. (1994) 'Buddhist Ethics in Western Context: The "Virtues" Approach,' *Journal of Buddhist Ethics* 1: 1–22. Online. Available HTTP: http://jbe.gold.ac.uk (accessed 15 March 2003).

Wilber, K., Engler, J., and Brown, D.P. (eds) (1986) *Transformations of Consciousness: Conventional and Contemplative Perspectives on Development*, Boston: Shambhala.

Williams, P. (1989) *Mahāyāna Buddhism: The Doctrinal Foundations*, London: Routledge.

Williams, P. and Tribe, A. (2000) *Buddhist Thought: A Complete Introduction to the Indian Tradition*, London: Routledge.

Yandell, K.E. (1993) *The Epistemology of Religious Experience*, Cambridge: Cambridge University Press.

—— (1999) *Philosophy of Religion: A Contemporary Introduction*, London: Routledge.

INDEX